David Brazier is spiritual teacher to the Order of Amida Buddha, a religious community dedicated to socially engaged Buddhism with an international membership and projects in Africa, Asia and East Europe. He is also a registered psychotherapist and holds a doctorate in Buddhist psychology. He is author of five books. Further information about his work can be found at www.amidatrust.com or by contacting the Amida Trust at Sukhavati, 21 Finsbury Park, London N7 6RT.

By the same author

A GUIDE TO PSYCHODRAMA
BEYOND CARL ROGERS
THE FEELING BUDDHA
ZEN THERAPY

THE NEW BUDDHISM

David Brazier

palgrave

First published 2002 by PALGRAVE™
175 Fifth Avenue, New York, N.Y. 10010
Companies and representatives throughout the world.

PALGRAVE is the new global publishing imprint of
St. Martin's Press LLC Scholarly and Reference Division and
Palgrave Publishers Ltd. (formerly Macmillan Press Ltd.).

ISBN 0-312-29518-9

Library of Congress Cataloging-in-Publication Data available at the
Library of Congress.

First published in the United Kingdom in 2000 by Robinson, an
imprint of Constable & Robinson Ltd

First PALGRAVE edition: May 2002
10 9 8 7 6 5 4 3 2 1

Printed in the United States of America.

Contents

Preface to *The New Buddhism*
Brian Daizen Victoria

In December 1997 I published a book *Zen at War* that sent shock waves through the Buddhist community in the West, for it revealed in graphic detail the way in which leading Japanese Zen masters (and scholars) had fervently supported Japanese militarism during World War II. Not only that, these Zen figures identified Japan's aggressive actions as the 'true Buddha Dharma' and an expression of 'Buddhist compassion'. Shortly thereafter I also revealed that perhaps the most influential Japanese Zen master in the West, i.e., Haku'un Yasutani, had not only been a militarist but an anti-Semite as well.

Among the many responses to my book was the pained reaction of a reader who asked simply, 'What the hell went wrong?' Upon reflection I had to admit that the reader was justified in having raised this question, for while I had carefully documented the war and violence-justifying stance of even such an imminent exponent of Zen as D. T. Suzuki, I had nevertheless failed to include an in-depth explanation of why these leaders had acted as they did. More importantly, I had failed to include any suggestions as to what reforms would be necessary were Zen to make a clean break with its militarist past. At the same time, I felt that these admitted deficiencies in my book were not altogether a bad thing. That is to say, it was my fondest hope that others in the

Buddhist tradition would go on to take up the challenge of explaining both the 'why' of Zen-supported militarism and proposing those changes necessary for a Zen renewal. To borrow a phrase attributed to Mao Zedong, it was, I thought, time for 'a hundred flowers' of Buddhist critique and reform to blossom forth.

Sadly, in the years since the book first appeared there has been little or no thoughtful critique of militarist Zen and its proponents, let alone proposals for Buddhist reform. On the contrary, utilizing the ancient principle of 'shooting the messenger who dares bring bad news to his sovereign', I have been accused of everything from mistranslating the warlike sentiments of this or that Buddhist master to simply fabricating their words out of thin air.

To be sure, some Western Buddhist leaders give the appearance of having recognized the serious implications of the material I presented. Accordingly, they have unanimously distanced themselves from the anti-Semitic statements of wartime Buddhist leaders like Yasutani while criticizing, as did now retired Roshi Robert Aitken, 'the incredible intellectual dishonesty of Japanese Buddhists who perverted their religion into a jingoistic doctrine of support for the emperor and imperial expansion during the period 1868-1945'[1]. Yet, accompanying this critique has been a parallel and more subtle attempt by Western Zen leaders to mitigate criticism directed toward those Japanese Zen master(s) in their own Dharma lineage who so fervently endorsed Japan's war effort. In Yasutani's case, for example, we are told that he may have acted as he did because 'his mother gave him up for adoption to a Buddhist priest when he was only five years old and he then grew up to be an angry youth and adult'[2].

A second American Zen master, Bernie Glassman, lifts (or lowers) the whole discussion of why to another plane when he informs us that we must do no less than redefine the very nature of enlightenment itself:

So if your definition of enlightenment is that there's no anti-Semitism in the state of enlightenment, you better change your definition of enlightenment. If your definition of enlightenment is that there's no nationalism, or militarism, or bigotry in the state of enlightenment, you better change your definition of enlightenment. For the state of enlightenment is *maha*, the circle with no inside and no outside, not even a circle, just the pulsating of life everywhere.[3]

Needless to say, I find that explanations like the above hardly begin to address the question of 'why'. On the contrary, they do little more than promote mental confusion, further obfuscating the deeper issues needing resolution. It was in fact my frustration with these 'non-answers' that initially led me to write the following in the introduction to my forthcoming book entitled *Zen War Stories*:

To my mind, a critical analysis of just how the Buddha Dharma was used to legitimate Japanese militarism is far, far more important than revelations about the militarist connections of any one Zen master. Nevertheless, since the appearance of *Zen at War* numerous Western Zen teachers have invested a great deal of time and energy in a futile attempt to defend their particular Zen lineage from the charge of war collaboration. Few if any of these teachers, however, have attempted to analyze, let alone criticize, the doctrinal interpretations of the Buddha Dharma used by the Japanese Zen master(s) in their lineages to justify the mass killing of their fellow human beings.[4]

It was only a few weeks after I had written the above that the British edition of David Brazier's latest book, *The New Buddhism*, arrived on my desk. The publisher thought I might be interested in this book since its author drew on the material in my earlier book for his own work. It was initially out of curiosity, and then increasing joy, that I read Brazier's work – here at long last a fellow Buddhist practitioner had honestly, forthrightly, and with great insight addressed the substance of the issues I had raised. Not only were the problems addressed, but 'solutions' were included as well.

In writing this, the reader may think that Brazier's book is no more than a thoughtful response to my earlier book. In fact, it is far more than that, for the author addresses a broad range of contemporary Buddhism's many 'ills', everything from a call for the reform of the teacher disciple relationship to a recognition of the contending definitions of the nature of enlightenment. What is perhaps even more surprising is that Brazier's frank and honest recognition of Zen and contemporary Buddhism's many ills, leads not to a denial of that faith, but a recognition and rededication to the teachings of the founder, Shakyamuni Buddha.

Although historical parallels are never exact, I suggest there is more than a passing similarity between Brazier's book and Martin Luther's famous Ninety-five Theses first published in 1517. Luther claimed that Scripture rather than the Church ought to be the ultimate authority in doctrinal matters, asserting as a corollary that justification came through faith alone and not through works. He also criticized the Church's sale of indulgences for, in effect, turning financial contributions into the prerequisite for escaping the consequences of past wrongdoing. In short, Luther was a reformer who sought to cleanse the Christianity of his day from those elements which he regarded as improper accretions to the Gospel.

While only history will be able to judge the ultimate effects of Brazier's proposals for the reform of Buddhism, his proposals are, if anything, even more far ranging than those of Luther. For starters, he calls on Buddhists 'to advance the radical social implications of some of its central teachings more effectively'. To accomplish this, he claims, Buddhism must first 'jettison much of its own conservative baggage acquired during centuries when the original message was buried under a series of compromises . . .' (p. 66).

But just what is the 'conservative baggage' Brazier refers to? Brazier critiques a number of allegedly Buddhist practices that he feels have long contributed to burying the original Buddhist message. One of these is 'the corruption of lineage' and a second, the abuse of the teacher-disciple relationship. In focusing on these closely related traditions, Brazier addresses what I have previously identified as the 'Achilles heel' of Zen. That is to say, inasmuch as Zen has traditionally claimed to be 'a transmission outside of the sutras', (from the mind of one enlightened master to another) what happens to the authenticity of this transmission when it includes masters who were demonstrably not only fervent militarists but ofttimes ethnic chauvinists, sexists and even anti-Semites?

Brazier points out that one of the most pernicious aspects of Buddhism's traditional conservatism has been its intolerance of dissent. His insight rings true to my own experience, not least of all because leading postwar Japanese masters have stressed that the master-disciple relationship transcends even the Buddha and Dharma in importance. Thus, postwar masters would never presume to criticize the wartime actions of their own masters, no matter what the latter had said or done. In stark contrast, Brazier castigates as 'complete nonsense' the idea that the enlightened master is 'a know-all who can never be gainsaid' (p. 76). On the contrary, Brazier claims a master is no more, yet no less, than a 'spiritual guide' who leads, not by coercion, but by personal example.

Brazier admits from the outset that his book is 'intentionally partisan' and 'makes no effort at academic dispassion'. He does, however, challenge those who disagree with his views to advance their own claims as long as such claims 'are well put and accord with the real world' (p. 13). No doubt one of the most interesting and important aspects of this book will be just how much debate if not disagreement it provokes.

Brazier clearly and repeatedly identifies nationalism in particular, and Sangha-State relations in general, as the key element behind what he perceives to be Buddhism's historic failure to advance the radical social implications of its central teachings more effectively. In claiming this Brazier is clearly within the camp of the advocates of today's 'engaged Buddhism' movement. This said, Brazier is unlike many of this latter movement's leaders who maintain that Buddhism need do no more than expand beyond its historic monastic focus and engage more effectively with the secular world. Instead, he recognizes, as noted above, that much of the problem lies within what has come to be accepted over the centuries as Buddhist doctrine and practice itself. All too often, Buddhism has been used in Asian countries as 'an instrument of state policy for subduing rather than liberating the population' (p. 66).

This is a very harsh critique indeed and, needless to say, it falls to scholars and practitioners alike to determine the merit (or demerit) of broad generalizations of this kind. Some readers might detect an element of 'Asia-bashing' in Brazier's remarks, complete or a suggestion of moral superiority on the part of the West. Yet Brazier is equally critical of what he identifies as the Western equivalent of the traditional four-tiered Indian caste system.[5] He means by this the contemporary concentration of wealth in the hands of the 'white caste' as compared with those of yellow, brown and black skin colors.

Brazier notes that whites enjoy more than three-quarters of the wealth of the planet while making up only a quarter of its population. Not only that, because of their relative wealth, white Buddhists tend to look to Buddhism for 'tantalizing spiritual experiences', bringing with it the serious danger that Western Buddhism will degenerate into a 'narrow, sectarian, small-minded and irrelevant pursuit of personal euphoria' (p. 26). This head-in-the-sand spirituality is, however, 'extremely remote from what the Buddha was concerned with' (p. 5).

But what, exactly, is this 'New Buddhism' that Brazier advocates? Brazier defines New Buddhism as: 'Buddhism finally liberated from the age-old demoralizing effects of having long ago become part of monolithic state apparatuses' (p. 70). In making this latter claim, Brazier reveals the degree to which his thinking has been informed by the 'Critical Buddhism' movement. In fact, two chapters of the book (nine and ten) are devoted to an explanation of this movement. Because he does not claim that his is a scholarly analysis, Brazier is able to take this movement beyond the confines of scholarly debate and assist the general reader in appreciating why the points it raises are so important to our understanding of Buddhism, East and West.

Ultimately, Brazier does not take a position in support of, or opposition to, the positions of such Critical Buddhist scholars as Matsumoto Shiro or Hakamaya Noriaki. Instead, he regards this movement as functioning more in the nature of a 'warning bell', revealing the way in which doctrinal tenets concerning Buddha Nature and inherent enlightenment can, depending on the context, readily become allies of socially repressive forces.

Like the Critical Buddhists, Brazier wants to identify, and rectify, those aspects of Buddhism that he regards as having harmed or even contradicted its original message of individual spiritual growth linked to radical social change. Furthermore, nationalism is not the only barrier to restoring Buddhism to its revolutionary beginnings. Brazier identifies a whole series of impediments to such a restoration, not the least of which is the 'cult of anti-intellectualism' (p. 12). Brazier asserts that those schools of Buddhism which eschew healthy debate and deride intellect are dangerous or hypocritical and sometimes both. 'Criticism of intellect provides a smoke screen', he claims, 'behind which the ills of the world at large can be ignored and malpractice can flourish, and no school that really advances the dharma can afford that' (p. 13). Coming from someone trained in the Zen tradition, as Brazier is, this is a drastic comment, no less so than his warning that 'we must not allow principles like "no-mind" to degenerate into sheer mindlessness' (p. 79).

Whatever faults this book may have, sheer mindlessness is most certainly not one of them. On the contrary, this book will and ought to provoke critical if not heated debate on a whole range of issues related to Buddhist doctrine and practice that have long been taken for granted. As the world once again reels in horror at the destructive power of religious fanaticism, this book is nothing less than a 'call to arms' for the renewal of Buddhism. It is this writer's sincerest wish that the 'peaceful revolution' Brazier calls for will grow and flourish for the good of the many, for the welfare of the many, whoever and wherever they may be.

Shalom

Brian Daizen Victoria, Ph.D. Senior
Lecturer, Centre for Asian Studies
University of Adelaide
Adelaide, South Australia
brian.victoria@adelaide.edu.au

Notes

1. Brian Victoria. *The Zen Life.* New York: Weatherhill, 1997, back cover.

2. Robert Aitken. 'Robert Aitken Responds' in *Tricycle* (Fall 1999), p. 68.

3. Bernie Glassman. 'Bernie Glassman Responds' in *Tricycle* (Fall 1999), p. 74.

4. Brian Victoria. *Zen War Stories.* London: Curzon Press, January 2001.

5. Traditionally, the four main castes in India consisted of: 1) priests, 2) warriors, 3) merchants, and 4) workers. At the very bottom, of course, were the so-called 'outcasts'.

Autobiographical Note

This book offers a radical, this-worldly, perspective on Buddhism. It is critical as well as constructive, and is concerned with both personal Buddhist training and Buddhist engagement in society. This note serves to situate the book in the development of my thinking and understanding as well as I can discern it from my present vantage point, and can be skipped without detriment to the reader's understanding of the main work that begins with Chapter One.

This text marks a shift in the tone and direction of my thought and, therefore, while it is in some respects a continuation from my previous writings, it is also a new departure from them. Looking back now, and wondering how this has come about, I have a sense of several distinct periods in the development of the thinking that informs this work and of my own continuum in the Buddha way.

As a young child I had spontaneous spiritual experiences that set me on a life-long spiritual quest. This started a first period, one of searching, that continued until my encounter with Buddhism in my early twenties. This search also led me to treasure what had been granted to me through experience. The search was for something in the world, or in the teachings of the great faiths, that might match with my own visionary experiences. These were visions of a world perfected: not visions of an other-world, so much as of the real potential of this world – of what this world should be, could be, and in some sense latently is. In childhood I assumed that what I sought would be found in Christianity, but, though I still have much respect for many individual Christians, and a love and admiration for a number of particular historical exemplars like Jesus of Nazareth and Francis of Assisi, the Christian path, for me, proved a disappointment. As time went by, it seemed as though there was a greater and greater gap between the things I treasured and the things I encountered.

By my early adult years I realised that I was deeply split between things that society and other people demanded of me on the one hand and things that I believed in and felt passion for on the other. This led to my life being lived in separate compartments with sharp dividing boundaries. Work and social life on the one hand and spirituality and social ideals on the other were kept apart. At times friends struggled to keep me from the excesses of spirit that sometimes broke out – as when, on one occasion, I determined to set fire to myself in Grosvenor Square in London, in imitation of and solidarity with the Buddhist monks who were at that time doing the same in Vietnam in protest at the war. I was persuaded – but only just – that the gesture would be futile. I was never completely sure whether the prudence to which I was persuaded at such times was really sanity or simply collusion with mass cowardice. When, soon after, I encountered *Soto Zen* and read the line in *Sandokai*, 'With the ideal comes the actual like a box with its lid', it seemed to resonate with a truth that was not so much deep as simply ubiquitous in my experience.

From the time of those first encounters with Buddhism, however, a new process took over. This second period was one of healing and of a search for harmony. In Buddhism, I found what I was looking for: the union of passion and enlightenment. However, there were still divisions in my life. For some twenty-five years I worked on harmonising. I sought harmony between the different teachings within Buddhism, between those teachings and my own experiences, and between Buddhism and the other disciplines that had become important to me, such as psychotherapy, social and community work. My assumption throughout that period was that truth, being unitary, all true teachings must be saying the same thing in different ways. My task, therefore, was to reconcile them. This period culminated in the publication of my book *Zen Therapy*, a book that was a synthesis of several varieties of Buddhism and psychotherapy.

Round about that time, a tide seems to have turned. Such turnings seem to arise quite naturally and demonstrate that we are a great deal less under our own control than we would often like to think. Under the harmonising, a fire still burnt. Although I did not realise it immediately, from there on I have once again become more interested in difference than in sameness. The book *The Feeling Buddha*, in which several basic Buddhist dogmas are challenged, was a first stage on this third path. The present work takes us a good deal further down the road of challenge. At a purely personal level, I can say that while I certainly needed the healing brought by harmonising, there comes a point when the healing is done, and one no longer wants to sit convalescent, but wants again to go forth into the struggle. This book, therefore, certainly returns to some of the spirit of my earlier youthful life – its protest and confidence, its contrasts and challenges – but does so, I hope, from the position of experience won, from the far side of the quest for harmony; a quest from which I learnt so much, but which ultimately could never fully assuage the heart's cry. An important theme of this book is that while healing is certainly needed in this world, it is not the only thing that is needed. There is also a place for struggle. The last words of the Buddha were, 'Strive on!'

Writing this book has proved to be a personal liberation. As I review the finished manuscript, I feel considerably unburdened. There are things here that I have felt for a long time, but have not until now found the words for. This is not the final word nor the perfect expression of it and I will no doubt go on to write more. It does, however, feel like a fairly clear statement. I imagine some will like it and some will definitely not. That is life. In fact, the assertion that our differences are valuable is a core message of the work that follows.

This book has many intellectual debts, but they are the gleanings of a lifetime. I have endeavoured to acknowledge a few as we go along. Basically, however, it is my own work, for better or worse. I do wish to acknowledge the help, patience and encouragement of my mother, Irene Brazier, my wife, Caroline Brazier, and of Mary Midgley with whom I have had many valuable, if incidental, philosophical discussions during this period. Also, of other members of our households at the Amida Buddhist Communities in England and France, and of my students and all those who have responded to my earlier books and thus given me encouragement to go further in these explorations. One of the greatest satisfactions I have found from writing has been the number and range of people that it brings one in contact with – both fellow spirits and adversaries alike. There is always more to learn.

Buddha's River

BUDDHA WOULD RECOGNISE OUR WORLD

Two thousand five hundred years ago, in northern India, Buddhism was born. The new socio-religious movement spread rapidly in its early days and it has become one of the most enduring and successful of such movements in history, older than Christianity or Islam and more international than Judaism, Hinduism or Confucianism.

Why did it spread so? Because of the depth of inspiration of its founder, the clarity of his message, and the personal and social implications of that teaching. Buddhism was an inspired protest against the oppressive conservatism, superstition, greed, racism and belligerence of the world into which it was born.

The word Buddhism means 'the way of enlightenment'. You can call it a religion, or a way of life, or a vision of human perfectibility. For 2,500 years it has been a light for those who would live the better life and create a better world with resort neither to superstitious escapism on the one hand nor violent coercion on the other. To be enlightened is to be compassionate, tolerant, reasonable, moral and engaged in a life that benefits humankind – that contributes to the emancipation of all sentient beings from avoidable suffering and exploitation.

Buddhism remains, to this day, a rallying point for those who seek a more peaceful and less greedy world. In the past hundred years Buddhism has spread into the West. Initially it was taken up, largely, because of the appeal of its contemplative traditions and disciplines. Increasingly, however, its social and this-worldly implications are coming into focus.

Many events have contributed to this. When India gained independence from Britain in 1948 and was partitioned into a Hindu and a Muslim state, half a million untouchables – those who occupy the lowest rung on the social ladder in the Hindu world view – dissented by converting to Buddhism. The first mass conversion occurred in 1956. What sort of Buddhism is this? people asked. This is the New Buddhism, they replied.

In the 1970s, Vietnam was engulfed in a horrific war, a war that was to prove formative in the politics of the modern age. In it, the world's most powerful nation was humiliated by one of Earth's poorest ones. It was an extremely savage conflict, supposedly between the competing ideologies of capitalism and communism, the former represented by the USA and its allies and the latter by North Vietnam. The ordinary people of South Vietnam, on whose land the conflict took place, however, were neither capitalist nor communist. They were, for the most part, Buddhist.

The newsreel pictures of Buddhist monks burning themselves to death while seated in serene contemplation are still vivid in the memories of many people decades later. These self-sacrificing protests against the war again brought home to the world at large that Buddhism is a social movement as well as a religious one.

In the contemporary world, one of the most widely respected of international figures is the Dalai Lama. The fate of the Tibetan people, and the failure of the international community to do anything effective in its aid, is one of the greatest causes for shame. The Dalai Lama's continuing search for peace and reconciliation in circumstances where most other comparable leaders would have opted for guerrilla warfare stands out like a beacon of hope in a dark world and touches the consciences of many.

The ills that Buddhism is concerned about are as prevalent

in the contemporary world as they were in the Buddha's own time. The New Buddhism is a call for a new enlightenment – an end to cruelty, grasping and self-aggrandisement by social groups just as much as by individuals. We should not, however, think that the New Buddhism is in any way out of keeping with the spirit of the original Buddhism. The Buddha would, without doubt, have approved of the conversion of the untouchables. He would certainly have disapproved of the Vietnam War; and there can be little doubt that the work of the Dalai Lama and others like him stands solidly in the spirit of the founder's own work.

The Buddha spoke on many of the social ills of his day and the problems he saw are also the problems of today. The nature of human delusion has not changed. The remedies that he offered are also worthy of serious consideration. It is my contention that the world urgently needs Buddhism or something like it, because we have the same problems that the Buddha discerned. Take, for instance, the question of racial prejudice and the division of the world into rich and poor nations.

One of the evils that most appalled the Buddha in his day was the caste system and it is possible to see many of his teachings as related to his rejection of it. He was himself born to be one of the system's beneficiaries, but he renounced it. He said 'No' to the privileges he could have had and, instead, aligned himself with the dispossessed. It is from this act of renunciation, more even than from his subsequent enlightenment, that Buddhism may be said to have sprung. The enlightenment confirmed him in his act, overcame his own inner obstacles, and gave him the will to propagate his renunciation. Buddha renounced both the social manifestation of caste and the whole metaphysical system of Indian religion that was held to justify it. He was one person alone and he said 'No' to the cruel system that ran the world of his time. In its place he offered a training in noble living that was intended to establish in the world a corps of people who would exemplify, work towards and lead others in a better way of life for all. That way of life was – and still is – a demonstration of that renunciation.

The Indian caste system was complex with four main castes – priests, warriors, merchants and workers. Each of these had numerous subdivisions. The origins of this system lay in the racial stratification of the country that resulted from earlier settlement as successive invaders imposed themselves on those who had arrived before. According to the caste one was born into one enjoyed differential social privileges, wealth, diet, health, longevity, work opportunities and so forth. It was not impossible for low-caste people to do well nor for high-caste ones to fall, but the scales were heavily weighted. Where you lived, who spoke to you, what you were allowed to do, what benefits you enjoyed, how much people cared if you died, all these things generally depended upon your caste. What your life was worth depended upon caste. And at the very bottom were those called outcastes who often lived the most wretched lives imaginable. Despite attempted reforms, this system still persists to this day.

What is even more important, however, is that this system was, and is, essentially the same as that which operates in the wider world today. Now we again have four castes – white, yellow, brown and black. Each has numerous ethnic and class-based sub-divisions that compete and struggle with each other. According to the caste one is born into one enjoys differential social privileges, wealth, diet, health, longevity, work opportunities and so forth. Where you live, who speaks to you, what you are allowed to do, what benefits you enjoy, your value as a member of society, these things depend upon your caste. Your chances of survival, your chances of going to prison, your quality of housing, the kind of job you are likely to get, and many other social discriminators, are closely related to your caste. It is not impossible for black people to make good, nor for whites to fall into poverty, but it is a steeply tilted playing field. The white caste makes most of the rules and enjoys more than three-quarters of the wealth of the planet, even though they make up only a quarter of its population. At the bottom of the system are the tribal and aboriginal peoples of the world who, when they survive at all, are widely regarded as simply getting in the way. The Buddha would recognise our world.

This is the relevance of the Buddha today, as a bringer of enlightenment to a world full of suffering based on prejudice and delusion, avarice and fear. If we see his relevance solely as a provider of a nice, comfortable, head-in-the-sand spirituality, then we have missed the point. Buddhism has spread in the white world on the promise of tantalising spiritual experiences. This is, however, extremely remote from what the Buddha was concerned with.

WHAT IS ENLIGHTENMENT?

It is enlightened to abolish slavery. It is enlightened to attend to the welfare of animals. It is enlightened to create the conditions for world peace. It is enlightened to help others in myriad everyday ways. It is enlightened to recognise others as brothers and sisters. It is enlightened to view yourself objectively and not collude with superstition. Basically, it is enlightened to be kind and to stand up against cruelty. Every enlightened action contributes to the emergence of a more enlightened world.

Visions of perfected worlds are found throughout the Buddhist schools. Their existence is common ground to all branches in one way or another. Sometimes the vision has become a promise located in a faraway place where the fortunate might be reborn in a future life or a place that only mystics see. Sometimes it is closer at hand. The Buddha established such visions firmly in the minds of his followers. He also acted them out in the way he lived and the way he treated those who came to see him. Kings and commoners were all treated the same, or, on occasion, those of low status were treated better. The better world vision that the Buddha dispensed was meant for this present earthly life.

White converts to Buddhism, of whom there are a growing number, are surprisingly oblivious to this central feature of the faith. So privatised has Western life become that the white Buddhist is often completely unaware of the this-worldly pretensions of this noble faith. Throughout the East, however, whether it be in Thailand, in Tibet, in Japan, in old China or in Vietnam, the revolutionary implications of enlightenment for society as well as – or even more than – the individual are not entirely lost. Buddhism is a social religion, not just a private spirituality.

Many white people have turned to Buddhism because they realise that they suffer, both individually and as a people, from a deep spiritual malaise. Instinctively, they see that the path of enlightenment offers medicine for their ills. Usually, however, they do not accept so readily that their sickness is a function of the conditions of life – the lives, that is, of those they oppress. This is because the caste system tends to keep other castes out of sight and out of mind. It ensures that people of different castes rarely meet, and when they do it may be in circumstances that the members of the higher caste are likely to experience with displeasure or that confirm them in their prejudice. We might visit the other castes as tourists, or as experts, perhaps, and these statuses keep us apart. Thus the caste system ensures that we never get too defiled by real contact. Nonetheless, the spiritual sickness of the privileged is a direct result of blindness to our own guilt. As the Buddha said, it is the failure to see what one is involved in that creates all the unnecessary suffering in the world. The spiritual sickness of the whites is but the other side of the same coin as the physical sickness and deprivation of the blacks. You cannot cure one without the other.

Enlightenment means to see what harm you are involved in and to renounce it. The Buddhist path, therefore, is open to people of every caste and there is nothing particularly esoteric about it. In their red, brown or orange clothes the Buddha's followers bear witness to a possibility for all humankind. They sow the seeds for a better world – for many better worlds, in fact. They are seeds of passion and of peace. 'Be impassioned for peace,' said the Buddha. These are not the downward pulling passions of lust, hate and arrogance that are the symptoms of the world disease. They are the passions for freedom, fellowship and harmony that live in the highest dreams of people of all faiths and races.

Buddhism is not an exclusive religion. There are Buddhists of all religions. Buddhism is simply the path of enlightened renunciation that bears witness to a better world, where the caste system is forgotten, and its associated machinery of wealth, power and oppression fall away.

Beyond this all-important act of renunciation, Buddhism is also a method of training that aims, metaphorically speaking, to wash people clean on the inside so that they may be healthy again. Buddhist training, however, does not end with 'inner work'. The whole purpose of overcoming one's inner obstacles is to be fitter to 'go forth for the good of the many'. Becoming healthy themselves they naturally go out to reduce the suffering in the world and bring great visions into actuality. Buddhist training is training in patience, calm, compassion, wisdom, confidence, selflessness and courage. This method is not limited to one or just a few techniques nor is it a retreat into a private bliss. It is whatever serves to heal the physical and spiritual sicknesses of the world.

THE RIVER

Rivers in India can be wide and difficult. In the Buddha's time the larger ones marked the boundaries between countries. The Buddha-to-be was born in the land of the Shakyas, one of these little countries, in the foothills of the Himalayas. He was brought up in affluence among people of his own caste. The walls of his father's palace kept the rest of the world out of sight and out of mind. When, as a young man, he eventually stepped out of the palace and saw the degradation of many ordinary people –

their sickness and hunger, the harshness of their world – he was unable to stomach his life of affluence a day longer. He cut off his long hair, turned his back on his heritage, went forth and crossed the river. Once he was on the other shore, he knew that he would never go back. He would never go back spiritually, that is. Many years later he would revisit his homeland and when he left the second time, half his kindred crossed the river with him. Crossing that river was the most important act of his life. It was even more significant than the enlightenment that followed some years later. Buddhism began with the Buddha's renunciation. His most serious disciples have all followed him in this step. We should see it in this light – as a repudiation of ignorance about how the poor majority of society live: of the refusal to see, certainly, but, more than that, as demonstrating the willingness and intention to commit one's life in the service of a better world.

Just as Caesar crossed the Rubicon and was thus committed to war and the pursuit of worldly power, leading in due course to his assassination and the spread of that same war throughout the Roman world, so Buddha crossed a river and committed himself to peace, and the path of enlightenment, leading in due course to the creation of a widespread movement for universal compassion. In this life there are choices to be made.

Crossing to the other shore was just the first step. He needed training. He needed to purge himself of the world's spiritual disease. Crossing the river got him going. When he thought of the luxuries he had consumed while others starved, was it any wonder that he undertook great austerities? Have you looked at the nutrition statistics for white, yellow, brown and black people recently? Eventually he realised that it was not by punishing his own guilt but by using the same energy to do some real good that the situation could be best redeemed. Not by starving himself would he help the starving, but by using the strength the food gave him to go forth in their service. But even then he faltered – such a true detail in the story this – he thought, 'What is the use?

Nobody will understand'. But, nonetheless, after this hesitation, go forth he did.

In so doing, his first thought was that he needed people to work with him. Eventually he drew a substantial following – not huge, but probably more than he expected. Soon he had 'sixty *arhats*' and, by the time he died, perhaps 500. Some accounts suggest many more. He opened their eyes to the presence of suffering in the world. He taught that it sprang from avoidable conditions – that while there is greed, hate and delusion, there will be starvation, war and anguish. He called this 'dependent origination'. The origin of one depends upon the other. The origins of the great mass of avoidable suffering in the world depend upon the conditions created by those who live lives of greed, hate and delusion. He called these 'the three poisons'. His teaching is not complicated. What stops people putting it into practice is not lack of understanding, but rather that they have not crossed their river.

The principle of dependent origination is the bedrock of Buddhism. The Buddha's most compelling insight into it is what is referred to as his enlightenment. The enlightenment simply confirmed the original renunciation. The Buddha left home because he could not stand to live in luxury while others starved. It was a gut response. Enlightenment revealed the process of dependent origination. This enabled him to engage in a purposeful ministry. The dependent origination teaching is his clarity about cause and effect in the ethical dimension of life. It begins with the assertion that not looking (*avidya*, in Sanskrit) is the root of all the misery in the world. If we do not look at the consequences of what we do, then we can carry on building our own ideas and chasing our own desires and pleasures, and while we do, we contribute to the oppression. We give rise to all this 'mass of lamentation and despair'.

Buddha's enlightenment had intellectual, emotional and visionary aspects. The texts that describe the night of his greatest struggle make this clear. He had the kind of experience that we can call mystical – a direct seeing of reality as it is and as it can be. This gave him the inspiration of the possibility of a world perfected. He also had the intelligence to understand the rationale of this vision and this produced the theory of dependent origination. Further, he had the courage to see that this all applied to him personally. He had to face his own personal greed, lust, hatred and folly and get beyond them, if he were going to be useful. Everybody has glimpses of this, but the enlightenment that Buddha had and to which he brought many others made it abundantly clear that what the world needs of us is not just a theoretical matter. It requires committing our life.

In our case, the palace wall is not always made of brick. Often it is real enough – the immigration checkpoint, the dress code, the application form, the language spoken in the right accent. Immigration control, though, also operates upon our minds. Of course, we have no alternative, we think. We have jobs and mortgages to protect. For centuries people have bent over backwards to build grand metaphysical theories out of the Buddha's teachings that would enable them to avoid the simple meaning of what he said. 'Stop and look', was his message. Stop and look at the person who is sick. Stop and look at the person who is old. Stop and look at the refugee. Stop and look at the person who has no social status. When you have seen the sights, as he did, do you not want to cross the river? Do you not twist inside?

Listen. Do you hear a scream? Over there – over the palace wall – somebody is being tortured. Listen. Do you hear a moan? Somebody is dying of malnutrition. Do you hear somebody crying? Across the world somebody is dying of a disease that you could cure in a few days with a medicine you can buy at the corner chemist. Do you hear a key turning? Is it to keep the prisoner in or the poor out? Shall we listen to the bombs? Planet earth is a paradise in the middle of a nightmare.

Buddhism is not a hobby. It was probably a struggle for the Buddha to cross that river. He certainly never forgot it. There were many days he never forgot. He lived that kind of life – full of unforgettable days. Unforgettable because he took courageous risks. He raised his voice for freedom, and he did not go back.

He put on a rag robe. He walked. He listened to people and he was always willing to help. He enjoyed a swim. He liked beautiful sights. He could laugh with company. He could give talks on *dharma* that made people's hair stand on end. He was difficult to ignore. He made a stir and not everybody thanked him for it. Several tried to kill or discredit him. He did not give in.

SOME FEATURES OF THIS BOOK

This book will do a number of things. It will outline what Buddhist practice can be and show its relevance to and inseparability from socially engaged purposes. It will offer a critique of those forms of Buddhism that have retreated from such engagement. It will stir our concerns about the condition of our world and thereby clarify the nature of and need for Buddhism's revolutionary visions. It will reinstate the central importance of struggle as a legitimate part of Buddhist methodology deriving directly from the Buddha's own example. It will invite the reader to find and cross the river.

It will use a broad perspective, for the most part. We will span two and a half millennia of history and take in a sense of the wider world. Here Buddhism is presented in its social dimension, not just as a private path. Here it will be argued that we should not confuse the goal of peace with absence of struggle, nor should we confuse harmony with uniformity. Religions seem to have an inexorable tendency towards a kind of monistic absolutism, often sanctified in the figure of an absolute god or some unifying metaphysical principle – the very things Buddha rejected. It will be argued that the strength and value of Buddhism lie precisely in its rejection of such reductionism. Instead of transcendental unity, Buddhism's principle of dependent origination leads to a cherishing of pluralism, richness and diversity.

In the process it will also contribute to re-establishing the importance of debate within Buddhism. This book is quite sharp in its criticism of some aspects of contemporary Buddhist practice. The Buddha encouraged us to use our intelligence and not to act blindly, simply because the people who tell us to do so appear exotic. He was willing to be sharp if he thought a shout might help people to wake up.

In the same vein, this book is opposed to the kind of extreme of anti-intellectualism that is praised in some Buddhist circles. Buddha needed his gut reaction and his universal vision, but he also needed to work out what was going on. It is true that a lot of time can be wasted on one concept chasing another, but we do need to use our intelligence.

The cult of anti-intellectualism has two sources. One is a common misunderstanding of the nature of the teacher-disciple relationship about which there will be more to say in a later chapter. Buddhism has been brought from the East by teachers who are not only trained in Buddhism, they are also immersed in the culture of their country of origin. This culture, in some cases, may be authoritarian, conservative, misogynist and superstitious. Western disciples who think that being Buddhist means closing down your critical faculties, believing every word your teacher says, and following his or her example in every respect, are at risk of acquiring more medievalism than enlightenment. The Buddha did not preach blind obedience, either to himself or to anybody else, nor did he advocate unthinking credulity.

Gurus are often charismatic. In consequence they are envied. People who are spiritually impoverished wish they could be like that. Such people are looking for something for them-selves personally rather than 'for the good of the many'. This is understandable, but far from ideal. Many individuals harbour the dream that they personally will be liberated into a wonderful transcendental state in which they will feel ever blissful, and all the world will fall at their feet. Longing for this, they themselves become willing to fall at the feet of the most unlikely characters.

All too frequently, the quest for enlightenment is driven by nothing more noble than the desire to be admired.

This is not to say that the whole process of learning from a spiritual teacher or guru is nonsense. Any movement that aims to train people needs trainers to do that job. Something has gone wrong with a discipline, however, when the highest position one can aspire to is that of teacher. The dharma, as the Buddhist way is called, is taught so that it can be implemented, not simply so that it can be taught again.

The second common source of anti-intellectualism is an idea that thought and intellect are themselves obstacles to enlightenment and that the truth cannot be expressed in words. Later in this book there will be more on this topic too. Let it be said at this point, however, that the Buddha himself appears to have had a great deal of faith in the power of words and ideas and clearly did see them as tools with which to change the world. He was a critic and this book is in favour of his kind of critique. It advocates a climate of healthy debate. It is in favour of intelligent thinking. Schools that deride intellect are dangerous or hypocritical and sometimes both. The very schools of Buddhism that most commonly scorn the intellect and thinking are among those that generally have the largest numbers of books in print, and most of these are intellectual to a point. More seriously, however, the criticism of intellect provides a smokescreen behind which the ills of the world at large can be ignored and malpractice can flourish, and no school that really advances the dharma can afford that.

On the other hand, neither is this book in favour of the kind of academicisation of Buddhism that renders it a subject only to be studied from a distance, like a specimen in a jar. This book is intentionally partisan and makes no effort at academic dispassion. Arguments are put forward. Evidence is mustered. It is expected that those who disagree will advance their own claims. This writer will be more than happy to entertain such claims, if they are well put and accord with the real world.

· 2 ·

Creating a Buddha Field

HEALED WORLDS

The Buddha was a visionary. In order to pass on his visions he told wonderful stories, stories that give glimpses of what is possible. He wanted to lift us out of the smallness of mind that so often hampers our best efforts. In the language of India, he was called *Lokavid*: 'one who sees worlds'.

Buddhism has many words for such healed worlds. They are called Pure Lands (*Sukhavati*) or divine resting places (*brahma vihara*). These promised lands, however, are not for just one tribe, one set of believers, or one caste. Non-exclusiveness is their essential feature. You do not need to be a believer to enter these lands. You do not even have to be good. For them to exist at all, however, there have to be those who become the vehicle for their manifestation. These lands are without boundaries. They are not one territory. They exist wherever there are people who have the insight to do what the Buddha did and to throw off the 'fevers' of avarice, aversion and self-deception. The concept is extremely simple.

The vision that we are talking about is one in which a small number of people, properly prepared, are seen as being capable of bringing about transformations that will benefit a great many. A few enlightened people working in cooperation can achieve things that bring changes for many others. The Buddha aimed to find and inspire those few 'who have but little dust in their eyes', that the few might benefit the many.

Another term used to describe this phenomenon is 'Buddha field' (*buddha kshetra*). The term Buddha field is a bit like the term 'magnetic field'. An ordinary piece of iron has no particular power. It is inert. When it is magnetised, however, it acquires a field of influence. The Buddha aimed to magnetise us so that we would each acquire a field of influence – so that we would each become an influence for transformation in the world.

What is the difference between an ordinary piece of iron and a magnetised piece? One might think that something must have been added to the iron to make it into a magnet. If you weigh the iron before and after it is magnetised, however, it weighs exactly the same. Nothing has been added. The magnet has exactly the same raw material as the inert metal. There is a great difference between the two, however.

The difference is on the inside. The effect, however, is on the outside. A magnet is made for a purpose. It is the same with us. By changing something on the inside, we become a force in the world that previously we did not even dream of. If we had dreamt of it, then it might have come to pass, for what the Buddha really awakens in us is the dream – the dream that has slept too long.

Let us go back to the magnet analogy. How does the metal become a magnet? First, it comes under the influence of another magnet. This is something that, in one sense, is transmitted from one magnet to another. However, nothing actually passes from one piece of metal to the other one. Nothing is transmitted, but there is an effect. One person has an effect upon another person, just as one piece of metal has an effect upon another. This is a good analogy for Buddhist training. One person can awaken such dreams in another. The Buddhist word for such dreams is *samadhi*. A sama-dhi is a 'consummate vision' that, when lived, creates a Pure Land. In Buddhism, there are many samadhis. These samadhis have names like: the samadhi of universal equality, the samadhi in which myriad buddhas stand before one, the samadhi of seeing infinite Pure Lands, and so on.

Those who live such dreams are called enlightened. Enlightenment passes like magnetism. Just as magnetism can be spread from magnet to magnet, so enlightenment spreads in the world. When there are several magnets together, a new piece of metal coming close gets magnetised very quickly. The dream multiplies.

The Buddha envisaged something like this. He established an enlightened culture and he wanted to see it spread. Those who had been magnetised by the Buddha were called arhats – enlightened ones. Their job was to pass it on. The aim was to heal the world by banishing ignorance and prejudice. Buddhism thus has quite a lot to do with the power of the right kind of leadership – a leadership by example.

Buddhism is, thus, intrinsically utopian, and the idea of enlightenment has little meaning in any other context. We are, therefore, invited to dare to hope and to dream. There is, running through all this, a profound faith in human potential running in parallel with a clear insight into the sick state of the world. The Buddha saw that human beings – and especially groups of human beings – possess enormous resources for good. They do not need to be given anything extra, but they do need to be magnetised, or woken up. When this happens it is as if giants who have been sleeping for a long time are roused. They rub their eyes and look around. They feel the air on their faces. They rise to their feet.

The giants that have been asleep are the societies that can be. They are the Pure Lands that we can bring into being. We will not create them by following an architect's plan. They will, when roused, rise of their own accord. There is no master plan. There are no plans for dreams, but dreams become realities nonetheless.

BUDDHA'S METHODS

As well as having dreams, the Buddha had methods. Outside their proper context the Buddha's methods are meaningless and, in fact, just become diversions. The purpose of these practices is to make people better vessels for the important work to be done. If attachment to the training practice were to get in the way of the task for which one is being trained something would be wrong. Buddha often warned his followers about this kind of mistake.

A basic misunderstanding is that many people have come to see Buddhist training as no longer being about bringing compassion to the whole world, and have, instead, started to see it as a means to a private and personal salvation. Enlightenment of this private kind may yield some limited personal satisfaction, but there is really little that is noble or honourable about it and if this is all that remains, then the main potential of Buddhism is dead.

Renunciation Means a Change of Behaviour

Buddhism began with renunciation. The Buddha left the palace of luxury. He cut off his long hair. He cast off his fine garments. He sent back his horse. He crossed the river and became a new person. In his new life he had given up the confines of affluence and taken on the freedom of travelling light and pursuing the spiritual quest without encumbrance. Renunciation is the first step on a journey. Each person has his or her river. It may be a different river in each case, but unless we renounce our old patterns of behaviour, our mind will just keep going back to its old ways. Modern people often think that the mind can be trained without a change of behaviour, but this is a mistake. It cannot be done.

Without renunciation, the whole of what follows is meaningless. There are many contemporary attempts to use Buddhist methodology to achieve things that have nothing to do with renunciation. We are all aware that modern life involves a lot of stress. There are those who teach Buddhist meditation as a method of stress management so that one can carry on in the same stress-generating life without becoming ill. Although in some respects the spread of such depotentiated forms of Buddhist method have enabled Buddhism to become more widely accepted in the privileged world, they are not what the Buddha had in mind. The Buddha did not just rearrange his palace.

Renunciation means saying, 'I renounce . . .' and meaning it. What does an aspiring Buddhist renounce? She or he repudiates ignorance. Ignorance, the Buddha said, gives rise to greed, hate and delusion – the three poisons. When we look around us in the world, we can see that there is rather a lot to be renounced. There is not much room for complacency. Oppression, prejudice, exploitation, expropriation and torture are realities. There is an unjust and cruel game being played and even within that game there is a lot of cheating. In alliance with the caste system, there is a huge system of institutionalised greed running the world – enriching some and impoverishing others. It is a bubble that periodically bursts, and when it does there is even more suffering. The physical suffering, of course, falls disproportionately upon those who are already poor and dispossessed, but the spiritual suffering stays with the perpetrators. A Buddhist renounces the whole business, both inwardly and outwardly.

Currently, for instance, a large swathe of the world's best agricultural land is devoted to growing crops whose only function is the manufacture of alcohol or cigarettes. Much of this goes on in countries where the workers in the fields are themselves suffering from malnutrition. In Latin America and Africa vast areas have been turned over from food to tobacco production, for instance, in order for countries to cope with the world financial system that keeps them perpetually in debt and impoverished. A Buddhist dissociates him or herself from this. Similarly, much of our economic life is based upon the presupposition that people will buy and buy – that greed is a basic part of what it is to be human. A Buddhist dissociates from this. The greed system depends upon demand. If one lives a cleaner and more frugal life, one ceases to be a cause for many of the ills that beset the world.

This greed system is backed up by a hate system. The hate

system is war and oppression. We are told that 123 of the world's 185 sovereign states routinely practise torture.[1] In the period of so-called peace, after the Second World War up to the end of the twentieth century, there were actually over 125 wars on the planet causing well over 40 million deaths. Many other lethal conflicts never get so far as being dignified with the name of war. In the five years from 1990 to 1995, the United Nations High Commission for Refugees concerned itself with thirty-nine armed conflicts *within* states that were substantial enough to produce significant displacements of civilian populations.[2] A Buddhist cares about all this, renounces involvement in it, and seeks ways to restore peace and friendship to heal this world. A Buddhist does not say, 'There is nothing I can do'. There is always at least one person one can reach out to. There are alternative ways to live a life and each has implications.

The greed system and the hate system are essential props to the delusion system – the delusions of nation, class, caste, gender discrimination, racial prejudice, and so on: the delusion that the proper employment of one's energy is in furthering the selfish interests of one's own group. A Buddhist renounces this approach to life.

Renunciation does not mean falling into hate oneself. To renounce what is false is a kindness. Renunciation is compassionate action. Renunciation is not animosity. It is like freedom from prison, like putting down the burden, like finding the way home, like finding water in a desert – said the Buddha. Enlightenment begins, therefore, with simply saying 'No'. This 'No' constitutes the first step. It may take many forms, but all Buddhist practices are designed to change something.

It is, therefore, crucial to the Buddhist project that this first step not be lost sight of. Buddhism does demand that we change our life in practical ways. When Buddhism becomes simply a set of entertaining forms of exotic practice grafted on to a basically selfish, consumerist, high-caste lifestyle as simply one more diverting hobby, then all is lost.

Discipline Means Courage and Perseverance

The greed and hate machines both employ extensive and thorough systems of training. By a mix of stick and carrot they ensure that people learn all the skills and attitudes that are needed to keep them wedded to the purposes of their caste and its associated governments and corporations. If people are going to renounce these, then they need similarly comprehensive training – more comprehensive, in fact. Buddha's revolution is not the kind to be won by a rabble.

Consider an organisation like Greenpeace, for instance. Greenpeace equipped a ship – *The Rainbow Warrior* – to collect data on the activities of the whaling industry and to disrupt that industry. The crew of this ship would sail inflatable dinghies into the midst of shoals of whales where the whaler ships were firing their harpoons, getting between the ships and their targets. This was courageous, dangerous work. It was every bit as dangerous as the work that a soldier might do. Buddhists must train to be like rainbow warriors.

Buddhist training focuses passion. It leads to the acquisition of that inner stillness that makes decisive action possible. The trainee becomes the living embodiment of constructive attitudes and values: the attitudes and values of enlightened, compassionate living. If we find a passion for this way of life then the necessary discipline will naturally grow in us. Discipline is, therefore, a product of inspiration and vision. It is inherently, as well as etymologically, connected with discipleship. We learn this discipline as disciples of the Buddha, inspired by his example.

Since Shakyamuni Buddha died a long time ago, it is valuable if we have somebody alive today who also embodies these values. Generally, it takes one magnet to magnetise another. Such a person may become one's personal teacher. There will be more to say about the proper relations between teachers and disciples in a later chapter.

What areas of life do Buddhist disciplines focus upon? An

important one is self-control. Trainees acquire the capacity for calm, even under extreme provocation. They need a highly developed capacity for patience – for inner and outer stillness. They train themselves to eliminate killing, cruelty, violence, theft and wanton destruction from their own behaviour. If they cannot do this, then they will contribute to the very things that they are seeking to renounce and overthrow. They need to have their own passions – their sexual passions and their ego passions – under control or they will quickly be discredited or seduced back into forms of life that leave them powerless to help. They need to learn a great deal about right speech. Nothing is achieved in a human context without control over communication. The manner in which a message is given is as powerful as the message itself – often more so. There is a lot to learn about speech. Finally, they need to learn to eliminate all that is addictive and compulsive. Drunken revolutionaries are worse than the old regime. The temptations of stupor have to be resisted. A Buddhist trainee is, therefore, somebody who has a thorough training to follow.

Mind Training Sustains Compassionate Action
The mind drives one's life. Mind is what minds about things. A small life is one driven by a mind that minds about trivia. A great life is shaped by a mind that minds about things that matter. A change of behaviour requires a change of mind. If one decides to change one's behaviour in the ways outlined above it will be because, at some level, one minds. One minds that the world is sick. The mind that minds about the suffering of others is the awakened mind.

Let us go back to the magnet analogy once again. What the magnet and the inert metal have in common are molecules, each of which has a power-field of its own. In the inert metal these all point in different directions and so cancel each other out. This is like the unawakened mind – it is internally conflicted and cancels itself out. An ordinary person tends to exist in a condition of stalemate because nothing matters enough to him to pull himself together.

In the magnet, these same molecules are all aligned. They all point the same way. Lined up in this way, they all add to each other's effect. Together they are powerful. This is like the trained mind. In the trained mind, there is the possibility of concentrated and sustained purpose.

Now the word 'training' may not be perfect here. We could also say the inspired mind. The most important element in any kind of training is seeing why it matters. When people know why they are learning something, they learn fast. This is why the most important element in Buddhism is the sense of vision. To mix metaphors: it is by holding to the dream that the mind is magnetised.

A controlled mind has the ability to be steadfast and practise forbearance. It enables one to remain positive and compassionate even towards one's opponents. Usually a revolution aims simply to destroy the 'bad people'. Buddhism is not that kind of revolution. Buddhism does not see any bad people. It only sees misguided, ignorant people. It sees that if that ignorance can be overcome, the world will change. It does not, therefore, aim to destroy its opponents, but rather to convert them and counter their influence with a better one. Even when dealing with people who are imprisoning or torturing us, Buddhists aim to convert them and counter their influence by living better lives. This conversion, however, does not mean fitting people into a mould. It means touching their heart. Whenever a person came to the Buddha he tried to find a way that suited that particular person. He sought to turn on that particular person's capacity for compassion. It is compassion power that creates better worlds. Those who understand this can give themselves to it immediately. Others will follow.

Understanding Reveals the World to Be Real
Because the awakened mind is not full of inner conflict, attention

can shift to the outside. It becomes possible to be objective. Buddhism is not really about subjective concerns, altered states of consciousness and so on. It is concerned with going beyond them to reach the real world. Dreams do not exist for their own sake, but in order to be lived. The Buddha's own training programme, as he taught it to his followers, commonly began with an examination of material reality. This is the world in which real people exist.

It is here in this world that we can be enlightened – here or nowhere. It is here in this world that our lives can be meaningful. If there are other worlds to come, the Buddha suggests that they will require a similar outlook and so learning it now will stand us in good stead there too. If there are no other worlds, then we must do what we can with this one. Either way, this is the time when we must do something, or we will simply have done nothing. Such was the Buddha's attitude. Buddhist wisdom, therefore, has a strong concern with the here and now.

It is not limited to the here and now, however. Buddhism understands the world in terms of causation. One thing leads to another. The condition of things today is a consequence of things past and what is done today creates the world of tomorrow. Actions are consequential and great transformations are, therefore, possible. This is a message of hope, for Buddhism is concerned with the future.

In the future there is the possibility of whatever we have the capacity, the wit and the concern to create. The Buddha told his stories to create myths of Pure Lands so that they could be created. He called people to dedicate themselves to this purpose: to make great vows and to fulfil them through devoting their energy to the service of all sentient beings.

Compassionate Action
Only action actually has effect. In Buddhism, we have the word *karma*. There are two different ideas of karma in circulation. One is a kind of fatalism. According to this idea, if something

23

goes wrong in your life – say you develop a crippling disease – people will say that it must be because you did something bad in a previous life. Perhaps in your last life you were a torturer and so now you are reaping the consequence. This sort of idea was widespread in India in the Buddha's time and it still is to this day. It lies behind the Indian caste system, for instance. One's social position in this life is a function of actions committed in past existences. This is not the version of karma that the Buddha taught.

The Buddha's interpretation of karma rejected the idea of fixed destinies. To him, karma is the fact that action makes a difference to the future. His concern is compassionate action. Compassion demands of us that we step out of our old identity, however comfortable, and make ourselves available for a greater work. It also asks us to give up a measure of our individuality and serve the wider good through cooperation with others.

Buddha's first teaching was called the Four Noble Truths.[3] The first of these asserts that it is noble to accept the afflictions in this world as real. The second is that it is noble to accept that associated with these afflictions are energy and a motivating power that can be turned to good or ill. The third is that it is noble to harness that energy. The fourth is the noble life that results from so doing: a life led by vision. From those visions come right intentions – intentions to renounce what is sick in the world without falling into malice oneself. From such intentions, or 'vows', there comes the ability to speak and act in constructive ways that cultivate improved ways of life. These are ways of life that contribute to the great work that is needed, work that requires effort and mindful care. Such a life contributes to the realisation of the comprehensive vision of universal peace and goodwill.

Compassion power is, therefore, the highest value in Buddhism. Compassion means concern about the afflictions suffered by others. Compassion needs wisdom in order to be effective. Compassion is highest, however. Wisdom is the servant of compassion.

Compassion tells us what needs to be done and wisdom tells us how to do it. Buddhism is not about disappearing into a magical wisdom world. It is surely about doing something real.

The most compassionate act is the act of renunciation itself. Renounce your colour. Renounce the 'rat race'. Most of the cruelty and exploitation in the world requires the consent of many people. The world is highly interactive. Often the kindest word is 'No'. Renunciation also makes a person free. Armchair Buddhists achieve little. There are many people who have learnt some discipline, who have practised mind-training for many years, who have acquired wisdom and feel much compassion, but because they have not set themselves free, in a straightforward, practical sense, little comes of it. They are like a fully equipped ship that is provisioned and cargoed and has a fine crew that sits in the harbour until it rots because nobody thought to pull up the anchor.

TIME FOR A NEW BUDDHISM

There is, thus, already a significant danger of stagnation in contemporary Buddhism. Too many Buddhists see the task as being like that of making the perfect ship in the simile just given, without any idea of ever taking that ship out on to the high seas. They do not know what the ship is for. Their Buddhism is a pursuit of bliss for their own mind only.

Buddhism has undergone a revival in modern times – in the East as much as in the West. Why has this happened? Because people see a need for a new path to salvation after death? Surely not. Because we need another orderly, conventional, nice, Sunday religion? No. Because we want an exotic pastime pursuing mystic experiences? Perhaps for some this is the answer, but it will not do. No, the real reason is because a wide range of people have begun to suspect and hope that in Buddhism lie things of value for this world: possibilities that restore our faith in life; possibilities of culture without war and intolerance; possibilities of compassion and cooperation in social organisation; possibilities of real community that is not rooted in oppression: possibilities of all the things that people know instinctively are right for this world, but hardly dare risk believing in for fear of yet another disappointment.

Buddhism has revived on the strength of this transfusion of hope, and become established in some quarters of modern life. It is no longer the frail flower that it was even thirty years ago. There is, however, a need for a correction of course, if this growing phenomenon is to realise a few of the hopes that have been invested in it. This book, therefore, is not just a programme, it is also a critique.

There is a serious danger that white Buddhism will degenerate – it already has in some quarters – into a narrow, sectarian, small-minded and irrelevant pursuit of personal euphoria. This danger is fed by many factors: among them, the tendency for different traditions to spend more time defending their own patch than advancing the overall cause; the authoritarian conservatism of many of these traditions; the common obsession with self-salvation in another lifetime and the doctrines and practices that underpin it; the tendency to model Buddhism upon institutionalised Christianity and to sacrifice the distinctiveness of the Buddhist message; the fascination of the exotic and esoteric; the watering-down of Buddhist ethics in the pursuit of popularity and the consequent weakening of renunciation and service to the community; the quest for respectability that inevitably involves subscription to establishment values alien to the main Buddhist purpose; and many related phenomena. These are all real dangers that we should be careful to avoid.

The Buddhist revival has many positive features. The tolerance, kindness and cooperation that are exhibited by many New Buddhists give one hope. The lightness and freedom of spirit that are characteristic of many, likewise; the dedication of some who have given their whole life to this gentle radicalism. There is much faith, sincerity and genuine enlightenment here. The current growth of 'engaged Buddhism' is also a sign that there is continuing evolution going on within the Buddhist movement. Much innovation is happening, relating Buddhism to psychology, social action and other constructive aspects of Western culture. These developments should not be viewed uncritically, but they are alive, important and promising.

This book aims to inject some critical spirit into the contemporary scene in order that Buddhism not die of complacency and rot in the harbour. The idea of Buddhist training is a potent force and its realisation is creating new possibilities. It would be a great shame if all these newly training Buddhists never set sail or just settle into a conservative complacency while there is an afflicted world waiting for their help.

· 3 ·

A Critical History of Early Buddhism

Siddhartha Gautama, founder of Buddhism, lived approximately 400–500 years before Jesus of Nazareth. Like the latter, he was a sage who was also a saviour, a leader with a view to universal emancipation rooted in the principle of unconditional compassion. Unlike Jesus, however, Buddha did not base this prospect in theistic beliefs, but in the capacity of ordinary mortals to become enlightened.

On the one hand, we seem to know a great deal more about the Buddha than we do about the Christ. The records of his life and teaching are much more extensive. This is in part due to the fact that he taught for a much longer period. Jesus had a ministry of only four years, whereas the Buddha's stretched over as many decades.

Nonetheless, there remains a fair degree of mystery. The balance of probabilities lies heavily in favour of the Buddha having existed and having taught a teaching that was then carried on and spread by those of his disciples who outlived him. Those disciples then passed the teaching, or dharma, as they called it, on to others, and did so so successfully that by the time 200 years had passed, the monarch Ashoka saw fit to make Buddhism the established religion of his new empire. This development is comparable with Constantine's adoption of Christianity, though it took Christianity considerably longer to reach this point.

To know for sure what Siddhartha Gautama's original programme must have been is now impossible. What we make of it depends upon what assumptions we make. The assumptions I am making in this book include the following. Buddha made an impact beyond his own expectations because he was willing to live out the implications of what he had understood. The full revolutionary force of what he represented came from the fact that he lived it – he did not just talk about it. Every step that he took across India was a demonstration that even someone from one of the more privileged castes can step out from the gilded cage and become fully human – living a life transparently based on compassion and not on calculation.

His teaching had revolutionary implications that were, in some ways, the more powerful for not having a militaristic revolutionary intent. Whatever the consequences might turn out to be, his conscience would not allow him to live the life prescribed for him by the social dispensation of his day – caste, wealth, political power, prejudice, superstition, oppression and so on. He acknowledged that some afflictions are the inevitable lot of everyone, but he clearly saw that there was a difference between a noble and an ignoble response to that reality. He offered something different from both the theistic and the materialistic philosophies around him, all of which he saw to be deeply implicated in a tacit conspiracy to maintain power and oppression. This evident willingness to walk his talk was what convinced many of his contemporaries to follow him and sacrifice a great deal for what then became a great cause. What he offered, and what he called people to, has undergone change and distortion over the years and the nature of some of these distortions and the motives for them are apparent. If we make allowance for them, we can probably get somewhere nearer to the original nature of the inspiration that the Buddha offered.

What the Buddha was calling for was a revolution in human

consciousness that would have this-worldly effect both immediately and in time to come. The Buddha repeatedly asserted that his only concern was the afflictions of sentient beings. It does not appear that the Buddha had strong views about metaphysics. He was willing to accommodate the metaphysical preferences of those who came to him, so long as they did not stand in the way of his aims. He was not averse to using them, even. He could show you how his programme would lead you closer to *Brahma* if that really was what interested you, or how it related to previous lives if that was your thing, but none of that was really significant to him, as is apparent from some of his discourses, like the one he delivered to the Kalama people, in which he says that his dharma will stand you in good stead if there is an afterlife and it will also stand you in good stead if there is none.

He simply lived an uncompromised life and he invited others to do likewise. He did not do this with a view to personal reward, neither social reward, financial reward, metaphysical reward, nor anything of the kind beyond the satisfaction of 'knowing that one had done what was to be done'. When people asked him to say what he believed would happen to him after death, he said it was not a subject worth discussing. People have made great mysteries of this, but the simplest explanation is that it was not what he was concerned about. What he was concerned about, as he never tired of saying, was the fact that people suffer afflictions and that if you live your life the way most people do, then you add to those afflictions for everybody. He pointed out to people that they could do differently. He did not call them to do differently in order that they might reap a special reward in heaven, or wherever. He called on them to do differently because of the consequences that one can see for oneself.

Many followed him and their sincerity created the momentum that still carries the Buddhist movement forward twenty-five centuries later. There were of course also pressures upon the movement that tended to undermine its integrity and purposefulness, and it will be argued here that it fell too far under these influences.

Nonetheless, the original message of Buddha is worth digging out, for its relevance has never been greater than it is today. There were forces acting upon the Buddhist community both from without and within. Here we will concern ourselves primarily with those acting from within. In the next chapter we will include a look at how the movement may have accommodated some of the external pressures and seductions. Throughout this examination, however, our purpose is not simply that of historical research, but rather to clarify a programme of enlightened social engagement that offers new hope for the contemporary world.

EARLY HISTORY

There were a number of crucial change points in the early history of Buddhism. One of these occurred just after the Buddha died. A second was marked by the Second Great Council a hundred years later (*c.*350 BCE). Another was when Emperor Ashoka (*c.*250 BCE) adopted Buddhism.

Before he died, the Buddha was asked to appoint a successor. He refused to do so. The Buddha clearly was a leader, but his supremacy appears to have been simply that of being the most respected. He was probably generally referred to as 'the teacher'. He would give instructions, but the power he had to enforce these depended upon the collective support of his followers. There were occasions when the community was in uproar over some dispute when the Buddha simply got up and left. He was, himself, always a *bhikshu*, a sharer, just like all the rest. He would go on alms-round like any other wandering mendicant. If people wanted to hear his teaching, he stayed. If they did not, he moved on.

The fact that the Buddha refused either to appoint a successor or even to create any procedural machinery to select one is clearly significant. We should not conclude from this that he had completely egalitarian views, nor that he was individualistic.

It seems more reasonable to assume that he believed that teachers and leaders would naturally evolve and that those who had been part of the movement for longer would offer guidance to newcomers, but that this should proceed and evolve in a flexible, open fashion. He would probably have been surprised to see what did in fact happen. As soon as the Buddha had died, his disciple Kashyapa took up the reins of leading the new movement and made it his main business to arrange the compilation of everything that the Buddha had taught, including the codification of every rule that anybody could ever remember him having made. Before Kashyapa died, he 'transmitted the dharma to Ananda' and thus a kind of apostolic succession was put in place.

At about the same time as the Buddha had refused to appoint any 'dharma heir', he also said that the 'lesser rules' could be abandoned or changed, but did not specify which rules were to be considered lesser. He relied upon his followers having some intelligence. The 'rules', after all, had been changed numerous times during his own lifetime as new situations emerged and had to be responded to. What actually happened after he died was that all the rules were retained. Indeed, the rules that were adopted were probably more comprehensive than had, in effect, operated in the Buddha's lifetime, and it looks, therefore, as though the dispensation in the Buddhist community immediately after his demise was more authoritarian, centralised and rule-bound than he had intended. Furthermore, the rules were now set for ever. In the Buddha's own time, it seems, rules were made and remade to suit the circumstances. In the early days of his ministry there seem to have been few rules at all.

What has come to be called the First Great Council, therefore – a meeting at Rajagaha of the 500 arhats three months after the Buddha's death – established a system that introduced lineage and a large quantity of rules as central organisational features of the Buddhist community. This was not quite a reversal, but it was a quantum leap away from what the Buddha taught. While this development did probably enable Kashyapa to get a grip on the immediate situation and ensure that the fledgling Buddhist movement did not fall apart with the death of its founder, the resulting loss of flexibility was, ironically, to be one of the main causes for later splits, dissension and fragmentation.

A second moment of change appears to have come at the Second Great Council 100 years later at Vesali, though the Council itself probably only put the official stamp upon what was already an irredeemable split. This split occurred over precisely this issue of whether the rules of the Buddhist order could be changed to suit circumstances. The conservative group won the day officially, but failed to carry the support of the majority. This was a major mistake. There can be little doubt that, had the Buddha himself been present, he would have been willing to change the rules, because he often did so in his lifetime. The problem was that by now there was no consensus and the conservative group that held official power feared what would happen once even the slightest flexibility was allowed to creep in. The movement split into the Party of the Elders and the Majority Group. Soon both these groups experienced further splits. The movement became fragmented. This development, however, ensured that Buddhism never, thereafter, had a pope and this has proved a blessing.

Buddhism must have continued to grow apace and these splits may even have aided this process by setting up rivalries between different schools and allowing a diversity that could accommodate more different kinds of people. One sees something similar happening in the West at the moment, where the number of different Buddhist groups has reached an unprecedented level of diversity.

By the time of Emperor Ashoka, another 100 years on, the movement was widespread. The new king's conquests had just made him the first emperor of the whole of northern and parts of southern India. He decided to adopt Buddhism. He became the first Buddhist monarch in history and this was, therefore, the first time that Buddhism had been an established religion. Ashoka declared himself protector of all the other religions too, but he favoured Buddhism. It is, in fact, a principle of Buddhism to protect other faiths.

This development furthered two diametrically opposite processes. The first was that of creating an orthodoxy. Ashoka favoured a certain kind of Buddhism. Not surprisingly, this was one advanced by one subgroup of the conservative tendency. From the orthodox established Buddhism favoured – and to some extent created – by the requirements of the Ashokan government, eventually came the *Theravada* School of Buddhism. An Ashokan mission was sent to establish this form of Buddhism in Sri Lanka and there it remains to this day. Sri Lanka became a bastion of this form of the dharma even after Buddhism had disappeared from India itself. Sri Lanka also became the launching pad for missions to other parts of Asia. Burmese, Thai and Cambodian Theravada Buddhism all derive substantially from Sri Lanka.

It is generally thought that the Theravada texts, written in the Pali language, are some of, if not the, earliest Buddhist written materials. Most scholars seem to agree that nothing was written down by Buddhists before about 100 BCE – that is, about 150 years after Ashoka. This is because there is a Theravada tradition to this effect. In passing, I can say that this seems highly improbable to me. Writing certainly existed in the time of Ashoka himself, since the first written references to Buddhism in history are on the pillars that he erected all over his realm to inform the population of his glory and his intentions for them, his subjects. Now clearly somebody was expected to read these inscriptions. If Buddhism, a movement that has always had the highest regard for education, did not have people who were writing at that time, it would be astonishing. And if they did write, but did not write about Buddhism, this would also stretch credulity too far. I think that Buddhist materials must have been written down much earlier than is generally acknowledged. If so, why is there an orthodox tradition that denies it? Presumably because those who wrote down the texts c.100 BCE wanted these to be seen as the originals. This almost certainly means that at least some of the materials that predated them were ones of which they disapproved. Unfortunately, we do not have those materials.

If our purpose is to try to ascertain the nature of Buddha's Buddhism – a question that has always fascinated me – then we now have some contributions to a formula. If you take the picture of Buddhism that emerges from the Theravada texts and you subtract from it those features that might have suited an authoritarian monarchy, further subtract what might have suited a rather authoritarian conservative priesthood, and add back something of the Buddha's original spirit – a spirit that was at once strongly ethical and organisationally flexible – you might be beginning to get somewhere near the original.

We do have, however, some further clues to consider. A substantially different tradition of Buddhism has come down to us through texts in Sanskrit, and is called the *Mahayana*. The Sanskrit texts were not recognised by the Theravada and so probably represent a range of varieties of Buddhism that were not approved by the Ashokan orthodoxy. There is really no compelling evidence that the earliest Sanskrit texts are any later than the earliest Pali ones and many of the Sanskrit texts, that are undoubtedly later in the form in which we now have them may still have earlier elements embedded in them. There clearly are layers in these texts. The *Lotus Sutra*, for instance, has prose and verse sections that are clearly of different date. The earlier verse sections are incomplete.

The history of Buddhism has been a history of witness to an alternative possibility for humankind. The Buddha's main teachings are a principled protest against much of the orthodoxy of his own time. Commonly the Buddha is thought of as meek and mild, but this impression is not borne out by reading the early texts. Many of the Buddha's discourses are full of scorn poured upon the ideas he disapproves. Invective is certainly not foreign to him. The Buddha was strident in his criticism of the religious, social and personal mores of his day, 2,000 years before Luther.

The Buddha saw virtue and wisdom as the only sound bases for authority, and compassion as the only worthy power in society. Virtue, truth and compassion were to be the way to a new world. He rejected all ideas of lineage, and most particularly the caste system and its associated metaphysics of a reincarnating soul and an ultimate divinity. The idea of a divinity is always useful if you want to maintain an unfair social system because you can say things are like this because God wants them that way. Since this is the way they are it must be the way he wanted it to be since he is all powerful, and so on. Buddha rejected all such oppressive ideas and clearly thought that people had the power to change their society. Sri Lankan Theravada has, nonetheless, accepted the caste system and given a distinctly metaphysical ring to the Buddha's own key concepts of enlightenment and *nirvana*.

The fundamental difference between the Theravada and the Mahayana interpretations of Buddhism lies in the area of what Mahayanists call the '*bodhisattva* ideal'. The Mahayana critique of Theravada is that it is essentially selfish. They would say that Theravada had become a Buddhism of individual salvation that had lost sight of the possibility of the salvation of all beings. It is this goal of universal salvation that probably became atrophied during the Ashokan period. After all, there is no need for any further revolution once you have got a Buddhist dictator on the throne, is there?

None of this, of course, means that actual Theravada Buddhists today are necessarily any less altruistic than actual Mahayana Buddhists today. It is simply that the nature of these early disagreements gives us some clues to what the pre-Ashokan Buddhist movement was like. From this, we may draw some inspiration ourselves. Whether our interpretation of history is precisely right or not will be less important than whether we can establish virtue, truth and compassion as the dominant powers in our own time. History can, however, provide the mythology that animates the future.

A GOLDEN AGE TO COME

The speed with which the movement grew suggests that it had something special to offer, which must have had direct relevance to life here in this world. My impression is that original Buddhism offered a utopian vision – the prospect of a new golden age – and my contention is that this is what it can and should offer today.

The clearest vestiges of the vision of a golden age are to be found in a genre of symbolic imagery generally associated with one branch of the Mahayana form of Buddhism. This brings us to a second effect of Ashoka's rule. While an orthodoxy was established, there were plenty of people who did not go along with it. The split within Buddhist ranks became much sharper and those who were not in favour had much more incentive to refine and develop their ideas. Quite a number had to relocate to countries outside the reach of Ashokan power.

This was, in all probability, the real beginning of the Mahayana as a distinct movement, growing out of the Majority Group (*mahasanghika*) that had formed after the Second Council. This group was probably particularly alienated by the fact that the Party of the Elders now enjoyed royal favour. They not only kept alive an alternative vision, they developed it. In the process they almost certainly also incorporated further non-Buddhist elements. The problem is to distinguish which are which.

There has been some tendency among scholars to assume that the elements that were most like the other schools of Indian philosophy were most authentic and those that were most different were least so. This seems to me to be completely the opposite of what is likely. There would have been constant pressure to assimilate features that were widespread in India, like the doctrine of reincarnation or ideas of a self or of divinities. Elements of all these ideas were incorporated. One feature of

Buddhist teaching that does seem more distinctive, however, is the image of a better world that runs directly against the conservatism of the caste system.

This is the imagery of Pure Lands, Buddha fields, or sweet realms. The Sanskrit name is Sukhavati (*sukha* = sweet, happy; *vati* = realm). The Pure Land Schools of Buddhism are still some of the largest in the world. They flourish in the Sino-Japanese cultural sphere primarily, and there is a tendency for scholars, especially Western scholars, to regard them as most remote from the original teachings of Siddhartha Gautama. This may, however, be a mistake, occasioned by over concentration upon one or two features – like the debate about self-power and other-power that has been a major feature of Far Eastern Buddhist controversy – and Western prejudice that has tended to favour the so-called self-power schools, like Zen, and to not see the relevance of the Pure Land movement. Pure Land imagery is, however, widespread and potent. It is not only found throughout most branches of Chinese Buddhism and on into Japan, Korea and Vietnam. It is also found in all the Tibetan Schools too, where Pure Lands are called *Dewarchen*.

Sometimes, the prospect of entry into a Pure Land has been reallocated to the time after death. Those who have sufficient faith may enter Sukhavati when they die. This should not be confused with the Christian idea of heaven, however. Buddhist Pure Lands, even when they have been allocated to a future life, are not located in a metaphysical dimension, nor in the sky. They are earthly realms – far away to the West, according to legend. They are other countries.

If Sukhavati was originally a this-worldly goal rather than an other-worldly consolation, it is natural that it would be thought – in a society that believed in rebirth – that those who had faith in it, but died before it was realised, might be reborn there at a future time; or be reborn immediately into another land where the revolution had been already achieved. It was also not unnatural to assume that the goal might already have been realised in some far away country. In any case, in whatever location such ideal lands are imagined, they inevitably provide models for what should be here.

The Pure Land scriptures purport to have been spoken by the Buddha himself. Although the form of the texts that we currently have is of later origin, there is no particular reason to doubt that this strand of Buddhist thought goes back to the Buddha himself in one form or another. Indeed, there is an interesting twist to this possibility to be found in the Pali texts preserved by the Theravadans, as we shall see shortly.

In the Pure Land literature, the Buddha tells a story of long, long ago when there was a bodhisattva called Dharmakara – 'maker of dharma'. 'Bodhisattva', in this context, means somebody destined to become a buddha. This Dharmakara made great vows to save all beings and kept these vows for aeons. At the end of an incalculable time, Dharmakara became a buddha called Amitayus, a name that means 'measureless life'. This name became merged with another, Amitabha, which means 'measureless light'. In the Far East today, Amitabha and Amitayus have become merged into a single figure called Amida. In the story, Dharmakara goes to see the buddha of his day who is called Lokeshvararaja (= royal creator of worlds). Lokeshvararaja gives him a vision of all the different Buddha worlds that exist and insight into the conditions that are needed to bring them into being. Dharmakara then asks what he should do. Lokeshvararaja says that he must already know. Dharmakara then pours out a long series of great vows in which he promises to make a Pure Land himself. By fulfilling these vows, many Buddhists believe, Amida did indeed succeed in creating a Pure Land which welcomed all beings irrespective of their past achievements, and thereby provided them with the speedy means to attain complete enlightenment. This, therefore, has all the makings of a mythology of creating heaven on earth.

The manner in which the Buddha tells such stories leaves one with the impression that they are lightly veiled allegories about his own experience and intentions. The maker of dharma, after all, was the Buddha himself. Dharmakara was a prince who left his kingdom in order to seek truth and an answer to the world's affliction. It does not take a lot of imagination to see that the Buddha is referring to himself.

The whole Buddhist mythos is actually shot through with this imagery. Before the Buddha was born there were prophecies that he would either become a great sage or a 'wheel-turning king'. The term 'wheel-turning king' indicates the kind of monarch who ushers in a golden age of peace and prosperity. The Buddha calls his own first declaration of his dharma, the 'Setting in Motion of the Wheel'. There really can be few other possible interpretations of this choice of designation than that the Buddha intended to usher in just such a golden age. The difference was, however, that he intended to do it by a transformation of popular consciousness, not by military imposition. Thus Dimitri Bakroushin writes: 'both Christianity and Buddhism had their social revolutionary aspect. The Kingdom of Heaven was to be realised in the world as well as in the individual. It is no accident that the first sermon of the Buddha was called the Dhamma-Cakka-ppavattana Sutta, or "Turning the Wheel of Truth Sermon." Freely translated, the title can be read "Revolutionary Doctrine".'[1]

At the other end of his life, when the Buddha is near to death, he is on a journey and is taken ill at the little town of Kusinagara. Ananda implores him not to die at such an inconspicuous spot. This is recounted in the Pali text called the *Mahasudassana Sutta*.[2] The Buddha rebukes Ananda for calling Kusinagara a miserable little town and tells him a story. This is the story of how, long, long ago, Kusinagara had been the capital city of a great wheel-turning monarch called Sudassana. The Buddha tells at length the details of the realm of this king. These details correspond to a striking degree with the details given in the Pure Land text's formalised descriptions of Sukhavati. The jewelled trees, ponds and nets, the self-playing musical instruments, the parapets and banisters are all the same. Although there are some additional features in the *Mahasudassana* story that are not in the Pure Land one and vice versa, there can be no doubt that either one of these stories derives from the other or both derive from a common source or this was a story that the Buddha told often with slight variations to suit local circumstances. At the end of the Sudassana story the Buddha declares that Sudassana was he himself in a previous life.

So we have the Buddha's birth, first teaching and death all associated with the notion of the wheel turner and hence – and in the case of his death, explicitly – with the establishment of a heaven on earth. It seems difficult to deny that this was the Buddha's objective. He did not necessarily think that it could be achieved in one lifetime, but the goal of achieving it must have seemed to him to be the only noble goal one could have in life.

The fact that this material about the perfect land to be created by the wheel turner is to be found all over the Buddhist world and the fact that the wheel-turning imagery is found throughout the Buddhist literature of all schools give strong evidence that this element was part of original Buddhism. That the schools that developed from Ashokan times onward had reason to play down the this-worldly revolutionary implications perhaps also gives us a hint that such implications were a lot stronger in the early days.

What the Buddha offered was an alternative to the wheel-turning king. This alternative was the wheel-turning sage. The notion of wheel turning as indicating revolution is fairly clear. This is a colloquial motif in many languages, including English. The dream of a golden age is ubiquitous. What the Buddha offered was a different method.

People have always hoped that a golden age could be created for them. They, therefore, pin their hopes on politicians. When an old order has been overthrown and a new politician has come to power by public will, there is almost invariably a 'honeymoon period' during which the populace at large feel elated and full of hope. This is a frequently recurring manifestation of this common desire that is seldom far below the surface of public life. Kings and even tyrants will be supported because initially people have hope. Napoleon, for instance, won several referenda by huge majorities immediately after his accession to power. Invariably the glitter soon wears off and the exigencies of power ensure that even the most well-meaning politician soon finds him or herself hostage to forces of self-interest, greed and old feuds. The path to heaven via the wielding of political power is fundamentally flawed. The Buddha, therefore, offered an example of the only real alternative. This is for people to have the courage of their deeper conviction and create Pure Lands by their own pure actions of virtue, truth and compassion.

THE SANGHA REPUBLIC

There is some evidence that the Buddhists regarded kings as, in certain circumstances, the least of a number of evils, but the Buddhist vision is really nonmonarchical. In the Buddha's time there were both monarchies and republics. The republics were not of the universal suffrage type that we see in the modern world. Constitutions varied. In tribal societies it is common for there to be a kind of parliament in which the leading members of each family or clan gather to consider issues together. The people who met were to consider the best interests of the whole tribe and to offer enlightened leadership – good counsel should prevail. For this to work, a value system has to prevail in which people feel some solidarity together and responsibility one for another. The problem was, however, that the growth of individualism was making these republics lose their cohesion. The rulers were no longer consistently motivated by honour. They were no longer noble, or even good. They were becoming self-seeking. In a self-seeking world, there is a natural tendency for competition eventually to yield all power to one winner and for monarchical or tyrannical government to ensue. It was not long after the time of the Buddha before all the significant republics had fallen under the sway of adjacent monarchies, and this process was in motion during the Buddha's own time. Although born in a semi-republic, he spent most of his life in the monarchical states of Kossala and Magadha.

We can see a background to the Buddha's political thought in these developments. In principle, the republic should have been a better form of government. In practice it had become weak through internal dissension due to the rise of individualistic principles. The word for a republic, in the Buddha's day, was *sangha*. The same word was used for the meetings where decisions were made in these republics – their parliament. The people would meet in sangha in order to make their decisions. The peoples who were governed in this way were referred to as the sanghas, as distinct from the monarchies.

The Buddha, therefore, established a new kind of sangha that could lead a new kind of society. This sangha was a meeting of persons who were not individualistic and not corrupt. It was to be a sangha of all those who were selflessly devoted to the common good. This was the vision that the Buddha was able to offer that had contemporary relevance, that inspired the highest aspirations of all who heard it, and that offered a wheel-turning prospect sufficiently compelling to induce a large number of educated young people to give up promising careers and the luxury of home life as well as to inspire an enthusiastic following from less well-off sections of society, too.

The genius of the Buddha's programme is that it is a revolution that does not involve a call to arms. It simply establishes a different kind of leadership and trusts to the power that this can have to inspire change. This revolution does not come out of the barrel of a gun, but rather the willingness of a proportion of people, suitably inspired, to put ideals into practice. The key elements are to inspire some people to follow the ideal and then to provide them with the necessary training to be worthy to participate in – and indeed to lead – such a project.

The Buddha was able to declare his republic within the interstices of the existing political dispensation. The new sangha had to adopt tactics of accommodation to the political powers of the time, but this could be done without sacrificing their core principles or objectives provided those who led it were immune to corruption and, if necessary, willing to suffer. To suffer is not ignoble, said the Buddha. What is ignoble is for a person who suffers to allow that circumstance to corrupt him or her. One who can contain his suffering and not be driven by it into losing his nobility becomes an example to the world and a true leader in the new community. They did not seek suffering, but they accepted reality. The Buddha could meet kings and advise them how to be more virtuous and he could easily convince them that his unarmed followers were good citizens who offered no overt threat to the realm, while still pursuing a programme that was ultimately more subversive than any attempted before or since. It was a humanitarian revolution.

Schism in the Buddhist Revolution

ENTERING THE STREAM OF ENLIGHTENMENT

The attainment of the kind of enlightenment taught by Shakyamuni Buddha was basically a two-step process. People who had taken the first step were called *sotapanna*. A *sota* is a stream or torrent, like the one the Buddha himself had had to cross. *Panna* means to go down into it. A sotapanna is, therefore, a stream enterer. People who had taken the second step were arhats. The word arhat comes from the Indian word for 'worthy'[1]. Arhats are those who are fully worthy of the term enlightened – they are worth listening to. A sotapanna has stepped down into the river. An arhat has emerged upon the other bank. Arhats have crossed the river. They have made the act of renunciation, leaving the caste system behind and dedicating themselves to the service of others. They are just as enlightened as the Buddha. The only distinction between the Buddha and his arhats is that the Buddha became enlightened without the assistance or direction of somebody who was already enlightened. He had nobody to help him across. The Buddha thus used the story of his own crossing of the river as a basic motif for structuring people's ideas about the way to enter an enlightened life.

In the Sanskrit texts, most of which were written a bit later in history, the term buddha comes to take on further meanings and Buddhahood becomes a more remote goal unlikely to be reached in this lifetime. In Theravada Buddhism, too, however, the goal of arhatship also, over the period of history, has come to be conceived as more remote than it was in the Buddha's own day. I will make some suggestions here about how this process of distancing enlightenment has come about. In order to understand this process we need also to understand the parts played in the original Buddhist community by those who were already enlightened and those who were stream enterers.

It will also be valuable to our overall purpose to look at their relevance to Buddhism in the contemporary world. In works on contemporary Buddhism, the terms stream enterer and arhat tend only to be used for people who died a long time ago. Arhat is often thought to refer to a state that is beyond real human accomplishment – though this was obviously not the Buddha's idea of it. The Mahayana term bodhisattva, which we will also examine below, is more widely used and one does hear actual people described as bodhisattvas, so this term has a somewhat different currency. It will be a necessary task in the evolution of the theory of the New Buddhism to reconcile the usage of these terms within a single set of ideas that is not heavily biased against either the Theravada or the Mahayana interpretations. What follows is not perfect in this respect, but it is a possible and useful schema.

In the simplest terms, a stream enterer, or sotapanna, is somebody who has faith and commitment and is beginning to make progress, whereas an arhat is somebody who has knowledge, vision and experience and is in a position to inspire others. The person who has faith is, however, in Buddhism, said to be 'irreversible'. They will not fall back completely into worldly ways (or, alternatively, they will not do so more than seven times, depending upon how you read it). There have been disputes in Buddhist history about whether this is always so or not. The doctrinal point need not concern us too much. People who have faith are on the way; those who know have arrived. They are the sotapanna and the arhat.

This distinction seems to recognise the fact that people differ in their response to the Buddha's message. Among those who accept it, there are some people who, as soon as they hear it, think, 'That's for me', and they immediately divest themselves of all the things in their life that might get in the way, and throw themselves into the work of enlightening the world: helping others to overcome affliction. There are others, however, who find it difficult to be so wholehearted. They are inspired, but not enough to give up their attachments immediately. They are like somebody who has entered the river, but is still hanging on to the nearside bank. They have gone beyond the position of the ordinary person who does not enter the river at all, but they are still impeded by attachments and old habits.

Then there is the bodhisattva. A bodhisattva is somebody who is approaching enlightenment – is nearly across the river. One could say that the bodhisattva is on the way to becoming an arhat. Mahayanists prefer to say the bodhisattva is on the way to becoming a buddha, but, again, to quibble over terms would be unnecessarily hair-splitting.

Then we should also consider the Pali term *sekha*. A sekha is somebody who is living the homeless life and training in Buddhism, but is not yet enlightened. The term *asekha* (a-sekha), meaning one who has completed their training, is synonymous with the word arhat. We thus have four key terms: sotapanna, sekha, bodhisattva and arhat. These form a sequence. This sequence begins with the sotapanna – the person who has found faith – and ends with the arhat, the person who has found knowledge. In between are the bodhisattva and the sekha in no particular order. The sekha lives the homeless life. The bodhisattva, originally, probably did not.

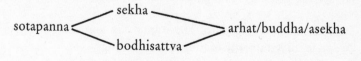

sotapanna ⟨ sekha — arhat/buddha/asekha
           bodhisattva

ENTERING THE RIVER

Let us first consider what was meant by entering the stream. The step of becoming a stream enterer involves courage. It contains elements of both faith and defiance. Early Buddhism does not use the idea of 'going with the flow'. 'Standing against the stream' is a much more characteristic metaphor. The river represents the 'deathward tendency' – the way of the world.

Buddhist faith is not subscription to a set of metaphysical propositions. It is the act of declaring for a better way of life. The image of plunging into a torrent with a view to reaching the other side gives us a good idea of what was meant. Once you are in the water you are in the struggle and fairly much committed. If you give up and return to your own side, you are defeated. If you reach the other bank you are accomplished.

If nirvanas are to come into existence, it requires some people to take the first step. The establishment of Sukhavati begins with an act of faith and commitment, just like any other project. Even though we do not yet see the goal, nonetheless, we take the first step. This is like laying the foundation stone of a building, or turning the first turf in a new field. A person who places strong faith in the Buddha's teaching enters the stream by acting upon it.

Faith is only meaningful in as much as it makes a difference to life. Such a person:

- understands the Four Noble Truths
- has made some progress in overcoming greed, hate and delusion
- trusts to the Buddha, dharma and sangha
- has stopped having faith in magical thinking.

Faith shows in their actions. These are really four ways of saying the same thing rather than four different things.

Happiness, Faith and Purpose

So a sotapanna is somebody who has lifted her or himself out of the ordinary way of going about life and found a better way. Such persons are purposeful and generally happy, like one who has put down a burden. They are engaged in intrinsically worthwhile activities. They have few personal desires and few enmities. They do not hold on to grievances and they do not regard their lot as an unfortunate one. Nonetheless, they are concerned about the delusion and suffering that is abroad in the world and this concern provides their motive and direction in life.

Such persons are attained the first stage in joining the free people. That is, they have freed themselves up enough to start to become of service to others. The Buddha wanted to bring about substantial changes in the world and this required the creation of a kind of peace army. There had to be people willing and able to work for the cause. Most people, even if they agreed and sympathised with what the Buddha was doing, were actually still not of any practical use. This is because most people are too tied down by involvement in conventional society, by emotional entanglements, pursuit of material accumulation and personal ambition, to have any serious amount of time or energy left over to work for the cause of great peace and world emancipation.

A stream enterer, however, has taken a substantial step in this direction. He or she has realised the futility of much of what worldly life consists of. Although he may still be hanging on to some worldly attachments, he has begun to see the importance of what the Buddha is doing and has freed himself from other commitments to some degree. The person who becomes completely free to devote total attention to the dharma work is an arhat. Before we go on to consider the role of the arhat, however, let us spend a little time upon the intermediate roles of sekha and bodhisattva.

BODHISATTVAS AND SEKHAS

The earliest use of the term bodhisattva was to refer to the man Siddhartha Gautama before he became enlightened and became the Buddha. In the Theravada tradition of Buddhism, this is still how the term is used. At an early stage in the wider Buddhist community, however, the term bodhisattva came to have a number of other uses. First, it started to be used to refer to anybody who is on the way to enlightenment, and especially somebody who is well along this path. Secondly, it indicates someone who devotes his or her life to the service of others.

In the early Buddhist community there were two types of lifestyle: householder and renunciant. The latter gave up the householder life and became full-time dharma-farers. There were also many followers of the Buddha, however, who continued to live a regular life in society while devoting whatever time and energy they could to the advancement of the Buddha's teaching and aims. People who entered the stream of Buddhism might follow either of these roles, bodhisattva or sekha, cooperating together to bring about what amounted to a complete revolution in the way in which society operated.

The Buddha's social vision includes the abolition of social class and of war. It envisages a society in which people make a living by engagement in wholesome activities and use whatever surplus they generate for the collective good. It sees a great increase in cooperation and community, mutually respectful relations between the sexes, and the banishing of superstition. It advocates that respect for people on the basis of the extent to which they fulfil the ideals of the spiritual life should replace respect based upon wealth or worldly status. It calls for an end to the exploitation of animals and so on. These principles are enlightened, are they not?

This was an agenda for a revolution. It was not to be a violent

revolution. It was to be a peaceful revolution. The Buddha was
the first prophet of nonviolent revolution. Of course, if you
start up-ending the social structure some people are going to
get angry about it. The people who carry out such a revolution
have, therefore, both to be disciplined to a high degree and to
maintain strong faith in the ultimate purpose. It is no good if they
themselves resort to violence under provocation. It was this aspect
of the Buddha's teaching that Gandhi was later to adopt.

Some of the Buddha's revolutionaries were renunciants. This
means they said, 'I renounce this society. Henceforth, I will live
outside it.' To become a renunciant is a revolutionary act. It is a
declaration of independence. The Buddha was interested in raising
people's consciousness to the point where they might make such
an act of renunciation, just as he himself had done by abandoning
a career in politics and the military that his father had lined up for
him. The people who had the necessary faith and who left their old
life behind in order to follow the Buddha in this way were called
sekhas. They were the ones who went to train under the Buddha's
direct instructions or with one or other of his senior disciples.

This raising of consciousness was a call to wake up. The Indian
word for it was *bo-dhi* – 'enlightened vision'. A bodhisattva was
really anybody who had the courage or spirit (*sattva*) to devote
their life to this work. In India people talked about liberation. In
the religious traditions of the Buddha's time, liberation meant to
liberate the soul from the confines of this world of suffering and
attain union with god. The Buddha radically reinterpreted this
term. Liberate yourself from the greed, hate and delusion that
keep you wedded to the shallow attractions of worldly life and
come to work with me for a better world, he called. We can speak
of Liberation Buddhism.

The rigorous training of the Buddha's disciples was, therefore,
undertaken in the service of the creation of a better world. They
called this better world Sukhavati – the sweet realm. With this
agenda, the work of the bodhisattvas and the work of the sekhas
went hand in glove. People were inspired.

Not all the Buddha's followers became sekhas, however. He also had friends, allies and supporters who continued to operate within the cities and the countryside. If you are going to wage a revolution, this is necessary. There have to be operations going on behind enemy lines as it were. The Buddha waged a subtle campaign. He did not set himself up as an easy target. He maintained relations whenever possible with the rich and powerful as well as with ordinary folk. He never ceased to advocate that they change their ways. He did not make the Marxist mistake of designating some people as 'class enemies' and thereby re-establishing the same oppressions that he meant to abolish. He himself came from the upper class. He saw that the revolution he had in mind could benefit everybody. He did not seek to destroy his opponents. He sought to convert them.

The followers of the Buddha who worked for the cause in the cities were the first great bodhisattvas. This is clear from texts like the *Vimalakirti Sutra* and the *Pratyutpanna Samadhi Sutra*. They were not renunciants (sekhas), in the sense of being people who physically leave society and live a mobile lifestyle. They were people who worked for the dharma in the midst of the ordinary life of the great cities. They devoted much of their time and wealth to activities designed to serve the wellbeing of the masses. They were supported by the sekhas who were like the shock troops of this revolution. The sekhas were free to go anywhere and do anything in the cause. In combination with the bodhisattvas, they could be a formidable force in transforming the world. They still can.

The term bodhisattva also came to mean a person who has been to Sukhavati and has come back from there in order to help 'ferry all beings to that other shore'. This usage reminds me of the famous last speech by Martin Luther King, when he said, 'I've seen the promised land. I may not get there with you but I want you to know tonight, that we, as a people, will get to the promised land. And I'm happy tonight. I'm not worried about anything. I'm not fearing any man.'[2]

Where Martin Luther King liked the metaphor of standing on the mountain top, the Buddha liked that of crossing a river, which must have been daunting in the India of his time. There were strong currents that might sweep you away. These, said the Buddha, are like the currents of greed, hate and delusion. He also likened his method to the making of a raft or a ferry to get people across. This was the job of the bodhisattvas.

Where the original bodhisattvas had been human beings, after some time, Buddhism adopted an array of celestial bodhisattvas too. This meaning of the term bodhisattva in part results from the repositioning of Sukhavati outside this present life. After a time, some Buddhists lost faith in the possibility of creating Sukhavati here in this world and they started to see it as a place to be reborn into after death. The Buddha, like Jesus some 500 years later, saw the possibility of peace on earth and a new world. The Buddha's new world would more likely have been a republic than a kingdom, but the parallel is still close. His inspiration faded with time, however. The goal ceased to be seen as something attainable and became displaced further and further into the future – many lifetimes hence. The further displaced from the here and now it became, the more people went back to the consolations of belief in other worlds and an essentially magical form of salvation.

When this happened, the two halves of the Buddhist community each began to see their way of training themselves as no longer being about training for a real task in this present world, but as a way of preparing the spirit for life in another world. The metaphors Buddha had used to point out the goal – nirvana, the other shore, and so on – now became names for other-worldly realms. In place of a sharp critique of this world, Buddhism became a belief in a mythical other world far away. Instead of needing each other, therefore, the bodhisattva path and the sekha path came to be seen as alternatives and even as rivals. The revolution was lost at that time through schism and loss of inspiration. The quest for individual salvation replaced cooperation. The original vision was, however, no less valid for that.

THE ARHAT: CREATOR OF NEW WORLDS

What then of the arhat? The person who was fully enlightened was already a citizen of Sukhavati. The Buddha was building new worlds in the midst of the old ones. This was not the kind of revolution that needed to pull the old down by violent insurrection. From where the Buddha was looking, the old one was wreckage enough already. In the midst of this wreckage, he would build communities of a new type. The full citizens of these communities – these sanghas of the enlightened – would provide example and inspiration to whoever had eyes to see and ears to hear. By simply acting from a position of virtue, truth and compassion, they would naturally draw others into their wake. This is precisely what we see happening in the accounts of the early life of the Buddhist community.

The prime characteristic of the arhat, therefore, was a shift of identity. An arhat is somebody who, going beyond the level of understanding of the stream enterer, realises that he or she no longer identifies with the roles and activities that sustain the old society at all. They have, as far as that is concerned, given up their old self completely. They have completed their preparation.

One advantage of this giving up of identity is that the arhat becomes free to travel. The new society is not in one place. It is potentially everywhere. The arhat's job is to take it everywhere. In order to do this the arhat has to be free. If the arhat is still thinking of him or herself primarily as a wife or husband or employee or father or mother or any of the other roles that are part and parcel of the structure of conventional society, then he or she will not be free to go wherever he or she is needed. It is thus intrinsic to the definition of the arhat status that it refers to somebody who has gone beyond those kinds of conventional roles. This really is the essential point in the identity of being an arhat. They are full-time Liberation Buddhists.

The arhats are, therefore, to be the bold creators of the new world. Their task is to spread the revolution – to turn the dharma wheel – far and wide. They are part of a great movement and they are the leading edge of it. An arhat is not simply somebody who lives such a pure life that she (or he) will attain her own deliverance. The function of the arhat is to be a leaven in society, effecting the great transformation that is necessary to overturn exploitation, oppression and war.

The arhats are the complete renunciants, and as such are the most complete revolutionaries. The arhat does not practise kindness towards his or her own family alone, but has become somebody who sees the whole world as his or her family. The arhat is, therefore, somebody who trains thoroughly in the way of the Buddha.

This does not mean that arhats are super human beings. There has been an unremitting tendency in Buddhism for the ideal state to be portrayed as more and more ideal until it ceases to be realisable on this earth. The whole point of the Buddha's work was that there should be arhats on this earth.

What has happened too often since is that Buddhism has become institutionalised. That is to say, it has been allotted a privileged place within the old society in return for giving up its social potential. The renunciant has become somebody who keeps 250 rules and wears certain clothes and lives in a monastery. Monasteries can be 'spiritual power houses' – as my teacher Kennett Roshi used to say – but, often enough, they can be just as much a part of the old society as other institutions. They can become bulwarks of conservatism. They can, in effect, be places where arhats are confined and neutralised. The 'worthy ones' whom the Buddha inspired were not the sort to be kept in a cage. The term monastery can cover a multitude of different kinds of community, only some of which really serve the Buddhist cause. Nonetheless, the spirit of the arhat ideal is not dead.

A REVOLUTION BETRAYED

In one sense the revolution that the Buddha started was lost through the loss of nerve of succeeding generations. Dilution of the original inspiration led to schism and allowed contamination by popular spirituality that destroyed the this-worldly goals of the movement. A second major problem was that the remarkable degree of success that the Buddhist movement did nonetheless achieve led to large sections of it being bought out by the establishment. This happened about 200 years after the death of the Buddha, when, in the year 250 BCE or thereabouts, the monarch Ashoka made Buddhism the state religion of India.

It has been a recurring problem for the peaceful revolution that, in certain political situations, powerful governments can see Buddhism as a valuable tool with which to pacify their realm. The same thing was to happen again in other Asian countries at later dates – several times in China and, perhaps most notably, in Japan at the time of Prince Shotoku (573–621 CE). The circumstances in these cases are quite similar. A violent monarch succeeds in slaughtering his enemies and then converts to the peaceful way. Of course, the successful warrior wants to stop when he is winning. Buddhism, as a movement that outlaws war, can thus, unfortunately, sometimes come in useful to a tyrant.

A hundred years before Ashoka, the Buddhist movement had been split between the Party of the Elders (*Sthaviravada*) and the Majority Group (Mahasanghika) at the Second Great Council. This had come about ostensibly because the Majority Group wanted some flexibility in the *vinaya* rules. The official differences between the two parties were, however, so slight that one cannot help thinking that this was a symbolic rather than a substantial issue.

The Majority Group criticised the Elders on the grounds that they were not perfect enough to be arhats, and the Elders criticised the Majority Group on the grounds that, if they wanted to change the rules, even slightly, they were obviously not made of the right stuff. Clearly what was happening here was a kind of competition in virtue: 'You're not as perfect as we are.' What probably lies behind this is the process referred to above in which the goal of the Buddhist effort was beginning to be seen as further away in the future than it had been. In a society where most people believed in reincarnation, it was easy to see the goal receding in this way.

As it did so, the idea grew that nirvana was not so much an emancipation for all as a personal reward to the virtuous. A competition in virtue resulted and sectarianism was born. It still continues today. The Elders came more and more to present themselves as the most virtuous. Where they had once seen themselves as there to serve, they increasingly restructured things in such a way that they saw the role of the laity as being to support and supply them, so that they could get on with the business of being ultravirtuous and thereby achieve their own salvation.

In this scheme of things, all that was left to the laity was the prospect that by being generous in their support for the 'arhats' they might accumulate enough merit to be born into that blessed category themselves in a future life. Some of the bodhisattvas, who had also been hard workers for the Buddhist cause, began to smell a rat in this new way of looking at things. This suspicion got expressed at the fringe meetings of the Second Council. Speakers commanded lively audiences with such allegations as that the Elders were not such great arhats as all that because they still had wet dreams. Although the Elders carried all motions in the conference hall, due to their control over the invitation process, the fringe meetings were where all the action really took place and the Buddhist movement was irretrievably split.

From here on, the Majority Group went forward convinced that it alone was concerned about universal salvation and compassion and many new texts were generated portraying the Elders as self-serving and the bodhisattvas as the only remaining representatives of the true message. It was, of course, a great shame that there should have been such acrimony, but division was probably inevitable and necessary to restore some of the diversity within the movement that the Buddha himself had been willing to live with as a natural state of things. A great movement is not going to be created by maintaining a rigid uniformity. It is necessary to distinguish between what is essential and what is not. The divisions that now occurred were a natural consequence of the initial attempt at centralisation that had occurred in the midst of the anxiety and grief immediately after the Buddha died. Given the nature of Buddhist principles, such rigidity could hardly have been sustained indefinitely.

However that may be, the resulting diversity can certainly be seen to have been a boon in times that followed. Whenever a branch of Buddhism has fallen into malpractice, there has always been another one available to offer criticism and an alternative example. When Buddhism has been driven out of a country, there have been neighbours to take care of the refugees and to provide a base from which this gentle faith can later be re-established.

Schism is not always an unmitigated failure. Although the Buddha made no provision for the appointment of a successor, he does seem to have made provision for the possibility of schism. If two groups differ, they should do everything possible to iron out the problem and arrive at truth and understanding, he said, but if this proves impossible and the difference is such as to be disruptive, then the two factions should simply agree to live separately. This was an enlightened and realistic attitude and it has saved Buddhism from the kinds of internal persecution that have spilt so much blood within other faiths that have had a less pluralist vision.

There were a lot of good people working for the Buddhist movement and the split did not vitiate it. For another 100 years it continued to spread. We can see, however, that where originally the arhats and bodhisattvas worked together for a transformation in this world, now the agenda was gradually becoming competition for entry into a world which was increasingly idealised and remote. Buddhism was becoming a religion of private salvation.

Ashoka's conversion gave this process an extra twist. It is, of course, a classic example of what is lost by buying into the establishment system. Buddhist historians represent Ashoka as one of the greatest and most humane monarchs in history, and there is quite a bit of evidence that, as absolute monarchs go, he was not too bad a chap. There is, for instance, the account in the *Biographical Sutra of King Ashoka* of how the king, like any good tyrant, had a secret police force and this was backed up by a singularly sinister torture chamber. In the text, it simply refers to this place by saying that 'King Ashoka constructed a hell'. We are told about some of the methods used in this hell. Nobody came out alive, apparently. Anyway, one day, Ashoka was talking to Upagupta, a Buddhist teacher whom he favoured. Upagupta, catching the monarch in one of his better humours, suggests to him that it is not really such a good idea for a Buddhist monarch to use torture as a major instrument of state policy. Ashoka is impressed by Upagupta's argument. A few days later he closes down the little hell, and, just for good measure, and so that nobody shall be in any doubt, he has the chief torturer boiled in his own glue pot.

Well, is this good news or not? Obviously it is a mixed bag. Ashoka did bring in many reforms that made for a more tolerant and humane society than was common in the world of 250 BCE. One might be willing to settle for that. Buddha himself had not been willing to. Siddhartha Gautama could have remained, or returned to being, an important politician and could have himself instituted benign social policies. He chose a different course. Really he chose to play a longer game. Even if he did not see the final outcome in his own time, he chose to start a wheel turning that would go on turning for a long time afterwards.

Ashoka's reign created the conditions for further developments in the Buddhist movement. On the one hand, with state backing, orthodoxy came into play. The Buddhism that Ashoka's missionaries took to Sri Lanka is still there in essentially the same form. Within the more cosmopolitan cities of Ashoka's own realm, as well as beyond his borders, however, the period of peace allowed further diversification. Buddhism came into contact with Greek civilisation in the area now called Afghanistan and developed forms that would permit the spread of the faith into central Asia and – with huge consequence – into China. Buddhism probably also spread as far west as Egypt, where it probably influenced the developments that led to the Christian desert tradition and hence Christian monasticism. This kind of diversification has given the world many riches of the spirit.

In these conditions, a new phenomenon arose. This was called *bhakti*. Bhakti means devotionalism. Buddhists have always been devoted to their teachers. The climate of the times began to allow the possibility of celestial teachers – a kind of rapprochement between Buddhism and popular spirituality, perhaps. There has been a lot of scholarly debate about whether this was a spontaneous development in central India around this time or whether it was an import from elsewhere – Persia, perhaps. In all probability it was a development within Indian Buddhism itself. Like many practices, devotionalism can be used in different ways. People need a way of expressing their love and dedication. All Buddhist schools have some element of devotion, therefore. Bhakti, however, carried this process much further and the transformation of Buddhism into an other-worldly system indistinguishable from theistic religion was gathering pace.

Bhakti became and remained a central feature of Indian religious life. Even after Buddhism had disappeared from India in the Middle Ages, bhakti continued. It came to be incorporated into the popular spirituality of the Indian subcontinent and is to this day a central element in what has come to be called Hinduism.

A LOST CAUSE?

It is possible, therefore, to see this as the story of a lost cause. The Buddha gave up his kingdom in order to start a movement to abolish greed, oppression and superstition from the world. Two hundred years later his followers endorse a rich tyrant and establish devotion to supernatural forces as a central feature of their practice. This, however, would be an unduly pessimistic assessment.

It is surely necessary to cut through the comforting rhetorical gloss that pious Buddhist apologists have put upon these events in order to get through the fat of religiosity down to the bone of Buddha's intention for this world. We are here, then, talking about a perennial revolution. This revolution will inevitably have its vicissitudes. There have been schisms, but these have had a positive outcome as well as a negative one. There have been sell-outs. Perhaps there will be again. This is not really all that surprising. The Buddha initially thought that nobody would be interested in what he had to say in the first place. The temptations of power are always there, as is the corruption that flows from complacent self-indulgence. None of this would have surprised the Buddha himself. He was down-to-earth.

The nature of a perennial revolution, however, is that while it can be betrayed many times, it can never be wholly defeated so long as there are sekhas and bodhisattvas, and perhaps even some arhats in the world. As long as this remains the case, the Republic of Sukhavati remains in being as an independent state. It does not have a delineated territory, but that does not mean that it is absent from the world. It remains a living presence that will always have the power to rattle the cage of oppression and to attract new people to enter its stream.

In the modern world, the message of Buddha is as fresh as it ever was. Buddhism is calling to our age. The sekhas and bodhisattvas of the modern age may not always dress as the ones of old did. They might not even be part of the Buddhist religious establishment. Could it be, however, that the dharma wheel is beginning to turn once again? Is the real voice of the Buddha still audible, somewhere behind the monastic building industry that we currently see all around? Keep your ear to the ground.

· 5 ·

Liberating Buddhism

What will a Western Buddhism be like? This is a question that interests many people and has many aspects. One approach is to say that since there are now white Western Buddhists, we can study what they do and think. Another approach is to say that it is too early to know – that the answer lies in the future. A third approach proceeds from first principles and leads immediately to a radical conclusion.

This is that a white or Western Buddhism is a contradiction in terms. If Buddhism means the life of enlightenment, then there cannot be a specifically English or American Buddhism and we should not be looking to create one any more than our spiritual ancestors should have wanted to create a Chinese or Thai Buddhism, specifically. Buddhism does not belong to countries and should not become caught up in national pride.

We need to understand that when you look through Buddha eyes, England and America do not exist. They are just conventional designations that have been blown up into a justification for some of the worst barbarities in history and currently stand as ramparts in defence of the world racist system. Do not be proud to be British, or American, or French, or any other nationality. As soon as you begin to feel any such sentiment coming over you, you should smell the blood of all those who have died for such folly –

and hear the cries of the excluded. Buddhism, therefore, should be profoundly non-nationalist.

People are conditioned to think that nationhood is inevitable and even noble – something to die for even – and certainly something from which to exclude nonnationals. That, however, is definitely not Buddhism. There have, in consequence, been repeated crises in history over whether or not the Buddhist sangha would recognise or acknowledge the supremacy of the state. On different occasions, this issue has gone different ways in specific cases, but the Buddhist position in principle is that the sangha does not recognise the state.

This principle has been compromised in many real-life situations. The subordination of Buddhist principles to nationalist ones, however, is generally extremely deleterious to the former. We will look at a specific example from recent Japanese history later in this book. The revolutionary nature of the Buddhist renunciation becomes sharply apparent in such controversies. Of course, much of the time this is an issue that never comes to a head. The sangha is no military threat to the state and its presence is often welcomed by the civil power because it brings peace, stability and social service of all kinds to an area. Buddhism does not seek to overthrow the civil power. It aims to make it redundant.

In Japan, it was not possible for the sangha to maintain its independence and a series of military governments regulated and subordinated the practice of religion to national requirements. In Japan, religion and state have always been closely connected. The word for a religious organisation is *matsuri*. The word for government administration is *matsuri-goto*. The state was a form of religious expression and religious expression was state regulated. Some of the schools of Buddhism that arose in Japan more than accommodated to this environment by advancing teachings with a strongly nationalistic flavour. It is these forms of Buddhism that have, in large measure, found their way to North America. Buddhism that places religion in a subordinate position to the state is actually being practised in a number of places, but this is not the original variety and should not be part of the New Buddhism either.

The original spirit of Buddhism is, on the one hand, positive compassionate action and, on the other hand, noncooperation with coercion and oppression. This spirit needs to be dug out from under the accretions of history. To ask what a Western Buddhism would be like, therefore, is already to have surrendered.

All this is symptomatic of the fact that people do not see the extent to which Buddhism is radical. It is common for people to think that a little bit of tinkering with the *status quo* will accommodate Buddhism quite nicely. This is, in turn, rooted in the assumption that most of what the *status quo* consists of is inevitable. Once you can persuade people to believe that something is inevitable, they will generally accept it, no matter how immoral or inappropriate it may be.

Karl Marx, for instance, argued in favour of economic determinism. This idea made his followers believe that history was on their side. Although Marx himself is now widely thought to have been discredited, his idea of economic determinism, in one form or another, still holds sway, particularly among his staunchest opponents. Margaret Thatcher, for instance, will be remembered, among other things, for her strident insistence that 'There is no alternative'. There is, in fact, a widespread sense nowadays that capitalist rather than communist economics have an historic inevitability.

History is full of such paradoxes. It is a further paradox that Marx was a living demonstration of the falsity of this central idea. Had he really believed it, then there would have been no reason to write the books that he did. In fact, his books gave hope to many of the world's oppressed and changed the course of history in ways that were not simply down to the relentless march of economic forces. Marx, like Buddha, went against the current. Each did so by establishing a new mythology.

It was not Marx the economic scientist who achieved this. It was

Marx the writer and speaker who created a mythology around the ideas of liberation and revolution. Liberation and revolution are key concepts in Buddhism too. The meaning attaching to them is different, and the suggested means are totally opposite – but the hope of a better world is not really so fundamentally different. The Buddhist revolution – the turning of the dharma wheel – is nonviolent. It is still, however, intended to cut through the hypocrisy of our world and establish a new order. The Buddhist liberation is inner as well as outer. Marx took away religion as the opiate of the people, but he left them hollow. A true revolution requires both inner and outer work – and it never ends.

Marx and his successors thought to impose the new order with weapons, but could only achieve and justify this by making it seem an historic inevitability. Corrupt myths are needed to support corrupt practice. Buddha saw that the only way to a better world was to renounce weapons. He was the first great proponent of nonviolence as the route to social change. He was a demonstrator in the strict sense of the word – he demonstrated what he meant. If you are going to overcome caste, then you must give up your own caste. If you are going to abolish oppression and violence, then it is no good employing those methods yourself. People who are willing to be so consistent are rare. When they are consistent in the cause of good they are precious indeed.

Most people place subordination to the state as the highest inevitability, and subordination to economic factors – even relatively trivial ones – as the next highest, and then try to fit their spirituality into whatever space is left – if that has not already been used up by the energy consumed in the dynamics of personal life. In consequence, spirituality means little to them and their lives are built on other principles.

The modern world maintains its caste system (delusion) by relying upon national rivalry played out through force (politics, hate) and money or debt (economics, greed). We think that our white countries are democratic and feel proud, for instance, but were there ever to be a worldwide election – for the United

Nations Security Council, say – where would the white caste be then?

As long as Buddhism's primary goal is subsumed within nationalism and national cultures, it will never be met. Unless Buddhism can help us to rise out of our local culture, caste and so on, no real enlightenment will occur. An enlightened person is a citizen of the world, not a citizen of Japan or Germany or Britain or any other local power structure. We have, therefore, to start seeing countries simply as organisations and not as part of our identity.

Ideas of historic or economic determinism are myths that seek to excuse what should not be perpetrated, and to lull people into thinking that the things that they knowingly do that are bad, or not the best they can do, are necessary and inevitable. Determinism of either kind is, simply put, a lie. There are better myths and a cleaner conscience is possible. If we cannot find better ways to live, then we will continue to make new nightmares.

There is now a hope abroad among many people that Buddhism just might be able to provide the world with what it needs to avoid the catastrophes to come. To do so, however, it will need both to advance the radical social implications of some of its central teachings more effectively, and to jettison much of its own conservative baggage acquired during centuries when the original message was buried under a series of compromises – some chosen, some coerced – with oppressive political systems in India, China, Japan and elsewhere. In all these countries, Buddhism has, at one time or another, been used as an instrument of state policy for subduing rather than liberating the population. It is remarkable, really, that so much of the pure spirit of Buddhism has, in fact, survived. It has done so, surely, because there have always been, throughout history, practitioners who did understand and who were willing to stand aside from the compromises.

I have heard many people say that it seems just too good to be true: a religion that does not require people to believe things they find incredible, that is not incompatible with modern science, that is not warmongering, that provides an ethic that applies right across the social spectrum, and that is still flexible and evolving to meet ever new social situations and applications in constructive ways. It is faith that urges us to protect the environment, to build harmonious communities, to avoid waste, to settle conflicts and live more simply, yet does all this without loading people with fear and guilt; a faith with a strong internationalist vision as well as thorough personal ethics – ethics that extend to our treatment of animals and plants as well our relations with other people. Many people nowadays are coming to have great hopes for the gentle path of the Buddha.

There is a close relationship between myth and reality in the sense that every religious ideology implies a social structure and that social structure has economic and political implications in turn. The implementation of a particular mythology, therefore, is a great experiment. The fate of the religion hinges upon the success of that experiment as much as the fate of the society hinges upon the merit of its religious ethos. All religions and ideologies are not the same.

In the world today there is much cruelty and oppression. Those who have power are cushioned against it. People of the rich countries reject people of poor ones and will not, for instance, tolerate those poor people coming to live in their rich countries. Within the poor countries again this oppression is repeated. The poorer members of the poorer countries are doubly oppressed. Such people can be exploited, starved, or even killed without anybody other than their own relatives caring. If ten people die from unnatural causes in London, it is a big news story. The same day, many more than ten have died in less regarded corners of the world and nobody even notices. We have discovered that even when genocide is going on in central Africa, all that the United Nations is likely to do is to save the handful of white people in the area. One of the things that a person in a rich country can do to help a person in a poor country is simply to write to them. The poor-country person is less likely to be subjected to gross oppression if they are known to have friends in richer parts of the world. This is because there is somebody in the power-holding part of the world who will notice if that person dies.

This is one important reason why the Buddhist project of Sukhavati must not become identified with one country. Stalin's 'Socialism in one country' was really a great setback to Marx's project. The same is true with Buddhism. Although it may seem a hard thing to say, there is a case for hoping that the Tibetans do not get back to Tibet for a long time, and that such people as Thich Nhat Hanh, the great peace activist from Vietnam, stay in exile for a long time – 'stay until *samsara* ceases'[1] as it says in a Tibetan prayer. When these people go back to what we think of as their own countries, the world may be much poorer. A real Buddhist will not go back to their worldly country, even when they physically reside within its borders. They are more use as an exile, whether metaphorically or literally. To be Buddhist is to be a refugee. When all the world are refugees of this special kind, then there will be no countries and no wars.

The Buddha taught us to recognise that identities are fluid. Look at the other person and see that he (or she) is human as you are. He does not like to be hurt. He needs to eat. Do not inflict upon others what you do not like. Do not say, 'But he's black' or 'She's not qualified' or 'That one has the wrong passport'. As you do so you sow the seeds of war and you give power to oppression. Why might you do so? To consolidate possession and territory and maintain the privileges of your caste. Buddhism, therefore, rests upon a bedrock of renunciation. Only when we renounce the primacy of possession and territory does the cause of war abate.

THE NEW IN THE MIDST OF THE OLD

In 1999 a collection of essays on engaged Buddhism was published to mark the sixtieth birthday of Bhikkhu Payutto. Bhikkhu Payutto is a Thai, Theravada Buddhist. He has worked to extend the scope of Buddhism in his country so as to make it a more active force in society. He has made particular contributions to thinking about educational method and the crucial role that education plays in social improvement.

Included in this collection is a perceptive article by David Chappell.[2] This is called, 'Engaged Buddhists in a Global Society: Who is being liberated?' One of the main points that Chappell is making is that before Buddhism is in a position to liberate society, Buddhism itself needs to be liberated. Further, a great deal of such liberation has already occurred as a result of the impact of modern society upon Buddhism. Chappell highlights the work of Thich Nhat Hanh, the Dalai Lama, Bhikshuni Cheng-yen, Sulak Sivaraksa, Ani Karma Lekshe Tsomo, Daisaku Ikeda and A.T. Ariyaratne as providing examples of people who, from a base in one or another branch of Buddhism, have become international leaders in advocacy and action for a more compassionate world.

All these figures have been able to operate effectively in the modern world and it is modernism that has made their work possible, he says. Modernism has provided the possibility for Buddhism to escape from state control. As Chappell points out, 'Throughout Asian history beginning with King Ashoka, Buddhist movements that organised and spread books were controlled and suppressed by the state-sangha' (Chappell, 1999, p.81). Chappell concludes that five conditions have provided the matrix within which a New Buddhism has come into being. These five conditions are: laws that provide some protection from the state, the humanistic enlightenment that encourages independent intellectual enquiry, modern communications, relative global peace and a global economy. These five are all major features of modernism.

In some quarters, Chappell's assertions will be controversial because some of these five factors are themselves targets of Buddhist critique. If we were to rename them as individualism, intellectualism, technology, Western political hegemony and materialist consumerism, then we would be sure to find a number of critical voices wanting to distance Buddhism from them as much as possible.

Nonetheless, it is precisely these conditions that Chappell sees as having provided the seedbed for a new *yana* – a new Buddhist vehicle. The characteristics that he attributes to this new movement are:

- action in society rather than reliance upon meditation and devotion alone
- a new morality encompassing nonviolence and ecological awareness rather than monasticism
- new forms of community exploiting the potentiality of new technology and mass media
- interreligious dialogue and a willingness to find allies among followers of other faiths
- a concern for mother earth and respect for the wild
- a search for a new economics at least to abate the destructive effects of wealth disparity and environmental degradation
- a gender inclusive approach
- a concern with institutional as well as personal reform.

This is an outline of the generally agreed programme of the New Buddhism, the Buddhism that has come about through the impact of modernism. One could call this a cross-fertilisation between Buddhism and modernism, or one could say that this 'New Buddhism' is really Buddhism finally liberated from the age-old demoralising effects of having long ago become part of monolithic state apparatuses.

This analysis is important because we need to distinguish between what is simply the product of a temporary phase of fortuitous conditions and what has the potential to become a lasting constructive socio-religious phenomenon. We also need to know what in it is truly Buddhist, i.e. enlightened.

For instance, if political changes permitted Thich Nhat Hanh to be welcomed back to Vietnam or the Dalai Lama to be welcomed back to Tibet, would these be instances of Buddhism coming into its own, or would they be occasions when Buddhism reverts to an unproductive conservatism?

Two tendencies are apparent. There is a powerful conservative tendency within Buddhism as well as a progressive liberation movement. These two are at present still closely linked to one another. Whether this link will remain in place indefinitely, however, will turn on events. The sheer fact that Buddhism as it *de facto* exists straddles such a wide spectrum, creates scope for experiences of disappointment and rejection.

Even those who appear to be pace-setters in the radical arm of Buddhism are often themselves, intentionally or not, also caught up in some profoundly conservative trends. In part this is a result of the fact that the revival of Buddhism in the twentieth century was in some respects a different phenomenon in the East and in the West. In the East, it was quite strongly associated – some would say contaminated – with nationalism. Many Buddhist centres in the West are linked to one or other Asian country of origin – Burma, Tibet, Sri Lanka, Vietnam and so on. These groups tend to be dominated by people from the ethnic group in question. There are a number of characteristic problems for what is sometimes called ethnic Buddhism in the West. The expatriate Asian group that holds office in such groups is often more conservative than members of their own nationality who live back home. Japanese priests coming from Japan to work with *Jodo Shinshu* congregations in North America, for instance, often find themselves faced with a staunchly conservative caucus. This is understandable. An expatriate community clings to its identity and this identity is set in the past. This, however, creates an even wider gulf between the Asian and the Western members. The real point at issue, however, for both these groups is whether Japanese or Tibetan or Chinese or, say, Vietnamese identity is more important than Buddhism itself.

Even groups that have achieved a strong reputation for progressive or engaged Buddhism are not immune. Thich Nhat Hanh,

Vietnamese by birth, is the best-known hero of the engaged Buddhist movement and he has certainly been inspirational for me. He is one of Chappell's prime examples. Hanh has established a sangha that is called the Community of Interbeing. The Community of Interbeing now has centres and communities in many Western countries radiating out from its headquarters in southwest France at a settlement called Plum Village.

The roots of Hanh's radical side lie in the extreme distress he experienced over the war that ravaged his country. He became an advocate for peace, and after the war worked hard to help the refugees called the boat people. The Order of Interbeing had its roots in this struggle. However, although the Order and its associated Community have grown fairly large and speeches by Thich Nhat Hanh commonly attract several thousand people, the Community of Interbeing does not actually take part in much that could be called socially engaged Buddhism anywhere in Europe. Plum Village continues to collect aid to be sent back to Vietnam and the whole focus of that community's attention is Vietnam. This is not wicked. Vietnam is one of the poorest countries in the world and certainly needs help. On the other hand, it is difficult to escape the impression that what is developing here is not a worldwide revolution. This is not entirely Hanh's fault. The fact is that few of his white supporters – a few areas of the USA excepted – have any real enthusiasm for engaged Buddhism. Rather, what many want is a form of religion that teaches mindfulness and gentleness in daily life and offers them freedom from stress and anxiety. They want their spiritual disease ameliorated without the trouble of attending to its social causes. Many Westerners are so alienated from the political process that they no longer see any connection between spirituality and society. Though radical by sentiment, they are effectively conservative in practice.

Hanh's establishment of the Order of Interbeing broke new ground in a number of ways. The concept of an order that included both monks and lay people, who would work for peace and social reconstruction on an equal footing, was bold. The Charter of the

Order of Interbeing specifies that within the Order there will be equality between lay and ordained members. This is, in terms of Buddhist history, a radical step. The reality, however, has proved different. In the Order and in the wider Community of Interbeing, effective power is now in the hands of ordained members, and this situation has become progressively more accentuated as time has passed. Furthermore, although a substantial number of white people have become ordained in the Order over the years, few have remained so. The Order of Interbeing is now largely an organisation controlled by Vietnamese monks and nuns, in which lay Westerners perform a variety of supporting roles. This does have the merit of reversing the usual caste gradient, and it is not inconceivable that this was the intention, but it has not really broken the hold of ethnic factors on the life of the community.

The name, Interbeing, implies a deep concern for ecology, internationalism and all those forces that work for cohesion and interdependence. The existence of this order provided a rallying point – a new mythology. Members of the Order take fourteen precepts as a basis for their way of life. These precepts are a reformulation of Buddhist traditional morality that catches the modern mood. The precept that traditionally forbade alcohol now reads as an advocacy for wholesome diet in general, for instance. The fourteen precepts are an example of the 'new morality' referred to by Chappell. The introduction of 'hugging meditation' endeared Hanh to progressive Western groups almost as much as it scandalised some of his critics back in Vietnam. His writings on social engagement have not, however, been as popular as those on personal practice.

What this means is that the Community of Interbeing, having started with some progressive modern ideas and a passionate commitment to social Buddhism, has steadily gravitated, in practice, back to a traditional Buddhist model in which the lay people's part is to support the clergy and the pressure towards such *de facto* conservatism has come just as much from Westerners as from the Vietnamese.

Hanh's movement is singled out here because it illustrates how even a movement that has been one of the more successful in liberating Buddhism from traditional forms and has played a pivotal part in the emergence of New Buddhism, still finds itself affected by a considerable gravitational field pulling back towards the old ways. Thich Nhat Hanh remains an inspiring example of someone who has attempted to liberate the progressive forces in Buddhism. If we were to analyse the progress of each of the other figures listed by Chappell, we would find similar crosscurrents. We are, therefore, here talking about a struggle that is ongoing and the difficulties should not be underestimated.

Will the New Buddhism reach escape velocity? Many existing movements may prove simply to have been booster stages towards the next rung of the ascent. Many other Buddhist groups have never even tried to get off the ground in the first place, but have remained ethnocentric, conservative, sectarian, exclusive and nationalistic. Hanh's movement is certainly one of the most progressive around. We must, nonetheless, continue to improve. Chappell's observation that something is afoot and a new movement is underway is not baseless by any means, even though that something may take a number of attempts to go into orbit.

FREE SPEECH AND THE VALUE OF DIFFERENCE

One of the most pernicious aspects of the conservatism of traditional Buddhism is its intolerance of dissent. Each group has its line – take it or leave it. There is a paradox here. Buddhism is often presented as a quest for harmony. What is often not realised is that harmony is not achieved by sameness, but by learning to handle difference in creative ways. The word harmony implies a relationship between notes of contrasting pitch. Competition between Buddhist groups seriously undermines the potential of the whole, not because different groups are different, so much as because they do not know how to talk to or cooperate with each other. Buddhist groups should not be seeking a purified, homogenous identity; they should be exploring the possibilities of friendship between those who have different things to offer. We should be seeking a symphony, not a monotone.

In recent years in Britain, a forum called the Network of Buddhist Organisations has come into being. Similar developments have occurred in other countries. NBO has done excellent work in creating a place where all Buddhist groups can meet and exchange news and ideas. It has also provided the infrastructure to support teaching tours by Buddhist leaders like the Dalai Lama and Thich Nhat Hanh when this cannot be managed by one group acting alone.

Nonetheless, activities of this kind are still viewed with a good deal of suspicion by many Buddhist groups. The primary reason for this is not just that each group thinks that its ideas are best and true – it is quite natural that they should think that and that they should each be capable of arguing for the correctness of their perspective – but rather that the tradition of free speech has not yet really taken hold in many quarters of the Buddhist world. This can be true even within some of the most seemingly progressive groups, let alone the avowedly conservative ones. It might not be surprising to know that the bookshop of the New Kadampa Tradition – a highly traditional branch of Tibetan Buddhism that finds the Dalai Lama too progressive – only stocks a narrow range of works. In fact virtually all the works available there are written by the leader of this school, Geshe Kelsang Gyatso. However, precisely the same is true in the bookshops of several of the organisations most closely associated with engaged Buddhism.

If this seems surprising to you it is because you have been brought up within the modern paradigm that owes so much to the Western 'Enlightenment' that freed up intellectual life in Europe in the eighteenth and nineteenth centuries. You might feel that these Buddhists have something to learn from the West here about the importance of free thought and intellectual creativity – about enlightenment, in fact. You would be right. This, however, overlooks the fact that there are also perfectly good resources within the Buddhist tradition itself upon which to base the overthrow of this kind of foolish narrowness.

Buddhism has flourished precisely in times of intellectual ferment. Buddhism in India developed a tradition of logic and debate while Europeans were still feeding each other to the lions in the Colosseum. It was axiomatic to this tradition that the other party's argument be respected and allowed to be heard clearly. There was a confidence that truth will out, and this bred a vitality that we should not be trying to stifle. This also requires a willingness to be wrong. Buddhism suggests that most of us are deluded. If so, then it is unlikely that we will be right about everything. Even if we are enlightened, we will still be able to learn. Actually, the enlightened are likely to be more open to the possibility of changing their mind than the deluded.

The books written by Geshe Kelsang Gyatso are, of their type, for instance, excellent. They are an important contribution to Western understanding of Buddhism and its traditions. They can stand on their own merit. That his organisation believes that its members must never be permitted to read anything else because they might then stray from the true path shows a lack of confidence that is completely unwarranted. Buddhism will be much richer when its various schools learn to see themselves as Buddhist first and as separate traditions second.

The trouble is that a mythology has spread suggesting that an enlightened person is a know-all who can never be gainsaid. This is complete nonsense. Consider the Buddha himself, faced with the question of whether or not to admit women to the Buddhist order. At first he refuses. Why? Because he sees that in the conditions of the times this will create a lot of practical problems that no one previously has succeeded in overcoming. For instance, if he creates an order of defenceless women wandering the Indian countryside, who is going to protect them? When Francis of Assisi was faced with the same problem in Europe more than a 1,000 years later, the women who joined the Franciscan order were cloistered behind high walls. Only the brothers were allowed to go walking across the world.

Ananda who, we are repeatedly told in various texts, was not enlightened listened to the pleas of the women and tried again to persuade the Buddha to change his mind, using a different line of argument. 'Do women have the same capacity for spiritual enlightenment as men?' he asked. 'Yes, definitely,' said the Buddha. Starting from this point, Ananda was able to change the Buddha's mind and admit women to the order. This did not go down too well with some of the senior brothers. Eventually a compromise was hammered out in which the new sisters would keep a larger number of rules than the brothers. Some of these rules were attempts to keep the sisters safe. Some were to prevent sisters from being exploited by the brothers themselves, and some were to ensure that sisters showed outward respect to brothers in order to pacify the social critics. Most of these additional rules are now anachronistic, and in some branches of Mahayana Buddhism they were dropped long ago. Such is the conservatism of the Buddhist tradition, however, that they remain in place in many branches of the Buddhist order to this day.

In passing, we can note that there is an interesting dispute about the interpretation to be put upon a short passage in the Pali account of this incident. In it the Buddha says that with women in the sangha, the dharma will remain in the world for half as long as it would if only men were allowed in. The patriarchal interpretation of this passage is to the effect that Buddha thought that allowing women in would ruin things much quicker – that the influence of worldliness creeping back was bound to occlude the dharma eventually and that this would happen twice as quickly if women were involved. If we see the Buddha's agenda as being to establish a Pure Land, however, and if we see the dharma as the means of achieving it, then the passage can be just as well taken to mean that with women involved as well as men, the job will get done in half the time.[3]

The primary point here, however, is not about the rules for

sisters and the shameful fact of their persistence in some quarters, nor the benefits of having both sexes involved in the life of the sangha – interesting and important as these are – but that this incident shows how the enlightened one is able to change his mind after listening to sensible, contrary argument. Buddhism developed within a climate of debate and it developed its own science of logic and argument. In many quarters this appears to have been lost. The dialectics have become a sham with foregone conclusions. Buddhism became overattached to orthodoxy. A spirit of suspicion of thought and rejection of the intellect became widespread. This spirit is oppressive, anti-Buddhist and anti-enlightenment.

ENLIGHTENMENT WEST AND EAST

The Western Enlightenment has come in for increasing criticism. Its blessings are thought now to have been very mixed. It has brought us space travel and nuclear bombs, freedom to speak and to starve, mod cons, modems and monoculture. If we include in its scope the industrial and technological changes that it made possible, it has been one of the most total revolutions in the human way of being since the invention of agriculture. Despite its drawbacks, however, few would really want to return to the days before it arrived.

The Buddhist enlightenment is a different affair. It is a project to create a harmonious world via the creation of a cadre of enlightened people. It begins and ends with ethics and compassion. It is not antiscientific, however. It is not wedded to ideas of a flat earth nor is it antithetical to theories of evolution. It is happy to see science advance and it wants that science applied for the benefit of all sentient life. It is happy to see intellectual freedom and it wants to see people using that freedom to debate the best ways of helping all beings rather than the best way to sell more soap. It is happy to see principles like freedom of information and equality before the law spread, and it wants the opportunity that these bring to be used to create communities where people can live generous, faithful and creative lives.

The Western Enlightenment without something like the Buddhist enlightenment all too easily becomes an alienating, antisocial, dog-eat-dog wilderness, in which each privatised individual fights for his or her personal survival, equipped only with selfish concern. The Buddhist enlightenment without something like the Western Enlightenment all too easily becomes an oppressive orthodoxy in which no one is allowed to think for him or herself and harmony is achieved by suppressing diversity rather than by capitalising on creativity. We must not allow principles like 'no-mind' to degenerate into sheer mindlessness.

The two enlightenments need each other. As modern people, we need to learn how to cultivate inner peace and outer compassion, to wean ourselves from addiction to chemically induced oblivion, to live simpler, kinder lives and to build wholesome yet fluid communities whose crisscrossing networks gradually grow strong enough to care for all the dispossessed of the world and make the tyrannous absurdities of state militarism into anachronisms. All this we can learn from Buddhism.

As Buddhists, we need to cherish what is wholesome in the modernist paradigm without becoming swept into the nightmares of selfish individualism, or those of doing everything that is possible just because it has become possible – whether in the realm of nuclear physics, biotechnology, or market economics. What is wholesome? Freedom of thought, freedom of speech, freedom of movement, facilities to write, to meet, to communicate – all these are wholesome. Equal treatment for people of all castes, classes, genders and so on – this is wholesome. The New Buddhism will arise from a merger of these two enlightenments, not from a return to Asian medievalism in the name of Buddhist tradition, nor a return to Western medievalism in the name of postmodernism. The vision of the two enlightenments needs to be fulfilled, not betrayed.

· 6 ·

Varieties of Enlightenment

HOW MANY KINDS OF ENLIGHTENMENT ARE THERE IN BUDDHISM?

The other day I was asked by a newcomer to Buddhism, which of the different schools of Buddhism that we see today is most like the original teachings of Shakyamuni Buddha? This was, of course, a good and very understandable question. Reflecting upon it afterwards, however, I thought that, although my friend could not be expected to know this, her question was really a bit like asking which supermarket brand is real home cooking.

Buddhism is being retailed in the Western world as a quest for enlightenment. Enlightenment has thus become an ultimate value. The question of what enlightenment is for is seldom asked. What has happened, rather, is that a mystique has been created. Under the spell of this mystique some questions can no longer be asked. As an end in itself, enlightenment is just a plaything. Unhooked from its social context, Buddhism ceases to be serious – unless, of course, and this is what has often happened, it is re-associated with magical and grandiose metaphysical pretensions.

Not only does enlightenment have a real, compassionate purpose, it also has causes. The basic teaching of Buddhism is that all things – and especially all spiritual states – arise in dependence upon causes and conditions. To read many books on Buddhism, however, you would think that enlightenment was a causeless state, self-subsisting, eternal, immutable and beyond this world. In this and the following chapter, therefore, we will take an iconoclastic look at some of the main forms of enlightenment that are on offer. In the process we will gain a slightly caricatured picture of the philosophies of the main schools of Buddhism available in the present day. We will imagine these schools as so many supermarkets, each retailing its own brand of enlightenment. Having sampled them we may be in a position to consider whether they do actually have anything in common with old Shakyamuni's home cooking. I am sure it is bad form for a Buddhist to look at enlightenment in this way, but that probably makes it all the more necessary.

It is quite easy to get a representative sample of contemporary products, that can be divided into two categories. The first consists of those forms of enlightenment associated with the schools of Buddhism that evolved within the sphere of influence of Indian culture. The second group consists of those that grew up in the Sino-Japanese cultural zone. The marks of the ambient culture are apparent in all cases, so this exploration will also provide us with a study of what happens to Buddhism when it comes in contact with powerful indigenous cultures. If we come to understand this process well, then that knowledge could stand us in good stead in trying to understand what is happening and what is likely to happen as Buddhism enters the culture of the Western world. By studying the mistakes and distortions introduced by our forebears, we may be able to avoid some of the pitfalls ourselves. The likelihood is, however, human nature being what it is, that we shall fall down just the same holes as those who went before us did. Indeed, it is arguable that we have descended into several of them rather deeply already.

In this chapter we shall examine the approaches that evolved within the Indian sphere: primarily Theravada and Tibetan forms of Buddhism and their predecessors. There is not, however, a one-on-one correspondence between schools and ideas. Different schools of Buddhism have been borrowing from one another throughout history, just as they have borrowed from their host cultures. There is a strong, though erroneous, tendency for Buddhists to assume that what is called enlightenment in one school is exactly the same thing as what is called enlightenment in another. This creates a situation in which borrowing is not only easy and frequent, but also often unconscious. Many Buddhists reading this and the next chapter will, no doubt, want to resist the notion that the enlightenments offered by different groups are not the same. The idea of a plurality of enlightenments may seem heretical. It is to be hoped, nonetheless, that this exploration will, on the one hand, encourage the reader to clarify what she or he does actually believe and practise and, on the other, that it will clear up some of the confusion that arises for many Western readers of Buddhism when they read material that appears to be part of a philosophy they affirm, but clearly does not correspond with what they themselves think that philosophy asserts or requires. So, without more ado, let us begin with enlightenment number one – E1 we can call it.[1]

E1: ENLIGHTENMENT AS ESCAPE

The first type of enlightenment for us to look at is Enlightenment as Escape. Escape from what? Escape from the suffering and misery of this existence. There are two basic beliefs or assumptions that make this kind of enlightenment meaningful. These are first belief in rebirth, and secondly the idea that this world is intrinsically a place of such suffering that any intelligent person who really understood the situation would ardently wish to be free of it.

This type of enlightenment is based upon the commentarial interpretation of the Four Noble Truths according to which (a) all suffering is a product of desire and (b) desire can be abolished by following a prescribed programme of spiritual training. The implication is, therefore, that it is desire that both creates the suffering in this world and that keeps one anchored to this world. If one follows the instructions, then one will eventually become free from all desire. This will be an immediate cause of happiness, but, more importantly from the perspective of the advocates of this brand of enlightenment, it will also be the cause of one not having to be reborn here again. What will become of you if you are not reborn here? Well, this apparently is one of the questions that ordinary mortals will never understand, so that part of the product description has been left blank.

The aim with this kind of enlightenment, therefore, is to ensure that this life is one's last, or, if one is not sufficiently rigorous in one's training to achieve that happy state, then at least to ensure that one reduces desire as much as possible so that one is born with a head start next time round. A head start towards what? A head start towards the complete extinction that results from becoming completely free from desire.

The person who achieves this kind of enlightenment has attained a state of bliss: the bliss of extinction. The instructions for this type of enlightenment say that it requires a huge effort at personal reform and that this takes a long time – a lot longer than one lifetime, usually. They also say that no one can make this effort for another, so this is an individual path of personal salvation. Fundamentally we are alone, but if we stick at it for a long time, we may be happy one day – if extinction is to be counted a happiness – and even achieve the *summum bonum* of never having to come back to this world again.

One of the attractions of this product may be not so much the final goal that it advocates, which seems heavily negative, but the fact that it promises degrees of relative happiness along the way proportionate to the degree to which the user has succeeded in reducing desire. This could, therefore, be seen as a useful product if taken in moderation.

An interesting feature of this form of enlightenment – one that is shared by several others we shall look at below – is that few of those who advocate it really expect to achieve it. There is much emphasis upon the idea that it takes a very long time, so the fact that the ultimate goal may not be very attractive perhaps does not matter too much. This idea that it would be immodest to think one could actually attain this enlightenment, however, is clearly out of keeping with the pronouncements of the Buddha himself. He aimed to enlighten his followers quite quickly – often in the course of a few days, even – and certainly did not offer them something only to be attained in a far distant future rebirth. He wanted them enlightened now, I suggest, because once they were there was work to do.

E2: ENLIGHTENMENT AS EMPTINESS

Supermarket number two offers a slightly different product. They claim that this is an improvement upon the type offered at supermarket one, which they tend to refer to as an inferior brand. E2 is called Enlightenment as Emptiness. Being a more refined item, the product description this time is longer and not quite so easy to get your mind around.

This type of enlightenment is called the realisation of the emptiness of all phenomena. At first this seems like a fairly clear definition. When you read it the second time, however, you realise that you might need a bit of help sorting out just what this actually means. What exactly is 'the emptiness of all phenomena'? one is inclined to ask. In fact, there is a distinct implication that when you do understand the wording, then you will, in fact, be enlightened – or, to put this the other way about, only those who are enlightened know what this kind of enlightenment really is. From a consumer's point of view this is not entirely helpful, but let us persevere.

If this were a supermarket, one might now go and ask one of the assistants for help. The trouble is, however, that there are some very different ideas around about what constitutes (if that can be the right word – which is doubtful) emptiness. Broadly speaking, we can see two different, almost opposite, definitions: 'emptiness as absence' and 'emptiness as presence'. We shall return to emptiness as presence in the next chapter. For the moment, let us confine ourselves to emptiness as absence. The obvious question is, absence of what? The answer, in the small print on the box, is absence of inherent existence.

This is beginning to look like a philosopher's puzzle – not surprisingly, since the people who came up with this form of enlightenment were the top academics of some of the world's earliest universities, most notably that at Nalanda in India, which was famous for its philosophy department. Among these philosophers there were basically two schools of thought about what emptiness of inherent existence meant.

According to the first view, emptiness of inherent existence is the result of carrying the logic of certain basic existential facts to their ultimate conclusion. These facts are the truths that (a) everything is impermanent, and (b) everything depends upon something else. These two are generally taken to be basic Buddhist axioms. Realising their truth and their application to all phenomena, then, constitutes enlightenment.

There is a problem here, however. Most people reading this are likely to say, 'So what?' It is difficult to see from a dry definition like this what all the fuss is about. Surely enlightenment is something more than comprehending an academic definition?

To understand why anybody might have got excited about this, one must first understand some of the context in which this kind of enlightenment was invented. Existence, in the terminology of Indian philosophy, had a rather different implication from what we now take the word to mean. In the Indian context, existence really meant what we would call eternal existence. We are talking here about the first couple of centuries of the Common Era or possibly slightly earlier. There was a widespread belief at the time that things, including people, had eternal essences. The eternal essence of a person was called the *atman*, or soul. Buddha had denied the existence of the atman, so Buddhist enlightenment was said to consist of a realisation of this truth, not just about oneself – though that is an important part of it – but about everything.

You see, if you believe in the atman, then you are doomed to go on circling through life after life *ad infinitum*. As with Enlightenment as Escape, this, apparently, is a fate worse than not doing so. This second approach, however, adds a special twist. This is the assertion that this circling is only apparent – that is to say, it is a delusion. If you think that it is so, then it will be so in your case. If you realise that it is not so, then it will not be so in your case. If this sounds like a logical fallacy to you, then that is because you are thinking like a modern person who believes that there is a reality that is separate from your subjective beliefs. The people who invented this kind of enlightenment did not believe in any such reality. Here, therefore, thinking makes it so.

So, let me try and restate this. If you think things have 'inherent existence', then that is how it will be for you and you will be trapped in a world of inherent existences indefinitely. Such a world is a world of suffering. With E1 escape was achieved by eliminating desire. With E2 it is achieved by realising that the world of inherent existences – and, therefore, of suffering – is a mirage. When one realises this, then the mirage disappears. This is enlightenment.

There is a second interpretation of the absence of inherent existence. There were those who took exception to the idea that this idea could be established by logic. After all, if everything is empty of inherent existence, then 'everything' also includes logic and the mind that creates logic. Now we really are getting into the realms of the *mysterium tremendum*. What this boils down to, however, is the idea that emptiness really refers to the impossibility of defining reality in words and theories. This is, of course, a popular idea, but, again, one runs up against the 'So what?' question.

Well, according to this definition, understanding this will radically change our lives. But I do understand it and my life has not changed, you might say. Well, then, you have not understood it deeply enough. It is not enough to understand this with your intellect. You have got to understand it with your whole being and in such a way that the realisation does not desert you at those times when it matters.

How might this work? If you really understand and experience that everything is empty of inherent existence, then you will not get upset about anything – because nothing is truly real. If you go even further and also subscribe to the associated idea that 'thinking makes it so' or, to put that differently, everything is just projection of mind, then you will be doubly immune to getting upset about outside influences. Instead, you will realise that whenever anything nasty appears before you, it is not because something nasty exists in the world, but, rather, because you have projected your mind in a nasty-making way. So this is a rather different kind of enlightenment from Enlightenment as Escape in that it is vastly more solipsistic.

Review

A short review is in order before we go on and confuse the picture further. E1 and E2 are both based upon the idea that the desirable goal is to escape from this world of sorrows. Escape is essentially a form of extinction. E1 sees this as being achieved by eliminating desire. E2 sees it as a matter of a change in the way one perceives the world. Both approaches are rooted strongly in the idea of rebirth. The two are different, but not necessarily incompatible. Advocates of E2 see it as an upmarket version of E1. E2, however, especially E2(b), is closely associated with the idea that the material world is only a projection of mind, whereas this is not the case with E1.

Both types are said to take a long time to accomplish and this assertion seriously undermines their claim to be the same as the enlightenment that Buddha and his arhats experienced, which generally came quickly. This problem is commonly explained away, either by saying that the Buddha was much better at enlightening people than anybody else has been – which is possible – or, and this is the more standard explanation, by saying that the people alive in the time of the Buddha were a special lot. They had apparently been waiting in various heavens for an opportunity to be born while a Buddha was present on the earth and now seized their chance. This kind of fairytale stuff seems to me to devalue Buddhism and I find it sad that the Buddha's efforts on humanity's behalf should have been so diminished. These stories, nonetheless, do have a charm for some.

E3: ENLIGHTENMENT AS ETERNAL LIFE

Supermarket number three offers a quite different product. This product sells well in some Far Eastern countries, but has made little headway in the West, largely because another Middle Eastern manufacturer got in first and cornered the market. Nonetheless, the launch of this product by a Buddhist firm in the East at around about the same time as the well-known Middle Eastern concern got going, namely, about 2,000 years ago, did mark a significant stage in the development of Buddhist thinking.

In the pre-launch publicity, supermarket three put it about that the products offered by one and two were only half-way houses. The idea was that this talk about extinction was all very well, but there is actually something much better on offer. Buddhists tend to avoid direct confrontation, so rather than denying another school's ideas outright, the usual thing to do is to construct a story that will explain why the Buddha might still have taught the idea that one actually intends to reject. This enables one's opponents to retain their place as Buddhists, even though one intends to show that their idea of what the Buddha really meant is inadequate.

So here the story is that Buddha only taught those ideas about extinction for the sake of people who were so bogged down in worldly life that they just needed a way to get out. Extinction was just window-dressing to get people to take the first step, said the people from store number three. According to this approach, the enlightenments that E1 and E2 advocate are themselves just a mirage – well, actually, if we are going to be precise, what the text in question calls them is an 'apparitional city'. This is all set out in a book called the *Lotus Sutra*.

If people have a long journey to make and the goal is out of sight, then they will probably never even start. So the Buddha apparently conjured up the appearance of a staging post half-way along the journey so that the weary could think they were going to get a rest. The travellers, of course, do not think this is a stage – they think it is the destination. When they have got that far, however, it will be possible to tell them that the real goal is to be found further on. This ultimate goal is not called extinction, it is called eternal life.

The launch of this third model of enlightenment was bitterly resented by the people loyal to stores one and two. They did not like the way that it suggested that they had been hoodwinked. You do not like changing your ideas because you are arrogant, replied the people from store three: it is not a case of hoodwinking, it is a case of skilful means. The Buddha would never have got people to start on the journey, had he not been a bit crafty about it. Thus, the term 'skilful means' (*upaya*) came to play a significant part in later Buddhist thought.

The idea of skilful means is both useful and treacherous. It is useful in providing an ideological underpinning for Buddhism's adaptability. Buddhism is the only Indian religion that has managed to break out of the Indian cultural world and become the established faith of large countries with quite different cultures in other parts of the world. Some of the world's most populous countries – China, Japan, Indonesia and others – have been Buddhist at one time or another. This achievement has required flexibility and this flexibility has been made possible by the idea of skilful means. On the other hand, the idea has also been carried to quite ridiculous lengths. There is a strong current in Far Eastern Buddhism that maintains that the Buddha was, in effect, superhuman. Apparently, when the Buddha cut his foot and was laid up for a few weeks suffering agonies from a septic wound, he did not really suffer at all. He just contrived this incident as a skilful means demonstrating to his disciples how to suffer with fortitude. Apparently, the Buddha did not have to die: he only did so as skilful means in order to give his disciples a sense of urgency. Apparently, he did not really need to practise asceticism before his enlightenment ... and so on. From this viewpoint, the Buddha's whole life and ministry was a put-up job. This line of thinking, which this author finds totally unacceptable, is nonetheless widespread in the East and provides a basis for the kind of religiosity that gives the Buddha a semidivine status.

So, to recap, the product offered by supermarket number three envisages a long journey indeed – eternal in fact. This journey leads to a place called complete Buddhahood for all sentient beings. Buddhas are those who have reached there, and we shall all reach there eventually. It is just a matter of time. In the meantime, the important work, for those who are in the know, is to spread the word and to help others along the way. These helpful people who are in the know are called bodhisattvas. Those who still think that extinction is the end of the journey are called *shravakas*. The word shravaka originally meant disciple. In this context, however, it refers to the people who shop at store number one.

Review

It is possible to discern a sequence from E_1 through E_2 to E_3. Each builds upon and contradicts some elements of the one before. The differences between them are strongly evident. They also do have some features in common. All three require personal discipline and strict morality on the part of the practitioner. The morality is not the same in each case, but all three do convey a sense that an enlightened person will act in certain ways and not in other ways. If we consider the three to be a spectrum then at the E1 end, the prescribed morality is based upon individual purity and merit making, whereas at the E3 end the prescribed morality is altruistic and more flexible. We cannot imagine somebody who is enlightened in the sense of E1 being anything other than celibate, for instance, whereas this is by no means so clear with E2 or E3. Before we go on to look at the forms of enlightenment invented in China, we have one last Indian product to examine. E4 is called Tantra.

E4: TANTRIC ENLIGHTENMENT

The origins of Tantra are lost in the mists of time. On the surface at least, this approach to enlightenment owes a good deal to magic. This is an approach that offers transformation through ritual. In the Buddhist form, this has, however, become a psychologically sophisticated method.

The essence of this approach lies in the idea that anything whatsoever can be transformed into enlightenment: an idea that is at once radical, intriguing and dangerous. Those who advance this approach would not quibble with this description. Tantra is not for the faint-hearted, they would say.

Thus, while the Buddha recommended various forms of abstinence – from sex, for instance – the Tantric practitioner believes that everything can be transformed into enlightenment – sexual activity, drinking alcohol and, in principle, even taking life, not excluded. This, of course, could and sometimes has been, a popular idea and at other times an infamous one.

It is not so simple as it might at first sound. While everything can in principle be transformed, actually doing it is not so easy. In fact, it can only be achieved by following long, disciplined training under the strict guidance of an existing master of the secret art. This, therefore, is an approach in which the guru-disciple bond takes on formidable consequentiality. Woe betide those who enter this path and then break or abuse their connections with the teacher.

The element of guru worship is absolutely central to this approach. In fact we could say that E4 is achieved when there is complete submission to the guru. Teachings are given not 'open-handedly', as with E1, but only after ritual empowerments. The more important of these are generally only given after the aspirant has completed practices or tests designed both to demonstrate sincerity and to accumulate the kind of merit that will ensure that the adept will use the powers they acquire virtuously. They also serve as an initiation that helps to keep the core teachings secret.

Tantra, like all the other Indian-based approaches, is rooted in the ideology of rebirth. Here, however, the focus is not so much upon escape as upon navigation. The tantric adept aims to acquire the skills to navigate the between-lives state – called the *bardo* – at will. The person in possession of E4, therefore, can and does choose where, and as what, he or she will be reborn in the next life.

The actual methodology of Tantra is a matter of controlling the projections of mind. To this end, elaborate visualisation techniques are practised. This approach shares with E2, therefore, the idea that the mind controls the physical world. Whereas in E2 this simply means that a person can, therefore, escape from misfortune by gaining insight into the illusory nature of their own projections, in Tantra this principle is carried much further, turning the practitioner into a virtual magician who can, in theory, do all manner of miracles. The shamanic influence in this approach is apparent. There are many texts that portray the Buddha as such a practitioner – able to fly through the air and walk through walls and so on. Not all Buddhists take this kind of material seriously, however.

Tantra is most strongly associated with Tibetan Buddhism where, in general, E2 and E4 are practised in tandem. This yields quite a promising hybrid since the Tantric element accommodates the passions, while the philosophy of emptiness component accommodates the intellect. The unification of the two is achieved through the ideology of the bodhisattva ideal. A bodhisattva is a person who is on the way towards buddhahood and who, in the meantime, lives for the service of other sentient beings. This altruistic spirit means that even though such people might acquire the insight necessary, as per E2, to leave this life of sorrows, they will not do so, but will choose to remain here to help other beings towards enlightenment. Having made such a decision, the bodhisattva, of course, finds the technology offered by E4 very useful. Now he can have a rebirth of his choice. This, of course, makes the work of staying in circulation and coming back to help others much more practical.

This is the basis of the Tibetan practice of *tulkus*, or reincarnated lamas. High-ranking lamas leave information before they die about where they are going to be reborn. This is generally in the form of a hint or a riddle. After they die, they may appear to their former associates in a dream and give them information about where the rebirth is to take place. Eventually the child is found and brought up as the new incarnation of the previous saint. This system has served Tibetan Buddhism well for several hundred years.

DISCUSSION

The interesting thing that emerges from all this is not so much the fact that different schools of Buddhism have markedly different ideas of what enlightenment is, as that the more sincere a Buddhist is, the less concerned he or she is with attaining enlightenment. There has been a striking tendency since the time of the Buddha to move enlightenment out of reach. It has become a goal that is out of sight over the horizon. This is in marked contrast to the picture given by the earliest texts, in which people are becoming arhats on every third page.

What seems to have happened is that for the Buddha and his immediate disciples, enlightenment was a means to an end. You needed to be enlightened in order to get on with the work that the Buddha had in mind. It was what you needed to do first. For later generations, however, enlightenment became the goal. It came to be the Buddhist equivalent to the Hindu apotheosis of merger with Brahma, the supreme godhead. What is indicated by the word enlightenment for these later generations of Buddhists is, therefore, completely different from what the Buddha meant by the term.

After the Buddha died, Buddhists had to defend their ideas against others and spread them amongst people who believed in rebirth and who believed that the round of rebirths finally comes to an end when one attains a state of perfection in which all one's humanness has been overcome and there remains no further obstacle to merging with the divine. It was naturally assumed that the Buddha must have been teaching something similar – he was a sage after all.

There was a constant pressure, therefore, to make the Buddha into a kind of god, to attribute supernatural powers to him, to see him as teaching a path of individual salvation, to see the enlightenment he spoke of as the word for such salvation and, therefore, to turn all his teachings into a path in search of that goal that everybody already knew was far, far away in the future. This was almost certainly a gross distortion of the Buddha's teaching.

Against this we can assert that the Buddha was not divine and did not regard being divine as desirable. Enlightenment was nothing to do with either extinction or merger with the divinity, but was in fact a waking up to the fact that relying upon divinities was a waste of time and extinction would simply be an ignoble escape. The fact that the Buddha was human like the rest of us is a vitally important element in the Buddhist story. He was human and enlightened. We are human so we too can be enlightened. Enlightenment is not, however, an end in itself.

We can assert that enlightenment is not a personal salvation, but is a waking up to the fact that self-seeking, either by the worldly route of self-indulgence or by the spiritual route of sacred procedures, is counterproductive. The selfish just end up lonely and unproductive. Buddha's vision was a vision of a noble life for all, not of salvation for the few. He chose a few not so that they could be privileged, but so that they could serve the many.

This examination, therefore, shows us how Buddhism has accommodated to one major culture. In the process, the goal of the religion has come to be reconceptualised a number of times in ways that, when formally defined, are completely irreconcilable with one another. Nonetheless, there is something that holds through all of this and that is the practice of service to others. Some will assert that service to others is only the hallmark of E2, E3 and, perhaps, E4, since these are associated with the bodhisattva ideal, but this is not really true. The desireless state of E1 is surely simply another way of expressing the same basic noble altruistic spirit that must have been the essence of old Shakyamuni's original dispensation. He might turn in his ashes if he saw what people had made of his teachings, but he would surely still be impressed by the fact that, whatever the doctrines they hold to, there are Buddhists of all schools who have continued to live lives of service, adapting to the conditions of their times. That surely is the real enlightenment that he was concerned about.

Let us now move on and look at what the Chinese, Japanese, Koreans and Vietnamese made of all this. As we do so we will encounter some further ideas of enlightenment, different again from those met so far.

Chinese Enlightenments

BUDDHISM IN CHINA

Buddhism was successful in China and this success was achieved by adapting to local conditions. Almost all the Indian schools of Buddhism were imported into China during the first 500 years of the Common Era. For the most part, however, they did not survive in their original form. Only the esoteric Tantric School made serious headway without root and branch revision at the hands of its new hosts. Completely new Chinese schools came into existence, however: *Tien Tai*, *Hua Yen*, Zen and Pure Land. These spread and further developed in the lands around China, most notably in Japan. This transition from India to China is important for us to study, both because it is an intrinsically fascinating story and because it gives us many more angles from which to look at what can happen to Buddhism.

The forms of enlightenment that developed in China are not the same as their Indian predecessors. In the West we are now exposed to forms of Buddhism arriving from the Indian worlds of Tibet, Sri Lanka, Thailand and so on and also from the Sino-Japanese world. Often Buddhists coming from these different lands use similar terminology while meaning different things by it. There is a tendency in Buddhism to gloss over these differences. It is, in many quarters, considered not quite nice to point out differences. It is much better, however, that we go into this with our eyes open. The Buddha would certainly have wanted it so.

On 3 May 1998 at the end of the three-day teaching on Tibetan Buddhism in New York, there was a meeting[1] between the Dalai Lama and Chinese Master Sheng-yen. Although, in general, this meeting was a polite affair in which the aim was to harmonise the Chinese and Tibetan approaches, finding their common ground and glossing over differences, several important statements were made in it by Shen-yen that indicate something of the spirit of Chinese Buddhism in general.

Shen-yen says, 'The realization of no-self is really the result of the practice of non-seeking, because as a person's practice advances, he or she ceases searching for individual enlightenment and concentrates on helping others' (p.35), and '. . . enlightenment does not end afflictions. Rather it is a state in which doubt with regard to the dharma is for ever terminated. Fully enlightened people may still have afflictions, but they will not manifest them verbally or bodily. They are not free from all afflictions, but they clearly know the path of practice they must follow' (p.36).

Shen-yen says: 'It is our hope to make the Buddha Land manifest in the human world. To make this vision come true, we must begin by purifying our minds and then purifying our actions. When our minds and our actions are pure, we will be able to have a profound influence on others, enabling their minds and actions to be pure. Eventually, in this way, our world will become a Pure Land' (p.24). This passage clearly reveals the this-worldly goal and practical nature of much Chinese Buddhism and shows how it is quite different in tenor from those approaches that focus upon escape from a world viewed as irredeemable.

The creation of a Pure Land here in this world was the one area where there seemed to be a real meeting of minds between these two leaders. It is interesting that Buddhists may be completely divided over doctrine and metaphysics, but still be united on an agenda for this world. The Dalai Lama responded to Shen-yen's statement by saying that liberation from suffering is a private affair but what matters is to create the 'nirvana of society' (p.37).

We will, of course, keep returning to this social theme which is central to the main argument of this book. Let us first pause to have a look at some of those 'private affairs', as they have appeared in Chinese forms.

E5: ENLIGHTENMENT AS REALISATION OF BUDDHA NATURE

When Buddhists reached China they discovered that there was already an enlightenment product on the market called the *Tao* as well as a well-developed social morality called Confucianism. The Confucians were more resistant to the Buddhists than the Taoists were. Some of the cost of acceptance in China was the adoption by Buddhism of a more Confucian style of ethics, and this included a strong emphasis upon filial piety, which brought with it a de-emphasising of ideas about rebirth. Chinese ancestors do not get reborn; they stay around to benefit or haunt their descendants.

The struggle with these two already established religions made a big impression upon Buddhism. At three points in Chinese history there were major persecutions of Buddhism. These were all carried out by emperors called Wu and so are sometimes referred to as the three Wues. Between the second and third Wu, however, Buddhism was effectively the state religion of China and a major force for carrying a new kind of civilisation across East Asia. As at other times, however, the allegiance with worldly power had its down side. As a state religion, Buddhism had to find a philosophy that would justify autocratic power. In this role, Buddhism itself started to take on an absolutist flavour.

The Buddhists not only accommodated to the powerful Confucians; they also recruited a lot of Taoists into their ranks. Taoists had their own brand of metaphysics that they brought with them. Some see this as having been an enrichment of

Buddhism, opening it up to harmonise with nature. Others see it as a dilution and distortion that took the edge off the Buddha's original message. Like it or not, however, the resulting cross-fertilisation of ideas produced a new kind of enlightenment called Realisation of Buddha Nature.

Chinese pre-Buddhist spirituality was much rooted in ideas of nature – both in the sense of the natural world and that of the underlying nature and right ordering of things. The underlying nature of things is the 'way', or Tao, of those things. Everything has its Tao. There is a Tao of making tea just as much as there is a Tao of running an empire, or ploughing a field, or killing an ox, or living one's spiritual life. The secret of a good and happy life, these people thought, is to accord with the Tao. The Chinese Buddhists, therefore, launched the idea that the Tao of a person was something called 'intrinsic Buddha Nature'.

You will remember from the last chapter that enlightenment E3 – Enlightenment as Eternal Life – had already established the idea that we are all inevitably going to become buddhas at some future point in time. It was not a big step from this to suggest that everybody already has buddha potential – or even that, in some sense, everybody is actually a buddha already, in some latent sense, if they did but realise it. There can also be a subtle implication in some of these teachings that in some sense we were all enlightened once before we fell from grace. This last notion, of course, has some appeal in the West now. It chimes with a long-standing Western myth set in a certain Middle Eastern garden, that nowadays sometimes reappears in the idea that everyone is endowed with an 'inner child' who is the fount of all purity and innocence.

This new type of Buddha Nature enlightenment proved popular. It had nearly all the advantages of E3 – but without the waiting. Enlightenment could be instantaneous. All you have to do is to wake up to the fact that you are already intrinsically enlightened. This was, of course, an instant hit.

Although this approach allowed for immediate results, it still required effort. The problem is that we do not readily believe that we are buddhas. Training schools thus came into existence offering methods of cultivating the mind towards this particular goal of reawakening one's inherent enlightenment. The method used is generally intensive meditation and strict discipline. The obstacle to realisation being the stubbornness of our minds, the mind had to be made to submit. No mind at all became an ideal. People are willing to engage in periods of such intensive training because of the attractiveness of the possibility of a sudden breakthrough to enlightenment.

Here, however, a catch arises. According to the instructions, it is precisely this desire for results that is what prevents people from having the realisation that they so much long for. This twist owes more than a little to the Taoist origins of this idea. Taoists have always had a predilection for mischief and paradox.

The framework of ideas that E5 rests in is very different from some of the earlier Indian models we looked at in the last chapter. Generally, the Indian models look to a future escape from a world conceived as depressingly afflictive. This Chinese model, however, implies that what is required is a return to an implicitly former or original state of grace from which we have somehow fallen. Escape from a world of suffering is not really even on the agenda any more and rebirth ideas may be given lip-service, but they have been side-lined in a typically skilful Buddhist manoeuvre that manages to affirm all previous positions while really totally discrediting them. The aim has become personal bliss.

E6: ENLIGHTENMENT AS NON-DUALITY

Product number six has a quite close relationship to number five. To realise one's Buddha Nature by a change of consciousness must amount to coming to see the world the way that a buddha sees it. What is that way? That way, apparently, is non-dualistically.

This idea of non-dual perception has grown up gradually over the period of Buddhist history and was not part of the original message. Nonetheless, contemporary Buddhism widely acclaims that enlightenment is a matter of attaining to non-duality, or, as it increasingly and significantly called, the Non-Dual. The sales literature for this form of enlightenment says that to be enlightened is to experience the dropping away of the subject–object distinction. When this happens one will, apparently, have a direct experience of the ground of being, the void, the true nature, the essence of mind, freedom from all dichotomy, the One, Ultimate Reality, the Absolute, and so on . . . and on, and on. Texts on this type of Buddhism tend to multiple terms for the eternal, the *dharmadhatu*, the primal mind, etc. *ad nauseam*. Reading them, one begins to have a sense that the authors must have thought that if you just know enough names for the Tao, the real essence, the *Dharmakaya*, the Non-Dual, etc. then you will surely start to believe in it, which, apparently, is what matters.

The so-called 'direct seeing into non-duality' experience is, in Japanese, called *satori* or *kensho*. It is conceived to be a 'seeing into the true nature of things'. In practice, Chinese Buddhism developed the meditation methods imported from India and merged them with Taoistic contemplation. The resulting technology included methods for inducing 'sudden awakenings'. During such an awakening, one may see visions, recall past lives and attain to an impressive vividness of experiencing such as one thereafter never forgets. Kensho, therefore, may also be thought of as not unrelated to shamanic initiation.

We can, therefore, see the presence of some significant Taoist components in this product. Non-dual perception is unconventional and illogical. This means that people seeking this kind of enlightenment need to be jolted out of their conventional modes of thought by startling or paradoxical interventions. The trainee does not understand what is going on, of course, but that is as it should be. There are a vast number of instruction manuals for this type of training on the market. Enthusiasts buy them eagerly.

The more they fail to understand what the book says, the more profound they assume it to be. If you say, this all sounds like so much hocus pocus, well, then that just shows how lacking in transcendent wisdom you are.

This product, like E2, relies upon the idea that there are 'two truths' – relative or conventional truth on the one hand, and absolute or ultimate truth on the other. Enlightenment then becomes a matter of breaking through to ultimate truth so that one is liberated from conventional reality. The rhetoric of this approach suggests that all the methods used by the other approaches are themselves simply part of conventional reality. It also fits well with the idea of a hidden world separate from and superior to this one.

The attraction of attaining to the Non-Dual is that it offers the possibility of being at peace with everything. Duality, after all, includes the human habit of making choices. E6 is presented as without difficulty, save that of avoiding making choices. There are, of course, pitfalls for one who is all-accepting and does not make choices. Many of these pitfalls lie in the area of ethics. The Non-Dual is capable of encompassing all things – including those that many people might describe as wicked. Detractors of this approach see it as weak in this area particularly.

The Non-Dual, like original enlightenment, is essentially a Taoist rather than a Buddhist idea. Accommodating it was part of the price Buddhism paid for acceptance in China. The idea had somehow, however, to be woven into the fabric of Buddhist doctrine. This was achieved by modifying the central Buddhist theory of dependent origination.

According to the theory of dependent origination, things arise from conditions. It is a theory of how one thing arises from another, or from a group of others. This arising is sequential. One thing leads to another. The purpose and merit of this theory was that:

- it provides a sense of purpose

- it provides a basis for ethics, since things have consequences
- it does away with the need for either a god above or a metaphysical substratum below.

The Buddha's ideology, therefore, was essentially constructive, moral and ontologically nonhierarchical.

Dependent origination provides a theory of how things are interrelated. The Chinese rewrote this theory along Taoist lines. In the Chinese version, the theory comes to be called 'interdependent co-arising'. Since this is quite a mouthful, the Vietnamese Buddhist Master Thich Nhat Hanh has recently coined the simpler term 'interbeing'.[2]

Interdependent co-arising is, however, a completely different theory from dependent origination. Co-arising is nonsequential and not really causative. The original Buddhist theory implies that all phenomena arise out of pre-existing conditions and each phenomenon can serve as a precondition for other subsequent phenomena. Thus we get sequences, such as very commonly occur in the Buddha's explanations of things. There is a sense from this that purposeful creativity is possible. It supports the idea of cumulative progress. We can represent the theory of dependent origination schematically like this:

$$O \rightarrow O \rightarrow O \rightarrow O \rightarrow O \rightarrow O$$

Each thing gives rise to the next thing. It does not necessarily follow from this theory that everything in the world is related to every other thing. It does follow that some things give rise to other things in a predictable and reliable way.

The theory of interdependent co-arising is different. It can be represented diagrammatically as follows:

$$O \sim O \sim O \sim O \sim O \sim O$$
$$\uparrow \quad \uparrow \quad \uparrow \quad \uparrow \quad \uparrow \quad \uparrow$$

All the apparently separate things arise together. They do not cause one another except in the sense that the left and right halves cause one another when you cut a piece of paper in half. In this second theory, the left and right halves 'cause' each other, whereas in the first theory it was the scissors and the hand that did the causing.

According to the second theory, things appear separate, but really they are part of one whole. This unity is, of course, the Non-Dual. This idea was popular in China because it was really an indigenous Chinese idea dressed up in Buddhist language. It was not original Buddhism. The same idea is now extremely popular in the West. This is in part because it tallies with popular versions of ecology that have been developing in the West for the past several decades as we have become more and more alert to the threat of environmental breakdown. Interbeing is thus a term that has hit a chord.

Before we swallow this idea hook, line and sinker, it would be wise to consider the question a little more thoroughly. Ecological thought, for instance, does not imply interexistence. Ecology took Darwin as one of its springboards. Darwin pointed out the effects of plant and animal species upon other species in a local environment. He showed, for example, that an increase in the number of domestic cats led to a reduction in mice that in turn produced an increase in certain pollinating insects that were then no longer having their homes eaten by the mice, and that that, in turn, changed the distribution of flowers in an area, permitting, in one particular instance, a profusion of red clover. One can say, if you like, no cats, no clover. What we are talking about here, however, is not a mystical unity, but a chain of dualistic interactions that are not particularly reciprocal. A good year for clover would not result in a multiplication of cats. This is not a case of cats and clover being part of a single greater unity, it is a case of one thing arising in dependence upon another as a sequence of conditional relations – just as the dependent origination theory would have it, in fact. This arising is not simultaneous. It is a sequence over time. These points are important if we are to understand what the Buddha is saying with precision rather than simply glossing it in a way that sounds mystical, but is not actually how it is and not what he said.

Dualism and sequentialism have advantages. They tend to be much more fruitful in the development of practical and constructive thought than spatial or temporal monism, which tends to leave us simply with a sense of unreality. Dualism also, contrary to popular prejudice, militates against reductionism. If the world is made up of contrasting principles, we can explain phenomena in terms of their interactions, rather than straining always to reduce one principle to the other. Take the issue of mind and matter, for instance. Modern science spends much effort trying fruitlessly to demonstrate that mental activity can be reduced to an understanding of brain chemistry. Eastern science has spent an equally vast amount of effort upon fruitlessly trying to demonstrate that matter is simply a manifestation of mind. This is wasted effort. People will make such efforts because they think that they would be happier if they could reduce the whole working of the universe to a single principle or a single substance. We should all ardently pray that they continue to be unsuccessful. Some of the current popularity of at least some branches of Buddhism no doubt rests upon the fact that it seems to offer a vision of primordial unity. This is unwarranted. We act upon one another, certainly. That we interexist is going too far. Cats will not be killed by a failure of the clover crop.

The real motive, and it is noble enough in itself, behind the search for a unifying substance or principle – a Non-Dual, or whatever – is the hope that this will eliminate conflict. This search for harmony through underlying uniformity, however, is counterproductive. Diversity is a fact – and it is a benign fact. There will be disagreements. This is not the end of the world – it is the beginning of it. Our pursuit of harmony must not be so stringent that we outlaw discord. There are ways to handle disagreements creatively and constructively, and it is better that we learn those methods than that we try to pretend that there is no need for them. If the French, the Americans and the Vietnamese, the Christians, the Buddhists and the Communists, had been willing to accept that they were different and that there could be a value in those differences, then there would have been no war in Vietnam. It was precisely because some groups thought that all people are the same underneath, and that they knew how that should be, that they set about butchering each other. Monism pressed too far can only prove oppressive.

Interdependent co-arising, as a theory on its own, leaves us rudderless. If we consider the three virtues of the theory of dependent origination, we see that interbeing undermines them all. Interdependent co-arising has the following characteristics:

- It is essentially a steady state theory rather than a progressive one. If things progress it is not through our agency.
- It does not, therefore, provide much foundation for ethics, since all things, good and bad, are a consequence of all other things, good and bad – there is no suggestion that good yields only good. The Taoist idea is that good and bad arise together and are mutually formative. Hanh has distanced himself from this aspect of the idea in other branches of his teaching, but this probably just introduces inconsistency.
- It cries out for a metaphysical basis – for some supramundane Unity or metaphysical substratum from which all things arise. This, of course, could be the Tao, Buddha Nature, or some divine source. Whatever it is, the effect is fundamentally disempowering of people as compared with the original Buddhist theory which allowed for diversity of action with corresponding diversity of effect.

If we represent the interdependent co-arising theory schematically and we give it such a basis, then it looks like this:

O ˜ O ˜ O ˜ O ˜ O ˜ O ˜ O ˜ O
↑ ↑ ↑ ↑ ↑ ↑ ↑ ↑

SOURCE OF ALL — PRIMAL UNITY

Now this primal source is, of course, what is being referred to by the term the Non-Dual. Quite quickly, in China, it came also to be identified with the Buddhist term *shunyata* meaning 'the void', or, as we should probably now say, the Void. The arrival of initial capitals in many of these terms and the transformation of words for qualities into entities, gives us a sense of how what this is really all about is the reintroduction of the metaphysical dimension of religion, that much of the original Buddha's teaching had been designed to take out.

You will remember that when we were discussing E2 reference was made to the possibility of emptiness as presence rather than emptiness as absence. The Non-Dual is emptiness as presence. It is shunyata present in all things. This is a new and different usage of the term. Emptiness has now become something that can be perceived and experienced.

There are clearly a number of variants here upon a single central idea. This idea is the unity in diversity. The appeal of this idea lies at two levels. It appeals to the common person because it suggests that we can all be at home in this world together, without necessarily having to do much about it ourselves. It appeals to those in power in society – especially those in absolute power – since they can identify with the Unity. The source of all, in China, could be represented by the emperor. This theory, therefore, is intrinsically conservative, whereas the original theory of dependent origination was not. Harmony in diversity is good. Unity in diversity is a deception.

Review
The two approaches to enlightenment that we have looked at in this chapter so far are related to each other in that they both posit a metaphysical basis to real world phenomena. The Buddha Nature is such a base for the individual person and the Non-Dual is such

a base for things in the world at large. To a Western world, that has a heritage of religion based on soul and god, and, though it may have lost faith in them, is still looking for credible substitutes, such ideas can have the appeal of comfortable familiarity at the same time as seeming daringly novel.

This novelty will wear off, of course. Anything new is radical in its first introduction. The most conservative ideas can seem outrageously progressive when they first enter a new social context. As Buddhism is introduced to the West, therefore, we need to be discriminating and to consider what is likely to come of the philosophies we are adopting when they have become more widespread and influential.

Despite the enthusiasm that many feel for these ideas currently, we should not be blind to the possibility that they will, if widely adopted, prove weak ethically, implicitly fatalistic, and yet supportive of oppressive degrees of conformity. The pressure to actualise the ideal by outlawing criticism is likely to outweigh other considerations. The soft, Taoistic, 'go with the flow' ethos is likely to prevail over the harder words of the Buddha – to stand against the current and cut the stream.

It is also possible, of course, that ideas of interbeing and Buddha Nature are popular in the contemporary West, in part at least, precisely because they are sensed to undermine individual ethics and because they are comforting rather than galvanising. The generation of people who were born immediately after the Second World War – my generation – has spent a vast amount of energy on discrediting the ethics of our forefathers. The fact that the old ways had led to war on an unprecedented scale was justification enough for this revolt. There is always the danger of throwing out the baby with the bath water, however.

The idea of Buddha Nature has come quite a way from its origins. To begin with, the idea of Buddha Nature was simply an assertion that all people *could* become enlightened. This usage is in line with the Buddha's original teaching. One can become enlightened. There has, however, been a shift away from the

CHINESE ENLIGHTENMENTS

original idea, first towards an assertion that all *will* become enlightened, then to one that all *are already* enlightened, and finally to the idea that Buddha Nature is a metaphysical, eternal element residing in each individual. By this stage we have reached a point that is remote from the Buddha's original intention.

E7: ENLIGHTENMENT AS IMPASSIVITY

Before finally leaving E5 and E6 we need to consider a further variant upon this theme that is nonetheless distinct enough to warrant its own section. Not long ago, an acquaintance of mine went to visit a Zen monastery. He asked one of the monks what the object of their practice was. The monk pondered for a moment and then he looked out of the window and pointed to a small Buddha statue that was sitting upon the wall opposite. It happened to be a wet day and the rain poured down over the stone figure. In some of the crevices of the figure, moss was growing.

The monk said, 'You see that stone Buddha, out there. He just sits there come what may. He does not budge if it rains or if the sun comes out. It is all the same to him. He gets on with his practice irrespective of changes in conditions. In just the same way, we are practising here in order to become like that. We sit in meditation just like the stone Buddha. Thoughts come and go, but we are not moved by them. Worldly circumstances are all transient. Our practice is to centre ourselves upon the Ultimate and so be beyond all that is transient.'

This description provides a nice picture of one important strand of Buddhist thought. If we adopt the idea of the Non-Dual, then really there is no reason to do anything. The only possible thing worth doing might be to wake other people up to the idea of the Non-Dual, but really there is no need to do anything at all. All beings, after all, are already inherently enlightened. Their only problem is that they do not realise it, but since it is already so, their non-realisation is just a delusion. In reality, all beings were, are and always will be perfect just as they are, so there is nothing to be done. As it says in the Zen poem, 'Sitting quietly doing nothing, spring comes and the grass grows all by itself'.

There is thus a form of enlightenment advocated by some Buddhists that is complete passivity, or, alternatively, in some versions, spontaneous irrationality. This is a matter of virtually giving up the idea of actions having consequence. Another friend talked to a prominent monk of a quite unrelated Buddhist school. He told the monk that he found the things that he read about in the news distressing. The monk's advice was, 'Don't read the newspapers'. The idea here is that there is nothing you can do. This form of enlightenment is the peace that comes from detachment. Detachment is a key word in this form of enlightenment.

This approach is widespread, and, in my view, is a pitiful trap that has sidetracked many creative intelligent people and seriously reduced the contribution that they could have made to the world. It is not limited to one school of Buddhism. In several schools there is the idea that all living beings are divided into two categories. One category is sentient beings. The other category is buddhas. The idea is that buddhas are beyond being sentient – Buddhas have no feelings. This is worse than nonsense.

How has this come about? This is the result of mistaking the method for the goal – something that has happened over and over in Buddhist history. We can easily understand how this happens. The Buddha wanted to see change in the world. To achieve these changes there need to be people trained to carry the work forward. This training is bound to include bringing people to the kind of fortitude where they can meet difficult circumstances with some equanimity and poise. Gandhi employed these methods to great effect in recent times. His followers were willing, if necessary, to go without food or to march into the clubs wielded by the police and to do so with dignity. Actions of this kind changed the destiny of the world.

The Buddha's disciples did not live in ivory towers. They went forth into the world far and wide. Many did meet with mishap in the service of the dharma. When the Buddha talks of his followers not giving way to anger even if they are being cut up with a two-handed saw, he was not talking idly.[3] The first Buddhists were courageous. Many were able to triumph over adversity impressively because of their training. In this context, training that increases equanimity and fortitude makes sense and is useful to the world. People immediately sense from those who have done such training a quality that is desirable. Soon people are pursuing such training without any thought to its purpose. Instead of training themselves to help the world, they are really training themselves in order to obtain a personal experience, or in order to be well thought of by others.

Unhooked from its purpose, Buddhist training still offers something. It becomes a form of character training. If this is walled up in monasteries devoted only to quietism, or is practised only by lay people looking for stress relief, it is largely wasted. And if it develops into a creed of dissociation from the problems of the world, then it has not only lost its original purpose, but has come to stand against it. This kind of training in impassivity can, therefore, lead people to make a good deal less of their lives than they might have done.

There is a further aspect of this approach that we should also consider. Once unhooked from its original compassionate purpose, techniques of Buddhist origin can sometimes be reharnessed to purposes that are completely opposed to the original Buddhist project. The discipline of intensive meditation training leading to imperturbability in the midst of turmoil has a strong appeal for the military man.

Zen became the preferred approach to spirituality of the Samurai. The ability to maintain a clear mind even in the midst of battle was much sought after. That this stood in direct opposition to the rule in the vinaya that Buddhist practitioners should not even stay to witness the preparation for battle nor participate in any military activity was recognised and seen simply as evidence that later Japanese interpretations were superior. Those early Buddhists were just not made of the right stuff.

Here, therefore, we encounter a form of enlightenment that enables one to be a more effective killer. With the completely purified mind one can act decisively in any circumstance. Some branches of Buddhism developed close associations with martial arts and the trainings of the two disciplines merged. Through several centuries of Japanese history many monasteries had their own armies and these were frequently in conflict with one another. Similar phenomena were not unknown in Korea and Tibet. Beware.

E8: ENLIGHTENMENT AS FAITH

Let us turn to a quite different approach. This is the form of enlightenment offered by approach number eight. Like product number three, this item has not made so much advance in the West, and for similar reasons, though this may slowly be changing. In the Far East, however, this is a best-selling brand. The popular appeal of this product is due to the fact that it is a lot less work than any of the others. It is sold upon precisely this fact: it is less arduous. In many respects this product has developed out of product number three. You will remember that in the scheme of things advanced by E3, there are buddhas and bodhisattvas around trying to help other beings. The line taken by number three is that one should, therefore, become one of those helpers. The line taken by approach number eight, on the other hand, is to say that since that would be far too difficult, what we should do is to accept fully that we are the ones who are to be helped. If we just recognise that we really have no capacity to save ourselves and, at the same time, place complete faith in the idea that there are buddhas and bodhisattvas who have pledged to help us, then we can be saved by simply having faith in them and their saving work. This approach, therefore, enjoins faith, modesty and gratitude.

It does not particularly require virtue or effort on our part. Rather we should accept that we are incapable of real virtue. This is called an 'other-power' approach and, from this perspective, all the other approaches are called 'self power'. The self-power approaches are criticised for being like trying to lift yourself up by your own boot-straps. This critique is a bit like the paradox built into method five – if you really want it then that very wanting will prevent you getting it. In method eight, if you try to save yourself then you are not really relying upon the saving power of the Buddha. Only when you reach the point of experiencing the fact that he does everything and you do nothing will the great turning around in your consciousness occur. You will then enter into a condition called settled faith. Your rebirth in the Buddha Land will be assured and from there you will be irreversibly guaranteed entry into nirvana.

Put like this, E8 has little appeal for Westerners and this is, in fact, the case. The Shin Buddhist schools that offer this approach are popular among even third- or fourth-generation East Asian immigrants to North America, for instance, but make little headway in attracting Caucasian followers. The paradox is, therefore, that Buddhist Churches of America, the Jodo Shinshu organisation in the USA, is the biggest and longest established Buddhist organisation in North America while also being the least Westernised and the one in most serious decline.

Those Westerners who have ventured over the threshold of the Shin Church are commonly left with the sense that there is something here that is of great value that is never going to spread in the West while it is presented in its current guise. The problem is that it looks just like Protestant Christianity and if that is what Western people want, then they are not going to go to a Chinese or Japanese import while Protestantism remains alive and well.

Some of the similarity between Shin and Protestantism is cosmetic and deliberate. The Japanese living in the USA were interned during the Second World War. They were all placed in concentration camps. When they returned to their homes or were resettled by the American authorities after the war, they were regarded with great suspicion by their neighbours. They might be second-generation Americans, but they were seen as the enemy. Jodo Shinshu made deliberate efforts to style its pattern of activity and worship to look as much like Christianity as possible. This enabled the Japanese to continue their own community and culture without looking any more conspicuous than they inevitably already were. This policy served them well for a couple of generations. Now it has become a liability. There would undoubtedly be much greater interest by Westerners in this approach to Buddhism if it were not wrapped up in a 'go to church on Sunday, live a conventional life and then go to heaven' framework.

Let us take a little time to look beyond the first appearances. In particular, we need to ask what made Shin Buddhism so popular in the East originally. The founders of this approach in seventh-century China – Tao Cho and Shan Tao – and those in thirteenth-century Japan – Honen and Shinran – were immensely influential in their own times. They were all unconventional figures who advanced Buddhism for the masses in the face of fierce opposition from those who had found positions of power and privilege through the alliance of religion and state power. These were people who lived virtuous lives that were not detached from those of ordinary people and who preached a message that the Pure Land can be entered through faith.

Nor are Pure Land approaches limited to China and Japan. In Tibet, as we have already noted, the Pure Land of Dewarchen appears in the teachings of all the four different denominations. The idea occurs all over the Mahayana world and the imagery of the Pure Land is also found in the Pali suttas. The mandala diagrams that have become such a widespread symbol of Buddhism in so many ways are also Pure Land imagery, the mandala being essentially a stylised map of the ideal city. We are, therefore, talking about a widespread phenomenon. Indeed, there is really more common ground between Buddhist schools on the question of a Pure Land than there is on the nature of enlightenment and this is probably significant. The creation of a Pure Land may be a more important agenda than the attainment of enlightenment.

A figure like Shan Tao was popular for a number of reasons. First, he lived a simple and good life with no pretensions to personal grandiosity. Secondly, he was human and certainly sentient. He was, in fact, an artist. He had been a monk in a strict branch of Buddhism and it did not suit him. Then one day he saw a painting representing the Pure Land. Suddenly a whole lot of things fell into place for him. He realised that Buddhism did not have to be austerely world-denying and nonexpressive. Over his subsequent life he painted hundreds of depictions of the Pure Land himself. These paintings he would give away and these images became the rallying points for popular devotion and fervour for the Buddhist cause.

Shan Tao portrayed the Pure Land as something with both this-worldly and next-worldly relevance. He also offered an approach to practice that could be demanding and refined for the few or could be extremely simple for the ordinary person. At the core of such practice, however, always lay the element of faith, and this faith is not so much a belief system as an amalgam of purity of heart on the one hand with longing for a better world on the other.

The appeal of E8 is, therefore, that it reflects the longing of ordinary people for something better. Whether the Pure Land that is depicted is in this world or the next is of less account than modern readers are likely to imagine. We are used to Christianity and so we think in terms of heaven lying in another dimension or being 'above' us. Heaven is thus associated with hierarchy, kingship and being 'on high'. The Buddhist idea is not like that. If the Pure Land lies after death, then it will be a rebirth in a world that, though better than this one, is not conceived as being in another dimension. Traditionally, it was simply a long way away in the West. One is, therefore, thinking of a realm like this one, only better.

In practice, along with the after-death and far-away aspects of the teaching there has always been a subcurrent represented by the idea that 'the Pure Land is not so far away'. The sense given is that the Pure Land is always close at hand and could even be here. Why then was it necessary to remove the Pure Land to a safe distance? The answer, historically, probably lies in the fact that the early Chinese Pure Land movement rose to prominence after the suppression in the year 713 CE of the earlier Three Ages School by the Chinese government. The Three Ages School had taught a doctrine that explicitly rejected the authority of the state and this occasioned its demise. Most members of the Three Ages School then went over to the Pure Land School of Shan Tao. They knew that a direct challenge to the state had to be avoided.

DISCUSSION

We have now reviewed eight different kinds of enlightenment. The first point to re-emphasise is that they are different. If they were not all called enlightenment or if they did not all represent themselves as being the pinnacle of Buddhist spirituality, then this fact would be apparent to everybody. However, many people are confused by the fact that such different ideals all masquerade under the same banner and label. It would be liberating for us all if the different ideas were seen more clearly as different. This would clear the way for the kind of genuinely open discussion that we are much in need of. We will probably not see the full potential of Buddhism unfold until such a debate becomes more possible than it is now. Buddhists should not be afraid of this. Historically, Buddhism has always flourished at times when there was active controversy between different schools and languished when such debate was suppressed.

The second point is that this great diversity of approaches is both a richness and a liability. The syncretic tendency within Buddhism has made it both a survivor and a preserver. Buddhism has preserved and brought forward into the modern world ideas of enlightenment from extremely diverse origins – Indian and Chinese, shamanic and chivalrous, this-worldly and metaphysical, solipsistic and altruistic, and so on. Each of these has brought a certain amount of baggage along with it. We have seen how the Indian approaches crystallised around the need to accommodate the theory of rebirth that was then quietly side-lined by the Chinese. We have seen how ideas of escape from this world vied with those of passive acceptance and those of active reform. We have also seen how each idea is linked to a set of ideas about the nature of reality. The Buddha's relative silence on questions of ontology created a vacuum that others have been only too willing to fill and refill. Is the material world really there, or is it just a projection of mind? And what is mind, anyway? And so on. Will Buddhism change to accommodate the West or will the West change to accommodate Buddhism? And which Buddhism? No doubt there is going to be some give on all sides. The real question, however, is not what will probably happen, but what ought to happen.

For many the appeal of Buddhism includes the fact that it does not seem to carry the same weight of morality as traditional Western religions. This is only half-true, however, and there is room for considerable confusion in this area because of our Western conditioning. We assume that morality goes with authority. This is wrong, but nonetheless it is widely accepted. A long history of theism has associated morality with divine punishment. This, however, is simply the idea that might is right and from the point of view of moral philosophy it is a completely bankrupt idea. Buddhism posits no such powerful god yet has a more extensive ethical system than any of the monotheisms. From a Buddhist point of view, ethical behaviour is not a way of pleasing a god but a way of liberating oneself from the gods. One should not do what the gods say, one should make up one's own mind. If one's god says go out and kill those people who belong to the other tribe over the hill, then one should say, 'No'. One should know and do better than the gods. Buddhism, therefore, is moral and not authoritarian. This is not to say that a Buddhist teacher does not have good advice to offer. It is simply that morality is not a matter of guilt and punishment, but of action and consequence and insight into that process. If we see what we do in all its fullness, morality comes naturally.

Some of the forms of enlightenment that we have looked at appear to take one 'beyond good and evil'. This is an area where great caution is needed. There have already been instances of Buddhist teachers in the West acting as though they could do no wrong and believing that even the wrong they do will have no evil consequence simply because they themselves are enlightened beings. They are few, but even a few is too many. This is a dangerous doctrine with distressing consequences and we should reject it.

So which of these eight forms of enlightenment is most like that of Shakyamuni Buddha? Every school will make the claim for its own. What I think we should conclude from this survey, however, is not that this or that enlightenment is the real one, but rather that there is a need to re-contextualise enlightenment itself. What is enlightenment for? The problems that have arisen are largely attributable to the fact that this question has not been asked enough. Enlightenment has been pursued as an end in and of itself. This pursuit is then meaningless. It becomes simply a chasing after experience and as such is self-seeking. Buddhism will never be understood by somebody who retains the greed for enlightenment. Like the Dalai Lama and Shen-yen, I suggest that the only noble purpose that enlightenment can possibly serve is that of creating a Pure Land here and now in this world. It is in this context and against this as criterion that the different forms of teaching and realisation should be assessed. If they are conducive to this goal then they are worthwhile. If not, then not.

· 8 ·

Utopian Studies

A UTOPIAN FANTASY

What is the paradise of Buddhism like? If we assume that the Buddhist ideal came to pass, what changes would we see? In asking this question, I am not trying to suggest that this paradise exists somewhere physically yet – though parts of it do. I am trying to draw out something that lies in the hearts of those who are inspired by the Buddha's vision. Let us, however, in time-honoured way, just imagine that far away to the West, beyond innumerable worlds, there does lie another planet where the teachings of the buddhas have won the hearts of the people. What is that land like? It is an important meditation exercise to visualise that land. Those who visualise it successfully will surely go there. What follows in this chapter is, of course, simply of my own imagination. It is just a story.

First, that land is traditionally called the Sweet Realm. It is a beautiful planet, similar in size to this one. Approaching it from space, it is amazingly beautiful and radiant with many kinds of light. There are several great continents surrounded by vast oceans. The land and the oceans teem with life.

The people of that land live in peace with one another and with the other forms of life. They are vegetarian. It has become unacceptable to kill animals. The idea of taking a life simply because the body of the other creature tastes nice, or because one might want to use the skin or scent of that creature, has come to be seen as horrific as it would be if the creature in question were you yourself. The people of Sukhavati remember that long ago their ancestors lived by killing, but that is now regarded as a barbaric time and people shudder at the thought of returning to such a primitive state. In Sukhavati, animals are not regarded as commodities. They are there for their own reasons in their own manner and are seen as friends. Humans and other animals share the planet. The humans have taken on some responsibility for regulating the balance of things, but, for the most part, there is a sense that the wild will sort itself out in its own way. Human habitation is restricted so that areas of wilderness are extensive, allowing animals scope to live their natural lives.

Because people are vegetarian, it is not difficult to produce the quantity of food needed. Voluntary fasting is quite common and praised as a spiritual discipline, but famine is almost unheard of. When people used to raise animals for meat, those grazing animals required huge areas of pastureland. Now, however, the same area produces six, eight or ten times as much food from vegetable crops. There is a lot of horticulture. People like gardening – not everybody, of course, people are not all the same – but it is generally felt to be healthy and pleasant. Consequently there are well-tended gardens everywhere, both for producing vegetables and ornamental gardens. There are many orchards. The hedges that line most roads are also full of fruit trees and when the fruit is in season it is so prolific that nobody thinks of it as being owned. The passer-by can reach up and help herself. Beauty is everywhere. To walk through this land is a fragrant and ever varied experience. The vast areas of monoculture that used to be necessary in the old days are now few and far between. People appreciate the diversity of life that a smaller scale brings. There are still some areas of the planet where a more industrial approach to agriculture is carried on, but it is simply less necessary.

The human population of this planet has fallen somewhat. They say that it used to be ten times as many as now. This is not because the human race is in decline. It is simply that people have chosen to opt for a better life. Buddhist teachings imply restraint in procreation and people have realised that a billion people is quite enough for a planet of this size. Because they practise restraint, they rarely experience want.

One of the most striking features is the forests. There are great forests. Humans having exercised restraint, the forests that had once seemed in danger of disappearing have regenerated. There is more oxygen in the atmosphere than there used to be. Deficiencies once caused by human pollution have gradually rectified themselves, in part because of the adoption of wiser methods of manufacture and in some measure because of the cleansing effect of there being many trees. The climate has changed and the area of desert in that world is much less than on earth.

The extent and organisation of manufacture has changed through a general appreciation of quality. Things are made to last. Many of the things made are labour-intensive works of art. People appreciate using beautiful objects in everyday activities. The age of throwaway products has passed. The discipline of learning a craft is also valued as a form of spiritual training and viewed as a kind of meditation. Further, once people realised that bigness and centralisation were not virtues in themselves, it was also realised that there was nothing inevitable about industry becoming larger and larger in scale. Some useful items, like aeroplanes and ships, need large-scale manufacturing works, but even in these, the progress of technology had made work forces small and more human in scale. It is realised that the main reason for growth in the scale of industrial units in the past had not been technical, but commercial. Big units were not more efficient, they simply had the power to dominate their market – to cheat, in other words. With more care to distribution it had been found that smaller-scale production led to a richer life, both in terms of the diversity of products and in terms of the quality of the working life of producers.

NO NATIONS

Sukhavati has a global society. What had once been national boundaries laced with barbed wire have become quaint anachronisms that one reads about in tourist guides. People stand at them and wonder that their ancestors could have been so foolish as to kill one another, and themselves be willing to die, for something so odd as an abstraction called a country. People now feel their identity is as universal beings and citizens of the world. They have become less concerned about territory. They have a confidence that there will be somewhere for them and do not have to grasp after security at the expense of others. In any case, Buddhists like to travel and like to receive guests. The existence of all those old boundaries had gradually just come to be felt as irksome.

Where their ancestors were impressed by the idea that 'We don't want those people coming here', the contemporary citizens of Sukhavati are much more conscious of the advantages of being able to travel freely and enjoy the whole of their beautiful world. The visitor from Earth who talks about countries is likely to be met with comments like, 'But that means that there are parts of your own world that you are not allowed to visit. How sad.'

Globalisation has not meant loss of diversity. It has rather increased it. Diversity is, in fact, cherished. Every corner of this world has its local tastes and specialities. People's energy goes more into creativity because there is less greed and hate. What remains of these archaic emotions has been sublimated into artistic and cultural expressions of great diversity and the making of worlds of great charm.

Difference is valued. There is an attitude that difference is to be considered the source of richness rather than the root of conflict. The more intellectual members of this society like to debate and the more physical ones like sports. Some of these are cooperative and some involve elements of competition. These are not professionalised, profit-oriented activities, however. They are fun. There is a sense that it is good for people to extend themselves and to have some obstacle to come up against. Life is not to be endlessly soft. Spirit is matured through the mastery of passion, not through its endless appeasement, and if it is to be mastered, then it must also be roused.

WORK AND COMMUNITY

People work. There is an expectation that people will contribute to the life of the community in some way and if people are idle then that time is given to meditation, study or travel. There is a sense that work is part of a person's contribution to life and also something that life gives to a person. Work is not just a means to an economic end and so has not become a tyrant. Enough is enough.

There are utility organisations that are, in most cases, under some degree of collective control. There are also many private enterprises. Buddhism is not opposed to commerce as such. The Buddha advocated that young people be usefully educated and then given the means with which to establish themselves in some trade or enterprise. When an enterprise grows large, however, it will be broken up into smaller units. This helps to ensure that people's work is not too remote from a direct experience of what it is for.

The plying of a trade is a discipline and is character building. On the other hand, it is not good when people simply become wage slaves. There is a general sense that 'small is beautiful'.[1] Things should be kept within reasonable boundaries. Here too there is a valuing of diversity. Efficiency has its place, but people should not feel like slaves and the quest for efficiency should not be allowed to go so far that it imposes uniformity. Consequently, many people have a number of diverse occupations and the institutions of this society approve and support this. A person may be an accountant in the morning and a carpenter in the afternoon, or may even hold four or five different occupations to each of which he or she applies several hours each week.

Generally people live in or are attached to communities. These communities all have an active spiritual life, though it varies from place to place. Buddhism encompasses many practices and it also shelters the religions it has displaced so that their contribution to society not be lost. Public festivities are popular. The calendar is marked by many ceremonial events – the commemoration of a variety of exemplary people, both real and mythological, the passing of the seasons, rites of passage and events from history. These give people a sense of collective life and of harmony between the many elements of the community. These ritual events are not performed to rigidly fixed patterns, but involve new creativity on each occasion so that the inventive talents of the people, young and old, can be put to good purpose.

Some degree of communal living is common, though it varies in intensity. An isolated or institutionalised old age does not lie in wait for Sukhavatins. Community life is seen as an exercise in striking the right balance between and the encouragement of personal training and the accommodation of idiosyncrasy. In fact, each person is rather expected to have some eccentricity. Just as a field is made glorious by a sea of many flowers, so each member of a community illustrates a different facet of the human condition and all have their special beauty. Marriage and celibacy are both valued and a variety of forms of marriage are accepted. It is thought more important that sexual unions be publicly declared, acknowledged and given the support of the community than that they conform to a particular pattern, so while the majority of unions are monogamous and heterosexual, there are also many that depart from this pattern. Children are brought up by their parents and relatives primarily, but have a lot more access to other adults than on Earth as a result of the communal arrangements and the smaller scale and greater diversity of occupations. Adults are more available.

Education is similarly variegated. Where monolithic states demand fixed curricula and fierce academic competition, Sukhavati has a completely different approach. Education goes on throughout life. Schools grow around teachers. There are sophisticated systems of both formal and informal education that facilitate individuals in finding the combination of studies or the means to research appropriate to that person's leanings. In fact there is no clear line between education and leisure. Again, education often involves travel. It is generally believed to be important that people from different parts of the planet mix frequently, learn from one another and learn to be creative together. Modern technology, however, has made much possible that previously would have been impractical. In Sukhavati, there is no obsession with qualifications. It is accepted that there is a greater benefit in having enthusiastic students pursuing unique routes to knowledge, skill and personal development, than there is in standardisation.

In all aspects of life, there is plenty of scope for people to affiliate to a number of different groups, networks and communities. These diverse forms of association provide most of the regulation and services that this society requires. Their existence makes the old national institutions redundant. For sure, this means that provision is not uniform – but then it never really was under the old system either. This society is complex and that is its strength. It can accommodate many different kinds of people – all the different kinds that there are. To accommodate this diversity, it has this wide range of forms of association. The pattern is constantly evolving and shifting. The extension of modern communicative technologies has assisted this process. Sukhavatins found that it was possible to form networks and communities that transcended the old national boundaries. They learnt about people on the other side of the planet and made friends with them. They learnt to help their new friends. They no longer wanted to exploit or destroy them.

Some people live and work within their living community. Others go out to work. A great deal of work is, however, done within the communities themselves since many have become effective economic units. There is, therefore, some degree of economic specialisation in many communities, but never so much as to create the kind of destructive monotony that used to be characteristic of the lives of people in the old society. Life as a community rather than its function as an economic unit takes precedence. There is not, among these people, any strong drive towards excessive wealth or luxury. There is plenty to go round and it would seem absurd to sacrifice quality of life too far in the drive to produce one more widget per hour. Quality of life has come to mean precisely what it says and is no longer simply a euphemism for quantity.

For instance, because there are many forests on Sukhavati, good-quality hardwoods are not in short supply. The furniture made with these woods lasts a long time. It is beautiful and treasured and will not generally be changed every few years, or if it is, this will be because it has been given to somebody else who admired it. Similar considerations apply to many things. The economic activity of those who live a householder life in Sukhavati is high quality and low turnover. Shopping does not play so large a part in their lives.

The polity and economy of Sukhavati is regulated by institutions that do not themselves have profit in view and 'national interest' has long since become a meaningless concept. People remember the end of the former age when their ancestors suffered a great catastrophe through the collapse of the old economic system that had been designed essentially by a small cabal to enable them and their friends to plunder the whole planet.

AN END TO IMPERIALISM

They remember how political imperialism had gradually given

way to an economic imperialism that, while it was promoted as liberation, was actually even more inequitable than what had gone before. Disease and starvation had spread in many parts of the planet while, in other parts, a proportion of the population became so rich that one wonders what they can possibly have done with it all. What they had done, for the most part, was to plough much of it back into schemes to make themselves even richer. These included some more sinister aspects. Keeping oneself rich commonly also meant deliberately keeping others poor. The old system held together as long as people continued to believe in a myth called 'the trickle-down effect'. Once it was realised that the flow in question was rarely as little as a trickle and was invariably in the upward direction, popular sympathy faded away and the system collapsed.

This collapse was a terrible time. Financial institutions fell and governments teetered. In any other world, this would probably have been the time when a great dictator took over and restored order in a ruthless way, so that the whole unpleasant process could start from scratch over again.

On Sukhavati, however, a movement of peaceful people had arisen. These people had been predicting this apocalypse for some time and had prepared for it by training themselves in calm and steadfastness. They had begun to put in place some of the features that are now worldwide in Sukhavati. These smaller-scale experiments gave people confidence that a different way of life was possible. When the catastrophe came, the peaceful people were sufficiently numerous to maintain the kind of dignity that was needed. They did not think of themselves. They simply went about doing what was needed, feeding the hungry and looking after those who suffered. Despite the efforts of the old oppressive class to discredit them, they stood firm and the world began to change.

The new world has been constructed out of the changed value system. Adherence to the new values is strong enough to ensure that the old bad ways do not regain much of a hold. The new values are embodied in the lives of those – a substantial proportion – of the population who have made these dharma values the first consideration in their lives. These people are those who have most completely renounced the ways of the old world. These renouncers are respected by the people. They perform the ceremonial duties attaching to community life – rites of passage and of communal solidarity and thanksgiving. They live simple lives with a minimum of possessions – merely the necessary requisites for life. They give an example of life freed from hate and greed. They are, in effect, the guardians of the wellbeing of Sukhavati. Principally they are able to be so simply by living the dharma life with complete sincerity themselves.

They are, however, instigators and facilitators of new developments. They spend a lot of time listening to people and so they know what is needed in the community. They also know who knows how to do what. They can bring together teams of people for particular purposes and these teams become an important part of life. Sometimes a project may be a few hour's work. Occasionally it might occupy a group for several years. Some groups may be small, some large.

STABILITY, VALUES AND LEADERSHIP

The main guarantee of the stability of this society is the respect people have for wholesome values. These are the values of quality, diversity and friendship. This respect is reinforced by the obvious benefits it brings. This is not a soporific society. It is lively. There are festivities. There is work. There are many communal occasions. People meet frequently. Generally, there is mutual respect and where this fails there are always people to call upon who are willing to help. There is adventure. People travel. Young people may spend periods in the wilderness. Occasionally one is eaten by a bear or a lion, and this is sad, but there is also a sense that if opportunity for serious adventure is missing, the life of the people will turn sour. People do not think that everything should be made perfectly safe. Buddhists accept that a certain amount of exposure to affliction is character building.

There are, however, also laws of a common-law kind. Hunting, for instance, is forbidden. If a person is caught killing animals, their weapons will be destroyed and they will be rebuked. Weapons are, in any case, prohibited. The animal will be given a funeral and the hunter will have to attend this, make some offering and ask the animal's forgiveness. If the person persists in killing animals, then they may be sent to live in another community where the opportunity to hunt is not so easy, in a city perhaps. In the last resort a person may be confined. This is a rarity, however, since all other avenues will be explored first.

Serious measures have been taken to wean people off alcohol and other drugs. People who steal are required to make restitution. The idea of punishment is alien to this society, but when people have done things that offend against social values that are essential to keep the society in being, then the task of reform is undertaken seriously. This task may include elements of removing the opportunity for repetition, re-education, attending to the offender's situation in the community so that they become better integrated, finding them more meaningful activity, restitution and, in extreme cases, restraint. The incidence of serious crime in such a society is low. The media are not permitted to use the image of criminals to whip up campaigns of hate. Imprisonment is regarded as a general, not simply an individual, failure. A person is confined when the whole community has failed to come up with a solution that will provide satisfaction to both the individual with his or her particular character on the one hand and the community with its needs on the other.

The business of personal reform is, therefore, taken seriously. Here a mixture of two principles is applied. The first principle is that a person is expected to train in ways that reduce their needs and graspingness, and they will receive guidance in this. This may be done by meditation, by the teaching of ethics, by living among others who give a good example, or by selection of appropriate occupational roles. Punishment is not part of the social thought of these people, but reform is. Buddhism is deeply noncoercive, but there are situations where people will be coerced inasmuch as they will be required to carry out work or activity that it is believed will expose them to improving experiences. The second principle is that effort will be made to find a niche for a person that suits his or her native aptitudes, abilities and passions. There are many different types of people and this society provides many different opportunities. A good deal of care goes into matching these to one another.

Young men, for instance, are often energetic and high spirited. People of this type will be encouraged towards adventurous activities on the one hand and will also participate in other occupations that help them to learn some discipline, restraint and care. Here, the principle of diversity of occupation plays an important part.

Not everybody in this society has to be an heroic saint. However, the shift of popular values has gone far enough to make a radical shift sustainable. There is a sense that environment is important. A person's rectitude is not simply a matter of their own personal willpower. There is a collective responsibility. If somebody goes off the rails, then this must in part at least be due to the circumstances. By creating the right conditions, it is possible to bring out the best in people and everybody has something to contribute.

Nor is this a society without any suffering or affliction. People still get ill and die. Not every business venture flourishes and not every public project is a success. It is, however, a society with little recrimination. It is also a place with a sense of fun. The people of this society enjoy learning and it is accepted that sometimes one has to learn the hard way. Sometimes, also, one learns from encounter. This is not the kind of utopia that is maintained by fiat and terror. It is maintained by respect and balance.

In order to sustain such a state of affairs, it is necessary to ensure that nobody is uncared for. The nuclear family system is sometimes adequate to provide people with their need for care, but in Sukhavati it has been recognised that this system falls far short of meeting all needs. Friendship is held as something to be highly valued and a widely differentiated vocabulary for different kinds of friendship has developed, giving social recognition to different kinds of friendly relations, such as those between people of the same or different sex and people of the same or different generations; those that involve different degrees of trust, intimacy and mutual reliance; those that involve different degrees or types of sexual contact; those that are intended to be short or lasting; and so on. Friendship is a subject of abiding interest to be thought about, talked about and experienced and its perfection is felt to be one of the central purposes of life.

This, therefore, is a society in which people can be different from one another without this being offensive, but it is not really a society that values individualism for itself. It values friendship. When two Sukhavatins meet, they are more likely to be interested in knowing, 'Who are your friends?' than 'What is your job?' Everybody feels that they have more to learn about friendship, which is seen as the route to the fulfilment of many of life's satisfactions. This is not to say that solitude is not also valued. Solitude is regarded as a higher value whereas friendship is seen as the common passion. People who choose and are capable of much solitude are admired, but, in the case of most Sukhavatins, this is admiration from a distance for the most part.

Nonetheless, opportunities for some periods of retreat and contemplation each year are also generally undertaken and expected. These are seen as falling within a category of what are called improving activities. Improving activities include the educational and spiritual dimensions of life. From those who take readily and naturally to the improving activities, the guardians of the society are recruited. They then receive a thorough training in a way of life that embodies all the highest values of the Sukhavatin society. They learn to think of themselves as the servants of the people, and their task, collectively, is to facilitate the wholesome development of society.

Leaving planet Sukhavati, we might reflect upon what is possible here on Earth. Of course, Sukhavati is a long way away beyond the sunset. Our own Pure Land might turn out to be quite different in many of its details. We cannot plan it. Dreams may, however, help to inspire us towards it. Do not just rely upon my dream, however. The dream of a world perfected lives somewhere in each of us. It may be out of fashion, but I invite you to let the dream and its associated longing grow. Who knows what might come of them?

· 9 ·

Critical Buddhism: Part One

A CONTROVERSY ERUPTS

So, now back to the real world ... In the 1990s a controversy
that had been brewing for a couple of decades came to the
boil in Japanese Buddhism and spilt over internationally. This
controversy has many implications for the way that Buddhism
should be construed. Different theorists have taken sharply contrasting stances in relation to the issues raised. These issues go
to the heart of what Buddhism is all about. Reflection upon
the rationale and implications of the different positions held is,
therefore, important.

In the 1980s, a Japanese scholar, Matsumoto Shiro, participated
in a working party on social discrimination within the Soto Zen
School of Buddhism. It was widely known that some Buddhist
denominations in Japan had a poor record in this respect, giving
tacit and sometimes overt support to a variety of Japanese
traditions and practices that discriminate against or disadvantage
women, the poor and ethnic minority groups. Some of the Jodo
(Pure Land) schools had taken steps to put their house in better
order, but Soto Zen had fallen behind in this respect and was
particularly vulnerable to criticism. Reflection upon this working
party experience led Matsumoto, himself a member of the Soto
School, and his colleague Hakamaya Noriaki to embark upon a
critique of Japanese Buddhism that has become ever more wide

ranging. Much of this critique was gathered together and published in Hakamaya's book *Hihan Bukkyo* (Critical Buddhism), published in Tokyo in 1990.[1] It is understandable, perhaps, that in a country that has followed a religion for well over 1,000 years, some local practices may have crept in and may need to be reviewed. The question that interested Hakamaya, however, was whether the Japanese way of interpreting Buddhism itself was faulty and whether this faulty interpretation was not the weak point through which oppressive social practices enter and become established.

The kinds of questions that this Critical Buddhism opens up are:

- What is the relationship between religious ideology and religious practice?
- What is the relationship between that and society at large?
- Are there forms of Buddhism that are intrinsically supportive of social oppression?
- Are those forms to be regarded as true Buddhism?

The answers that Matsumoto and Hakamaya give to these questions represent a radical departure from the dominant Japanese interpretation of Buddhism. Since that mainline interpretation is also widespread in the West, Matsumoto and Hakamaya's arguments also represent a sharp challenge to Buddhism as many of us have received it.

The Critical Buddhists argue, for instance, that the teaching of Buddha Nature 'is not Buddhist'. They assert that the idea of Buddha Nature and several other closely related and widely held principles introduced into Buddhism half a millennium after the Buddha's own time actually function as a rationale for turning a blind eye to social oppression. They argue that these concepts were an accommodation by Buddhism to popular spirituality first in India and then, particularly, in China.

To lift this argument out of a purely Japanese context, we can consider the Critical Buddhist view that there is, just about everywhere in the world, a common form of popular spirituality. The structure of this popular spirituality is fairly constant from place to place, though terminology varies. The main elements of this popular spirituality are:

- Belief in an underlying, eternal, transcendental unity in the world called God, Tao, the Great Spirit or whatever. This belief has its roots in the idea of a god that favours a particular race. In Japan this god is the sun goddess who is regarded as the ancestor of the emperor.
- Belief in an underlying, immortal, transcendental unity in the person, called a soul, spirit, atma, self, etc. This belief has its roots in the idea of there being a chosen people who were specially privileged and protected – those who have something of the god in them – those who were 'god's own'.
- Belief that these metaphysical entities are superior, magical and more real than the things of the ordinary world.
- A sense that although bad things may happen in the world, it is all right really because of the existence of the metaphysical realm.
- A belief that those who believe in the metaphysical world will be 'saved' and that belief is therefore more important than anything else.

This, with local variations, is the basic structure of 'popular spirituality'. At the same time, there are those in every society who reject this whole structure of ideas and swing to the opposite extreme of materialism, declaring that since there is no metaphysical realm it matters not what one believes, nor what one does. Pleasure is therefore the only guide to action. The Buddha rejected both these positions. This is why Buddhism is called the Middle Way. The problem, as Vasubandhu said sometime round about 300 CE, is to distinguish the middle from the extremes. Buddhism is not rooted in ideas of chosen nations and chosen people: it is universalistic and nontheistic. In Buddhism a person does not consist of an eternal essence: a person is what they do. People are not 'chosen', they create the future by their deeds.

The drift back to popular spirituality is, the Critical Buddhists argue, a constant danger for Buddhism. People like it because relating to a parental deity puts them in a less responsible position, and knowing that they can be, or already have been, 'chosen' takes the question of salvation out of their hands. People assume Buddhism is a form of popular spirituality and so import these ideas into it without really thinking. These intrusions into Buddhism, Hakamaya believes, have introduced ethical weaknesses into Buddhist practice. Popular spirituality can effectively absolve many socially unethical norms on the grounds that the metaphysical realm is unaffected by them, the faithful will still get to heaven, and anyway God or the fates must have wanted it that way or it would not be like that. It can also actually support social discrimination, since these ideas advance belief in a metaphysical realm that is itself hierarchical and discriminatory, and those who believe come to think of themselves as a privileged class, not just in this world, but eternally, and see nonbelievers (and for 'heathens' you can often read 'foreigners') as second-class citizens or even subhuman. Further, since these ideas have their roots in an association between religion and race, all manner of prejudice may ensue. In Japan, this kind of popular spirituality has generally come to the fore in times of war. The suppression of Buddhism and the rise of popular spirituality in wartime are phenomena that have been seen repeatedly, not just in Japan, but also in many countries across the Buddhist world. The common criticism of Buddhism is that it weakens nationalist institutions, and this is perfectly true.

The Critical Buddhists argue, however, that elements of popular spirituality have also invaded Buddhism itself as a consequence of Buddhism's search for social approval and that these tendencies have reached unacceptable levels in the distinctively Japanese approach to Buddhism which, they therefore argue, is no longer the real thing. They are most strongly critical of the Soto Zen School, which is the school to which both Hakamaya and Matsumoto belong.

These assertions are, of course, highly contentious. They have been advanced on a number of fronts – textual interpretation, ethics, social criticism, religious practice, institutional organisation and historical interpretation. These advances have been made in a deliberately combative style uncharacteristic of Japanese academia. This style is consistent with the critical message, which includes the idea that the theories they criticise are part of a conspiracy of niceness that prevents anybody in Buddhism standing up for what they really think or against what is wrong. Buddha was a critic, they assert, not a conformist. Because he was against war does not mean that he was noncontentious. Buddhism is a nonviolent struggle for a better future.

In the background to this debate are specifically Japanese concerns about such issues as who in the Buddhist establishment did, and who did not, collude with the fascist government during the Second World War. There are also contemporary social concerns about, for instance, ethnic prejudice and the Japanese caste system. The arguments, however, have much wider implications well beyond Japan. The tacit alliance between nationalism, popular spirituality, prejudice and war is a phenomenon that can be seen in many countries, and Buddhism, with its reputation for tolerance and kindness, commonly gets invited into some sort of accommodation with such ideas. They can, however, be the death of the kind of enlightenment that Buddha offered, namely, a world view that is pluralistic, noncaste, radically nonnationalistic, free from any idea of being divinely chosen, in which we are what we do, and the word spirit refers to the spirit in which things are done, not to a ghost whose destiny is of particular concern. To be enlightened is precisely to abandon such self-concern.

This debate, therefore, also invites us to look closely at what happens to Buddhism when it crosses from one culture into another: from India to China and Tibet, from China to Japan, and now, from the East to the West. The contention that all spiritualities are essentially the same is not true and can be dangerous to the peaceful purposes that Buddhism exists to promote. In the West, for instance, many people are allergic to the whole idea of religion and spirituality because it is closely associated with war and oppression. For Buddhism to align itself with such creeds as just another religion may be a serious mistake. Buddhism is a critical countercurrent that can arise within many different religious contexts, in much the same way as, say, existentialism.

CRITICAL BUDDHISM AND TOPICAL BUDDHISM

Over the centuries Buddhism has spread through many lands. Along the way it has adapted. Some of these adaptations have been creative ways of repackaging the same original message for different peoples. Some of them may have amounted to a distortion or even reversal of that original message. But which is which?

The writings of Hakamaya, Matsumoto and some of their colleagues have brought this question to the forefront of people's minds. Hakamaya has carried the debate into a wide-ranging criticism of Buddhist social practice while Matsumoto has made a more forceful impact in the academic world. They refer to themselves as Critical Buddhists and designate those they criticise as 'Topical' Buddhists.

Scholars of both Japan and North America have responded in a wide variety of ways to the assertions of Critical Buddhism. There is general agreement that this development has sharpened people's thinking and made the holders of particular positions work harder to clarify precisely what it is that they do think. Some, like Tsuda Shinichi and Ueda Shizuteru, have strongly rejected the Critical Buddhist position. Most commentators, however, feel that the Critical Buddhists have some important points to make, but argue that they are overstating their case. In general, Buddhism's record on human rights is better than that of most religions. Maybe so, but in Japan, at least, not good enough, say the Critical Buddhists. Many papers have been written criticising details of the Critical Buddhist position without really confronting the main Critical Buddhist thesis. A Western scholar who has attempted to do so is Sally King, who has written a direct rebuttal of one of the main planks of the Critical Buddhist position. There is thus a good deal of debate going on.

It will, therefore, be helpful to clarify the issues that divide Critical and Topical Buddhists. Critical Buddhists are critical of what they call Topical Buddhism. What is Topical Buddhism? The term topical is here derived from the term *topica* used by the Italian philosopher Giambattista Vico (1668–1744). Vico's topical philosophy, in turn, was in large measure a critique of Descartes. The emergence of Critical Buddhism, therefore, is part of a new stage in the cross-fertilisation of Eastern and Western thought, with Japanese Buddhists offering contrasting critiques of each other's positions along lines drawn from their own interpretations of European philosophical divisions.

Topica refers to a place or locus. It is the Latin word that occurs in the word utopia. A utopia is a nonexistent country where all is well. The Critical Buddhists see many of the forms in which Buddhist teaching is presented as assertions that underlying manifest reality as we encounter it – a reality in which many things are far from well – there exists a more fundamental, unifying, metaphysical substratum that is more real than the ordinary world. This posited substratum they refer to by the Sanskrit word *dhatu*. All the manifestations of Buddhism that make assertions of this kind, they, therefore, group together under the heading of *dhatuvada*. Topical Buddhism and dhatuvada are thus more or less interchangeable terms. Dhatuvada is what Topical Buddhism teaches.

DHATUVADA

The Critical Buddhists assert that Topical Buddhism is not

Buddhism. They say that Buddhism is the criticism of dhatuvada; that this was the main thrust of the Buddha's teaching; and that dhatuvada is simply the popular, corrupt, deity-oriented, sacrificial Indian form of spirituality that Buddha rejected reappearing in Buddhist terminology. Not only Indian religion; the dhatuvada line of thought is also seen as characteristic of Taoism and indeed of popular spirituality in many parts of the world. Forms of Buddhism such as Zen that have been most strongly influenced by Taoism are thus seen as prime targets for critique.

So how does dhatuvada appear in Buddhist form? There are two particular widely used concepts that Hakamaya sees as 'not Buddhist'. These are the concept of Buddha Nature and the concept of original or inherent enlightenment. Matsumoto, meanwhile, has focused essentially the same line of argument upon the concept of *tathagata-garbha* (= the womb or embryo of enlightenment). The two concepts attacked by Hakamaya were evolved in China and do not date back to Indian Buddhism. They are generally believed to have been an adaptation for Chinese consumption of the concept of tathagata-garbha. This latter does derive from Indian Buddhism, the Tathagata-garbha Tradition being one significant strand of Mahayana thought. The Critical Buddhists believe that:

- The tathagata-garbha concept was imported into Mahayana Buddhism to appease people who wanted to follow Buddhism, but did not want to give up their Brahmanical ideas.
- The Buddha Nature concept was derived from the tathagata-garbha idea in order to please Chinese people who wanted to follow Buddhism without giving up their Taoist ideas.
- Inherent enlightenment gave even fuller expression to Taoist (non-Buddhist) thought in China.
- In Japan the idea of inherent enlightenment was extended to include even nonsentient objects through the adoption of the popular religious slogan that 'the grasses, trees, mountains and

rivers all attain Buddhahood', an idea that is more Shinto than
Buddhist and has no basis at all in Buddhist canonical texts
but is often cited as the epitome of the distinctively Japanese
approach to Buddhism.

The question arises: does it matter? If the Critical Buddhists are
right that tathagata-garbha, Buddha Nature, original enlightenment, and the idea that even nonsentient beings are destined for
Buddhahood are all imports into Buddhism as it spread across
Asia, could we not simply regard them as enriching the Buddhist
tradition rather than subtracting from it. No, say the Critical Buddhists, we should not. Why? Because, first, this would
neutralise the force of everything that the Buddha said about
personal responsibility, karma and clarity of understanding,
and, secondly, these forms of dhatuvada are deeply implicated
in the kind of smug, and essentially nationalistic, spirituality that
makes accommodation between religion and oppressive worldly
powers easy and in the rationalisation of a wide range of actual
discriminatory practices in contemporary Japanese society. Are
they right?

INTRINSIC ENLIGHTENMENT

The Chinese term *pen-chueh*, 'original, or intrinsic, enlightenment', arose in China probably in the fourth century CE, first
appearing in the text: *The Awakening of Mahayana Faith*. This
work is widely regarded as a foundation stone of Mahayana
Buddhism, translated into Chinese from Sanskrit, and attributed
to Ashvagosha. There is now general agreement that Ashvagosha
was not a Mahayanist and did not write this text and that there
almost certainly never was a Sanskrit version. *The Awakening of
Mahayana Faith* was composed in Chinese.

The idea of intrinsic enlightenment grew out of the concept
of tathagata-garbha, which means the womb of Buddhahood

or Buddha-embryo. The tathagata-garbha concept does have an Indian genesis. This idea occurs in several Mahayana Buddhist Sanskrit texts of which the *Srimaladevi Sutra*, the *Tathagatagarbha Sutra* and the *Mahaparinirvana Sutra* are most significant. These texts are unusual among Indian Buddhist texts in using a 'positive' language to describe the ability of all beings to attain enlightenment. Tathagata-garbha is this potentiality. In the *Tathagatagarbha Sutra* the Buddha is represented as saying, 'All sentient beings, in all destinies, in the midst of their *klesha*-bodies (i.e. in the midst of their corrupted nature) possess the tathagata-garbha eternally free of corruption'. It was this idea that was seized upon enthusiastically by Chinese Buddhists and developed into the idea of 'original enlightenment'.

It can, of course, be argued that to treat tathagata-garbha as indicating some kind of soul is a complete misunderstanding of the text – that all the text is doing is making the point that even corrupt people can become enlightened in the future and putting this in a slightly poetic way. In Tibet, there are two readings of this text commonly taught, one following each of these possible lines of interpretation. The nonsoul interpretation is regarded as the older.[2]

In China, however, the intrinsic enlightenment concept soon became virtually synonymous with another Chinese-coined word – the term Buddha Nature.[3] This term came into prominence through the text called the *Fo Hsing Lun* (Buddha Nature Treatise), attributed to Vasubandhu, a leading Indian Mahayana Buddhist, and translated into Chinese by Paramartha. Again, many scholars believe that this text had no connection with India, nor with Vasubandhu, but was actually composed by Paramartha himself. There may never have been an Indian version.

The ideas of Buddha Nature and of intrinsic enlightenment are, therefore, principally of Chinese origin. They came into prominence during the struggle to establish Buddhism, an Indian and Central Asian import, in the very different cultural climate of China. It is interesting to see that the term Buddha Nature is also enjoying another surge of popularity now that Buddhism is being imported into the culture of the West – another culture with a strong tradition of belief in the soul. The question whether this is a valid Buddhist concept or, as the Critical Buddhists would hold, a corruption of the original message with serious deleterious consequences for the social impact of Buddhism, is a relevant one for us.

Intrinsic enlightenment thought was appealing to the Chinese because it reflected ideas that were essentially Taoist. The idea of intrinsic or original enlightenment had close echoes of the Tao, envisioned as the source of harmony in the universe. The Buddha Nature idea was useful to the Buddhists, especially Buddhists who preferred to align Buddhism with Taoism, because it was a popular concept with which to counter Confucianism. Confucianism promotes social order and explicit morality and is in direct contrast to Taoism's sense that all will be well if one just refrains from interfering. This Confucian moral order involves three particular virtues: *ren*, or human kindness, *yi*, or appropriate balance between individual and collective needs, and *li*, social rules, rituals and etiquette. These three ensure that people live according to their 'nature'. Confucian 'nature' is a state in which parents behave like parents and children like children, boys like boys and girls like girls, kings like kings and subjects like subjects, and so on. When everyone conforms to their nature all will be well in the world. Buddhists were able to counter the conservatism of this philosophy by adopting the slogan, 'everybody has Buddha Nature'.

Originally, therefore, Buddha Nature thought offered a counter to the kind of conservatism that would have excluded Buddhism on the simple ground that it was not Chinese – not part of Chinese nature; and an appeal to groups in Chinese society that were influenced by Taoism. It was among these groups that the new religion found many converts and sympathisers. The presentation of Buddhism in the terms of intrinsic enlightenment and Buddha

Nature thus became well established and spread wherever Chinese Buddhism went – to Korea, Vietnam, Taiwan and Japan, and, now, via Japan, to North America.

In India, however, Buddhism continued to develop without these ideas. As already noted, the nearest that Indian Buddhism came to the notion of Buddha Nature was the idea of tathagata-garbha. This concept originally appears to have had no more implication than that enlightenment is possible. On that early interpretation, ordinary people have tathagata-garbha, i.e. potential for enlightenment, whereas buddhas do not, i.e. they really are enlightened. Only later in Tibet did a doctrine that equated tathagata-garbha with something like Buddha Nature arise – not just a potential, but an underlying eternal reality – and this may have been an import from China.

As for dhatuvada, the term dhatu has a number of meanings. One of these is that dhatu indicates a basis or substratum to something, and especially the kind of underlying factor that may be said to be a single essence or ground for a number of diverse things. The most classic examples would be (a) the idea of Brahma as the only reality behind all the diverse phenomena of the world, and (b) the idea of the soul or atman lying behind all the diverse phenomena that make up a life. Using the term in this sense, the Critical Buddhists have coined the term dhatuvada to refer to all those tendencies in Buddhism that they see as reintroducing into it ideas of an 'eternal' or 'only real' essence or substratum to empirical existence. Dhatuvada, therefore, includes all those forms of Buddhism that revolve around the concept of original enlightenment, Buddha Nature and tathagata-garbha, as well as all the derivatives of these. Although the word dhatuvada is used as a target by the Critical Buddhists, it has a fairly clear meaning and is not intrinsically pejorative. Some people might be proud to call themselves dhatuvadists. It seems quite possible, therefore, that this new word could enter general usage in Buddhist circles, perhaps along with the term Topical Buddhism, about which similar observations could be made.

The orthodox mainstream of most non-Buddhist religions is avowedly dhatuvada, though most of those religions also have their dissenters.

The rejection of dhatuvada presents Buddhism as more distinct from other religions. It also amounts to a root and branch critique of Japanese Buddhism and much of Chinese Buddhism too. The Critical Buddhists are particularly strong in attacking their own Soto Zen School. This is in part because this is the area that they know best, and in part because the Zen schools have, in general, lagged behind other Buddhist institutions in Japan in doing something about institutionalised forms of prejudice and oppression. Many of the ancestral teachers of Zen, or Chan as it is called in China, are prime examples of teachers of dhatuvada. Thus, Hui Neng, the sixth patriarch of Chan and the speaker of the *Platform Sutra* is one of the heroes of the Zen tradition. The *Platform Sutra* is full of such terms as 'essence of mind' that clearly come within the sights of the anti-dhatuvada party and Chan was one of the few Buddhist schools that was not repressed by the Chinese military authorities in the Chinese Tang Dynasty.

The Critical Buddhists are, therefore, arguing that Buddhism should not be compromised by an influx of popular spirituality, either in its wishy-washy 'be nice about everything' variety or in its more sinister nationalistic guise. Nor should bases of legitimacy within Buddhism be established other than straightforward conformity to the Buddha's teaching on and practice of universal compassion.

Critical Buddhism: Part Two

WHAT CRITICAL BUDDHISTS ARGUE IN FAVOUR OF

According to Critical Buddhism, the fundamental Buddhist teaching is 'dependent origination', with no underlying dhatu, no entity of a divine, transcendental, eternal or metaphysical nature to lie behind, make sense of, or justify the manifest phenomena of this world. According to dependent origination, one thing leads to another in unending succession. The things of this world are real in the sense that there is nothing 'more real' lying behind them – what you see is what you get – but they are not eternal ultimates either, for in this view there is no 'eternal ultimate'. Reality is diverse and should be appreciated as such. Buddhist mysticism is an uncommonly naked encounter with reality, not a flight from it.

The teaching of dependent origination is, itself, as we have seen, open to varieties of interpretation. Critical Buddhists assert the sequential interpretation and reject the co-arising version. Dependent origination is the basic Buddhist teaching and it has implications. These include, first, the teaching of nonself or *anatma*. Critical Buddhism is an *anatmavada*. Buddhist ethics are not, they assert, about retiring from the world in order to rediscover your original enlightenment, they are about acting unselfishly in the world. They include, secondly, a strong and particular emphasis upon karma. Karma is to be seen as implying responsibility for one's actions in this life. It is not to be seen as implying that all the disparities of this life are really all right because they just reflect good and bad deeds in previous existences.

Thirdly, dependent origination is to be seen as the primary teaching and the concept of *shunyata* (emptiness) is to be seen within the context of dependent origination, not the other way around. They suggest that what has happened in the history of Buddhist ideas is that:

- The Buddha taught dependent origination and this implies that there is no underlying dhatu behind phenomena. It is a horizontal teaching rather than a vertical one. One thing leads to another in succession.
- This absence of an underlying dhatu came to be talked about as emptiness, shunyata.
- People who thought in terms of a vertical model, then, simply assumed that shunyata was the new Buddhist word for the underlying eternal essence of everything. The shunyata concept was thus corrupted into its opposite.
- In the context of this second interpretation of shunyata, dependent origination came to take on a different connotation. Since everything was now seen as really arising from the hidden essence, dependent origination was reinterpreted to mean the simultaneous co-arising of all phenomena or even the 'co-arising of the dharmadhatu'. Hakamaya, therefore, argues that shunyata in the context of the original teaching of dependent origination is a valuable concept, whereas shunyata transposed into a code word for dhatu is a corruption of the Buddhist message.

Fourthly, in the context of dependent origination, nirvana is not to be seen as a transmundane, ultimate, absolute or anything of that kind. It is to be seen as a change in life resulting from understanding. In many books on Buddhism one will encounter such statements as samsara is the ordinary conditioned world whereas nirvana is the unconditioned, the timeless, the supramundane. Nonsense, say the Critical Buddhists. Nirvana is just as much 'in' time as anything else and it arises from conditions just as everything else does too. It is for precisely these reasons that enlightenment and nirvana are attainable.

In addition to basing their philosophy upon dependent origination, Hakamaya and Matsumoto assert the value of criticism, logic and intelligent discourse over mere rhetoric. They have been engaged in writing an impressive quantity of studies on many aspects of Buddhist teaching and life, identifying and challenging all those points at which the ideas of dhatuvada have, as they see it, illegitimately, crept back into Buddhism.

They see Buddhism *as* criticism. They argue that the Buddha was a critic. His mission was to criticise the cosy yet corrupt certainties of his time. Criticism is seen as having a positive function in itself. The first reaction of many people to reading the materials put forward by the Critical Buddhists is to think these people are rocking the boat in an unbuddhist fashion. Their very criticalness seems to go against the grain. The Critical Buddhists themselves, however, are well aware of this and frequently refer to it in their own writings. Their contentiousness of style is a deliberate tactic.

The second reaction of many readers, after they have got over the shock of what is being asserted, is frequently, it appears, a sense of freshness. Whether they agree with the Critical Buddhists or not in detail, there is no doubt that many who have read them have been stimulated into greater clarity – where they disagree as much as where they agree. The Critical Buddhists seem to appreciate this kind of response. Hakamaya has written appreciatively of many of those who have offered further critiques of his own work.

They will point out that sharp debate for the purpose of

establishing the truth has an honourable place in Buddhist history and they will quote the numerous instances in the Sutras, both in Pali and Sanskrit, where the Buddha himself is precisely and devastatingly critical of philosophies he disagreed with. Most importantly, however, they argue that dhatuvada exits primarily as a device to stifle dissent and to provide a 'nice' camouflage for discrimination and oppression, both in society and in Buddhist institutions. It is this paralysing niceness, as much as anything, that they want to expose.

Dhatuvada is closely associated, for instance, with the idea that the real truth cannot be expressed in words. Critical Buddhists regard this as simply a blunt way of stifling debate. They will point out that the Buddha did not seem to have a lot of trouble using words to indicate what was a good path and what was a destructive one. He was a master of words. Critical Buddhists assert that words and intelligence are important. If they are suppressed in the service of a belief that all goodness resides in the unspeakable 'essence of mind' etc., then nobody will be able to stand up and say anything sensible and social dissent will be smothered.

IS DHATUVADA OPPRESSIVE?

The structure of dhatuvada, they say, is to posit a 'good', singular, ultimate, eternal substructure or essence lying behind the multiplicity of actual phenomena appearing in the world. These actual phenomena are not necessarily nice, good, elevated or anything of the kind. Some are. Some, however, are cruel, unjust and oppressive. From a dhatuvada perspective, however, it is possible to justify anything because, after all, the bad things are only superficial and 'unreal'. What is real is the dhatu behind it all. The one (imaginary) good thus subtly justifies and unconsciously sustains the many (real) evils. It also inculcates a value system that implies that that which is the same is more important than that which is different and, thereby, feeds conformist prejudices. In terms of Buddhist analysis, therefore, the contention is that dhatuvada is just the sort of ignorance-generating mechanism that the Buddha discerned as the root of all social problems – the factor that permits 'nice' people complacently to collude in nasty social effects and keeps people spiritually immature.

This niceness and collusion are associated with pursuit of unity at all cost, and the cost is usually social oppression. Buddhism was established in Japan by Prince Shotoku in the eighth century. His clan had just subdued all their rivals and now needed an ideology that would establish good order across the country. Buddhism seemed ideally suited to the purpose. One of the first texts to be introduced was the *Srimaladevi Sutra*. Japanese Buddhism can, therefore, be seen as having been a dhatuvada from the beginning and at least some of the motive for this choice was to establish unity and harmony as supreme values in Japanese society in order to suppress resistance to the power of the throne. Hakamaya sees this as 'nothing more than political ideology pure and simple'.[1]

The centrality of 'harmony' to Japanese social relations has remained firm to this day – often to the frustration of foreigners who cannot understand why the Japanese will never give you a straight 'No' for an answer. One can perhaps also appreciate, however, that the Japanese were willing to accept Shotoko's reforms because they represented something better than what had gone before, which had been a terrible civil war. The cost, however, can be that a national consensus about unity can ensure that nobody ever speaks up for the oppressed, nor against those who commit the kind of crimes that many in the Japanese establishment were involved in during the last war.

Critical Buddhists are, therefore, rocking the boat. They have been likened to Liberation Theologians in Latin America. The latter criticise the Catholic Church for taking a 'God is in his heaven so all must be well' attitude, while the poor starve. The Critical Buddhists see ethnic discrimination in Japanese society being glossed over as a result of the idea that the oppressor and the oppressed all have Buddha Nature so there cannot be anything wrong really. The difference in people's social positions must just be another example of the mysterious working out of the original enlightenment of all, and anyway, good Buddhists should not criticise, so bad practice should not be exposed.

They argue that a dhatuvada style of religious discourse leads to withdrawal from concern with the problems of the world into a pursuit of unity with the soul, Buddha Nature, Tao, godhead or whatever else the dhatu is called. People sit on their meditation cushions emptying their minds of concern while the world starves. This, they say, is what a lot of Japanese Buddhism consists of and, they assert, it is not Buddhism. Buddha did not leave his palace for this. People are encouraged to devote intense effort to the attainment of an experience of 'satori', that Hakamaya regards as no more than a personal indulgence.

Even if one accepts the general drift of what Hakamaya is saying, an important further question needs to be considered. Is dhatuvada intrinsically oppressive or has it only become so in the context of Japanese society? This is a big question.

Sally King has made one of the clearest counterarguments to Hakamaya. She accepts that concepts influence practice, but she argues that the influence is not always in the same direction. She is struck, as any Western observer must be, by the fact that the concepts that the Critical Buddhists focus upon as pernicious – intrinsic Buddha Nature and so on – are precisely the same ones as are favoured by some leading figures in the contemporary engaged Buddhist movement. She says, 'Buddhist social activists specifically cite Buddha-nature as their justification. Thinkers and movements as diverse as Rissho Koseikai, Soka Gakkai, and Thich Nhat Hanh all assert that it is an important part of practice to manifest one's Buddha-nature through bodhisattva action in the form of concrete acts of compassion and social activism'.[2]

Her way of explaining this is to say that the same concept can mean different things in different contexts. In a modern Western context, the concept of Buddha Nature can be a basis for ethically sound and socially constructive initiative even though this may not have been what it was used for by premodern Buddhists in another part of the world. She calls this a problem of hermeneutics – texts yield different meanings in different contexts. She concludes, therefore, that the Buddha Nature tradition of thought has valuable resources for the purposes of those who favour an engaged approach to Buddhism.

King's argument, therefore, is that:

- Concepts do affect practice, but they can do so in totally different ways according to the context.
- The Buddha Nature concept is in fact used to support social activism, so the charge that it leads to ethical laxity must be wrong.

There is some merit in this argument, as far as it goes. It is true that advocates of engaged Buddhism coming from traditions where the Buddha Nature concept and the related idea of interdependent co-arising are central have used these concepts to justify their approach. At the level of rhetoric, almost total flexibility can be achieved in the use of concepts according to one's purpose and they have found that these concepts work in a Western context.

We could, therefore, conclude that we in the West are safe to use these ideas to the full and that they will not lead us into the kind of troubles that the Critical Buddhists highlight as having happened in Japan. To draw such a conclusion on such grounds, however, is quite close to asserting that the concepts are meaningless in themselves and can be turned into whatever we want to turn them into. If this is so, then much of their force must be lost. This, however, is clearly not correct.

The reality is that the ideas of intrinsic enlightenment and Buddha Nature are powerful concepts. They certainly strike a chord in many Western people. They perhaps are striking a different chord in them from the one that they strike in Japan

– or perhaps not. What the concept of Buddha Nature really stands accused of, I think, is that it induces complacency. The sheer fact that Western engaged Buddhists use the concept is not alone enough to exonerate it. We have to ask, if they use it too, does it induce complacency in them? Is it a nice idea that lulls people into moral laxity?

It will probably take a longer time span to gain an empirical answer to this question. It may be that the idea of inherent Buddha Nature (to merge the two concepts) inspires people to act compassionately on the grounds that others have the same nature as oneself and therefore they should be helped. Of course, it can be said that a higher moral principle would be to help people whether they have the same nature as yourself or not, but in practical terms, the idea of Buddha Nature can sometimes function as an encouragement.

How are we to explain the different uses of these words? The first stage in the introduction of Buddhism to China is often called the stage of 'matching of terms'. What this means is that, at that time, the Chinese had little understanding of Buddhism, so what they did was to map the new Buddhist concepts on to concepts that they already had, many of which were drawn from Taoism. When a Chinese person of that period used the Buddhist word, what he or she meant was the Taoist meaning. After a time, this started to cause enormous confusion and logical discourse became almost impossible. There was then a big job to rethink what all these new words really meant. It seems quite plausible to assert that we in the West are at our own 'matching of terms' phase of New Buddhism. When we say 'interbeing', we do not mean 'interdependent co-arising' – we do not even know what that is – we mean ecology, compassionate community and so on. In a similar way, when Western people use the term Buddha Nature, they are probably not thinking of a particularly Buddhist meaning. What are they thinking of, then?

In a Western context, the ideas of original enlightenment and Buddha Nature look remarkably like the concepts in humanistic psychology of 'self-actualising tendency' and 'actualising tendency' respectively. These, in turn, could easily be argued to have their roots in popular spirituality and the idea of the soul.

These concepts are central to the earlier work of Abraham Maslow and the work of Carl Rogers, two leading American humanistic psychologists. When originally introduced, these terms seemed attractive. They seemed to offer an ideology of unlimited human potential. Maslow, however, was soon to give up on them specifically because he saw that, in practice, they led people into a form of narcissism. What had seemed initially to be a promising and liberating concept became ethically corrosive once it became widespread. It became, in other words, an ideological basis for the direct opposite of selflessness. It bred smugness and self-indulgence. The 'self-actualising tendency', of course, is clearly and self-declaredly an atmavada (a path of self). The history of the idea of self-actualising tendency in Western thought, if it is equated with the dhatuvada ideas – and many people do quite naturally equate them – strikes a definite note of caution.

Rogers's ideas have been criticised for being blind to the nasty side of life. This criticism is probably unfair on Rogers himself, but it is not so wide of the mark when we consider the effect of his theories divorced from their originator. It would also not be difficult to discern a strain of complacent dogmatism in the movement that has sprung from his ideas, even though these qualities, too, were absent from the man himself.

When first introduced, the idea of self-actualising tendency, along with the idea of human potential, seemed liberating. For a time, these concepts were usable in the cause of love and peace. In practice, however, they generated ever-increasing narcissistic concern that steadily eroded the original idealism and led directly away from the kind of care for others that Critical Buddhism would see as the foundation of a good society.

Is it too far-fetched to consider the possibility that the ideas of Buddha Nature and of inherent enlightenment will have a similar effect, gradually transforming from within those socially active groups who have adopted them and converting them from radical, constructive social movements into passive and introspective fraternities where social criticism steadily loses ground in the face of the overwhelming inertia of self-salvation? Time will tell.

Critical Faith

A superficial reading of Critical Buddhism can lead the unsuspecting Westerner to think that this is a resurgence of logical positivism, of rationality and doubt over faith. This interpretation is, however, completely wrong. Hakamaya, for instance, is scathing about academic objectivity, seeing it as simply another form of self-congratulatory smugness. Critical Buddhism has more the quality of an existential faith than of scientific rationalism.

The heroes of the Critical Buddhists are people of faith, like Descartes in the West, and like Dogen and Honen in Japan. One of the refreshing things about this approach is that it brings together odd bedfellows. Dogen and Honen, both thirteenth-century reformers of Japanese Buddhism, were critical of one another, but they were both men of faith. They each advanced their interpretation of what the Buddha stood for in the face of social attitudes that preferred a more comfortable unity-based approach. They were also, each in different ways, advocates for the rights of lower-caste people and of women in the face of the hierarchical and chauvinistic character of the society around them.

The confusion for Westerners arises from the fact that, in the West, faith is associated with a vertical metaphysic, that is, with dhatuvada. In the West, faith tends to mean faith in the transcendent ultimate. In Buddhism, however, faith is really the faith to live without that comfort.

Faith in Buddhism could just as well be called clarity. Clarity can sometimes be clarity about propositions in words, but it can also be something that is not articulated at all. I have faith that this chair will support me. I do not think about it. I may never have thought about it. If I do think about it, then this is after the event. The faith consists, not in my thinking or talking about it, but in the fact that I do sit down on this chair.

It is the same in Buddhism. To have faith in the Buddha, dharma and sangha may, of course, be something that I have talked about. Whether the faith exists, however, is not a matter of my skill in definition, nor of my eloquence. It is something that shows or does not show in the way I live.

Faith is also a matter of commitment. It is subjective. This piece of writing, for instance, is not objective. It is my reading of the matter. A critical community, in the sense that the term critical has been used here, is one in which there is respect for differences when these are expressed in a straightforward way. The pressure for everybody to agree all the time is oppression and the pressure to be nonjudgmental can simply produce collusion and frustrate reform.

Critical writing depends upon being able to pass judgments. It also depends upon being willing to have the judgments one has made subjected to scrutiny. If I assert that racial prejudice is wrong, I am being judgmental. If I am told that I should not be judgmental, then, of course, the person who says so is also being judgmental. The problem with believing that one should not be judgmental is that it boils down to an assertion that 'One should not say should, should one?'

If one has faith, one has commitments. If one has commitments, one makes judgments. One is willing to assert, 'I declare this to be right and I declare that to be wrong'. If we are not willing to do so, then we are in danger of becoming spineless. Of course, people fear that those who disagree about what is right may fight. Buddhism, however, is committed both to truth and to nonviolence. Neither of these commitments should overwhelm the other. What is important, therefore, is to have faith in truth (dharma) and to be always open enough to listen to new argument and new evidence.

Buddhism is, therefore, both criticism and faith. Or, we could say, in Buddhism, faith and criticism are compatible. To criticise racial prejudice, for instance, may take a lot of courage in some situations. It requires faith. This is the kind of faith that Buddhism is. In a similar way, Buddhist faith is also the faith to doubt. Those who cling to dogmatic certainties are not people of faith – quite the contrary. It takes faith to live with uncertainty.

COULD IT HAPPEN – IS IT HAPPENING – HERE?

Critical Buddhism has attempted to open our eyes to a danger. It is a warning bell. The Buddhist message is of great importance to the future of our world, but not all that appears under the Buddhist banner is the real thing. Buddhism came into the world vigorously refusing cooperation with a number of gross oppressions: the oppression of the caste system; the oppressions of racism, sexism, and other forms of deluded and unenlightened social practice; the oppression of the poor and powerless by the rich and powerful; the oppression of animals; the Buddha gave a personal example of giving up worldly power and working ceaselessly for the wellbeing of all.

In the service of this anti-oppressive agenda, Buddha offered a philosophy that was radical. It offered a metaphysic that was essentially flat. The gods were demoted. The actions of all persons, not just the 'chosen', nor ones of a particular caste, were seen as consequential. Buddha called people to wake up and make a difference. He preached against oblivion, whether through alcohol, drugs, indulgence, comforting illusions or simply a head-in-the-sand attitude. He praised the giving up of wealth. He encouraged people to abandon the motive of self-seeking. He criticized meat-eating and sacrifice. He preached against war. The Buddha was willing and able to make strongly stated judgments on all these issues. He never implied that his path was comfortable or easy. This was not a 'go with the flow' message. He talked rather of standing against the current, going upstream, and cutting through the torrent. He was anything but complacent. One of his most-used words was 'Strive!' The duty of a Buddhist teacher is to 'advise, inform, instruct, urge, rouse and encourage'.[3]

He pointed out that actions have consequences and that it is therefore possible for people to have an effect. He taught ethical ways to act and he taught mind-training methods that supported those ways of acting. He recruited a following of dedicated people who were willing to give their lives to this agenda. These people were 'renunciants' – that is, they renounced the conventional society driven by greed, hate and delusion and set about creating a better world. The Buddha sent his renunciants forth 'for the benefit of the many'. They were a courageous band.

As can so often be the case, however, when such a movement starts to have some success, more conservative forces can infiltrate. The original ideology can be undermined by more comfortable ideas that are less threatening to the *status quo*. People arrive who would like to experience the elevated state of mind without the trouble of changing their way of life or the society they live in. Instead of seeing enlightenment as a basis for creating a better world, they see the worse world as an annoying distraction from the business of getting enlightened.

In the case of Buddhism, we now sometimes see the mind-training methods that were designed to strengthen the renunciant resolve being used in the service of withdrawal from engagement with the world. We see that Buddhism has picked up a lot of transcendental philosophy that encourages such withdrawal by placing the goal in the metaphysical realm. Buddhism has too-often ceased to be an activism and become a quietism.

By importing the kind of ideas that the Critical Buddhists identify as dhatuvada, Buddhism can start to assert a monistic outlook that can become an oppressive force in its own right, or become a tacit or even overt ally of oppressive forces in society at large. Self-perpetuating priestly monopolies of power are created. Monastic centres become rich and powerful and their leaders become the more powerful for being seen as the guardians of mysteries too abstruse for ordinary people to understand.

In the West, Buddhism is just getting established. The position is very different from Japan. Here, Buddhist values as yet have little influence upon social policy. This is changing, however. It is important that if Buddhism spreads it does so because of its intrinsic merit and not on the basis of pouring Buddhist wine into the old bottles.

If you are involved with a Buddhist group, therefore, it would be as well to ask yourself whether you can imagine this group putting its weight behind any significant resistance to social oppression. Is it already doing so? In some cases the answers will be negative. Some Buddhist groups do not see that as their job. Why not? Is it because they are in the business of helping people to realise their Buddha Nature, not in the business of changing social conditions? Is it because they assert that this world is not real and that salvation lies in a future life? If so, beware.

There is a Zen saying that the perfect way is without difficulty if one avoids picking and choosing. This idea that one should not make choices is a characteristic strongly associated with dhatuvada. If everything has the same Buddha Nature, what is there to choose between? However, this surely is a mistaken interpretation. Buddhism involves choice. Buddhism is a choice. Buddhism is a teaching that asks us to change the basis of our choices, not one that says no choices should be made. Will you choose to take life or to save it? Will you choose to speak the truth or to lie? If everything is the same in its Buddha Nature, then there is no reason to do anything. There is a lot of rhetoric within the dhatuvada approaches to Buddhism that asserts that one should not choose and this is where the Critical Buddhists start to see the ethical weakness arising. Buddhism is not about not choosing. It is about choosing in an enlightened rather than a selfish way. It is not about being without purpose. It is about being without a selfish purpose. These are not the same.

As Sally King says, words can be used for different purposes and the key terms that we have examined in this chapter – Buddha Nature, original enlightenment, tathagata-garbha, interdependent co-arising, dharmadhatu – are all capable of being construed in different ways, especially when one's intention is rhetorical rather than scientific. As science, dependent origination is a defensible concept where interdependent co-arising probably is not. As rhetoric, the latter can be used to assert compassionate community between all species on the basis of underlying sameness and this may sometimes be constructive. A sounder basis for harmony, however, is probably provided by acceptance and appreciation of diversity and difference than by assertion of sameness. This basis is sounder because it does not imply that difference is bad, nor suggest that uniformity is an ideal. After all, if the reason that we should love each other is said to be that we are the same underneath, the implication is that the more alike we are the more we will love each other, and this is a doctrine that can readily degenerate into exclusion of those who are different – of those who are not like us.

Popular spirituality abhors difference. Buddhism, on the other hand, is pluralistic. Popular spirituality needs a metaphysical substratum and sometimes a celestial overlord as well. Buddhism keeps the responsibility with us and teaches us to use that responsibility in enlightened ways. Popular spirituality sees things as being in the lap of the gods. Buddhism believes in consequential action. These are different. If concepts like Buddha Nature and tathagata-garbha are used to mean that everybody can become enlightened, then they are Buddhist. If they are used as substitute words for soul, god, divine essence and so on, then they are not. The message of Critical Buddhism is usefully disturbing and should not be ignored. Buddhism has a relatively good record, but it will only stay that way if the main message is neither diluted nor subsumed under ideas that support uniformity. We should not ignore the lessons of countries where that uniformity has become supportive of a nationalistic agenda. We will see some of the consequences of the latter in the next chapter.

· 11 ·

The Corruption of Lineage

THE YASUTANI AFFAIR

Hakuun Yasutani (1885–1973) was a Zen Master legitimated by the lineage system of the Soto Zen School. He received the transmission from his master Harada Daiun Sogaku (1870–1961). He stood, according to Zen tradition, in direct line from Shakyamuni Buddha and this was his claim to legitimacy. The Buddha, himself, however, refused to appoint a successor and also said, 'Do not know them by their lineage, know them by their deeds'.

As a younger man Yasutani had been a school teacher. He became a Zen priest and studied under Harada Roshi. In particular, for the eight years from 1935 to 1943 he engaged in serious Zen training with Harada. He made the kind of progress that pleased his teacher and in due course became a teacher in his own right. His friend Nakagawa Soen, in due course, invited him to go to the USA to help spread Zen practice there.

He was known as a strong-minded individual and a vigorous teacher of Buddhism. Many of the leading teachers of Zen in North America are dharma successors or were disciples of Yasutani Roshi. Yasutani's disciple Philip Kapleau Roshi, who was half-Jewish, wrote the book, *Three Pillars of Zen*[1] under Yasutani's guidance and this is one of the most-read text books on Zen in North America. The book largely comprises teachings given by Yasutani and descriptions of enlightenment experiences obtained by disciples under Yasutani's guidance. The Three Pillars, the reader is told, are called teaching, practice and enlightenment, in that order. The teaching is a recipe. The practice is the cooking. Enlightenment is that you get to eat the dish.

The teaching is that one should sit in meditation in the correct Zen posture and strive with all one's might, sparing no effort in the attempt to realise one's Non-Dual Buddha Nature. The book is full of descriptions by disciples of how long, painful and frustrating weeks and months of sitting in Zen meditation are finally rewarded with explosions of cathartic euphoria. It is clear that the appeal of this book to American readers lay in the tempting possibility of getting a dose of this spiritual crescendo. Having studied Zen myself in another tradition, I can testify to the hold that this appeal can have. Yasutani travelled many times to North America and had many American disciples. He has been one of the most significant teachers in the transmission of Buddhism from Japan to North America.

In 1997 the book *Zen at War* was published.[2] This book reveals how senior Zen clergy reinterpreted Buddhist teachings during the Second World War in order to support Japanese aggression in Asia. Even more recently, a book has come to light written by Yasutani Roshi himself in 1943. Yasutani's book[3] reinterprets the writings of Dogen, the founder of Soto Zen in Japan, in a manner designed to support the war, deify the emperor, promote the superiority of Japan, foster anti-Semitism and encourage people to exterminate the enemy.

This book is full of militarist and anti-Jewish propaganda. It also includes a commentary upon the first precept of Buddhism, the one that forbids killing. This commentary includes the passage, 'Failing to kill an evil man who ought to be killed, or destroying an enemy army that ought to be destroyed, would be to betray compassion and filial obedience, to break the precept forbidding the taking of life. This is a special characteristic of the Mahayana precepts' – a special characteristic indeed! Two months after the book was published, Yasutani received formal dharma transmission. Of this event, Kapleau writes: 'Yasutani-roshi was fifty-eight when Harada-roshi gave him his seal of approval and named him a dharma successor. This signal honor implied that his spiritual insight was deep, his moral character high, and his capacity to teach proven.'⁴

In general, people found Yasutani a kind person, generous in many ways to his students and associates. He also remained a man of right-wing political views throughout his life. He supported the American War in Vietnam and clearly never excluded the idea of violence being a legitimate way of settling political differences. The paradoxes and apparent contradictions in a man who could write hate-filled anti-Jewish rhetoric and also have Jewish disciples who became leading members of humanitarian and anti-war movements is striking and perplexing. The merits of a system that gives a person its highest seal of approval and spiritual authority when he is confirmed in murderously warmongering attitudes are surely less difficult to access.

If we take the case of Yasutani to be one of a legitimated Buddhist teacher who practises some grossly anti-Buddhist activities and sentiments, then it is not an isolated one. It is simply a salient example. During the last fifty years, which is the period during which Buddhism has been making important progress in the West, there have been a small, yet disturbingly significant, number of cases of Buddhist Masters who had been legitimated by the lineage system of their particular school, going off the rails. Baker Roshi at San Francisco Zen Centre and Osel Rimpoche in the Kargyu Tibetan tradition are two of the best-known examples. A few years ago I attended a conference called by the Network of Buddhist Organisations in the UK precisely to discuss the problem of what to do about cases of this kind, and this was before the Yasutani affair had become known to anybody in this country.

This phenomenon raises many questions. These include how to prevent it happening, how to help those who suffer as a result, and how to help the so-called Buddhist teacher in question. With help, Baker Roshi, after all, managed to pick himself up from his disaster and in due course became a better Buddhist teacher than before. Others have not done so well. This is certainly not simply a question of rogue individuals. It is a problem in the system. People want to have gurus to idolise and they, therefore, want some system to tell them who the gurus are. Generally this system is the lineage system. This system, however, is of questionable merit. What I think is impressive about the Buddhist world in the West is the fact that, on the whole, there has been, in all these unfortunate situations, a good measure of compassion in evidence for everybody concerned and the predictable recriminations have not got out of hand. On the one hand, we do seem to be mature enough to handle these things a little better than the population at large, but we still hold to the systems that create the trouble in the first place.

It has to be said, however, that there are degrees. That a Buddhist teacher, once in a while, strays from his vows of celibacy in company with another consenting adult is inappropriate and disappointing. That a person writes a book that advocates killing and seeks to justify that killing on spiritual authority is surely considerably more serious. That a church whose highest principle is supposedly enlightened compassion should confer the highest legitimacy that it has to offer upon the author of such a book is a folly of such magnitude that it is hard to comprehend.

THE LINEAGE QUESTION

Lineage can have a number of meanings. It can simply mean that every Buddhist today learnt his or her Buddhism from other Buddhists who learnt it from others in turn and that in this manner one can trace a succession back to the Buddha in India. In this form, the idea is unexceptional.

Generally, however, lineage means more than this. It refers to the certification of one Master's enlightenment by another of a former generation. This act of transmission certifies the legitimacy of the succeeding teacher to be a teacher and leader. This is the manner in which a priestly succession and a priestly monopoly of power is maintained in many schools of Buddhism. There can be considerable power and status attached to being a dharma successor. This system could be seen as a means of ensuring that only properly certified and, therefore, genuinely enlightened people are allowed to teach, or it could be seen as a system for maintaining priestly power and creating mystique.

The transmission and lineage system is intended to impart legitimacy. Why would a school or a teacher need such legitimacy? Presumably because what they have to offer is non-obvious. I do not ask for a certificate from my greengrocer, I just ask if he has cabbages for sale. I do ask for certification in the case of my doctor, because if I try to find out whether he is any good by practical experimentation it may be too late before I realise he is lethal. A certification system assumes that dharma teachers are in the same category as doctors and not in the same one as greengrocers.

It is worth noting at this point that the Buddha put himself in the greengrocer category. Come and see and try it out, he said. In other words, if you like what I sell, buy it. If not, not. The Buddha did not appoint a successor. He did express his opinion about whether this or that person was enlightened or not, if asked. There is a charming passage in which his disciple Ananda keeps asking him to do so and he rebukes Ananda for being tiresome, then tells him how to see for himself whether they are or not. He did not issue certificates as credentials. The test of whether people were stream enterers or arhats was whether or not they kept the discipline. The Buddha seems to have thought that the matter was obvious, not non-obvious. If a person was enlightened, you could tell from what he or she did.

This is a bit like the system that seems to have operated in premodern China where wandering monks were admitted with little formality to the visiting monks' hall of large monasteries.

They might even give a pseudonym. They were not asked for ordination certificates. The test of whether they were real monks was whether they rose at three in the morning, sat in meditation for long hours, worked hard, knew their scriptures and kept the discipline. If they did so, then it did not really matter much whether they had been properly ordained or not, they were monks. A monk is somebody who does what a monk does.

So much for individuals. What about schools? Lineages are not just ways of legitimising individual teachers. They are also, more importantly, ways of legitimising whole schools of Buddhism. Ever since the split between the Elders and the Majority Group at the Second Great Council, there have been competing claims to legitimacy in Buddhism. There have been polemics between schools. The teachings of different schools differ.

The School of the Elders, the Sthaviravada, and its only surviving descendant, Theravada, rely for legitimacy primarily upon their claim that they keep closely to the original lifestyle of the Buddha. This manner of establishing legitimacy is rather like the method of the Buddha himself. In this case, it is taken rather literally and rigidly, perhaps, so that some of the rules that Theravada monks are expected to keep today are anachronistic. Almost all Theravadans recognise this, but they do not change the rules. To do so would be taboo because the whole Theravada claim to legitimacy rests precisely upon them not being changed. Theravada also has a lineage system. This second system, however, is open to much criticism. In Sri Lanka, for instance, there are separate lineages for different castes. What would the Buddha have thought of this? He would have disapproved. Why then does it persist? Lineage is a system with its own highly conservative momentum and mystique.

The reason the Theravadans keep anachronistic rules as well as sensible ones is that what marked out the other party, the Majority Group, or Mahasanghika, at the Second Council was just this: they were willing to change the rules. Once the process of changing the form has been established, it can, of course, result in all manner of diversity and this is precisely what we see in Mahayana Buddhism, which is, in many ways, the descendant of the Mahasanghika.

Once the form has started to change, some criterion other than orthodoxy is required to establish legitimacy. This, really, is where the lineage principle starts to dominate. Lineage serves to show that even though the way that a particular school of Buddhism does things does not look like what Buddha did, nonetheless, it is directly descended from and derived from what he did. Furthermore, it suggests, all the changes that have been made along the way have been made by enlightened beings, so what you see now is at least as good as, and perhaps even better than, what the Buddha offered.

Lineage, therefore, becomes a way of legitimising something non-obvious. The more non-obvious it is, the more the idea of lineage may be relied upon. That is, the more that the present practice of a school differs from primitive Buddhism, the more importance that school is likely to place upon lineage.

Lineage is, of course, a form of 'argument from authority'. Western logic (but not Western popular opinion) has long regarded this form of argument as fallacious. The fact that somebody holds a certain position does not, of itself, ensure that he or she is right. The Buddha himself seems to have been of the same opinion. Do not believe something because of the position of the person who told you it, he says – and he clearly even includes himself in that. Things are not true because the Buddha says so, they are true if they are true and as regards the things that really matter, you may need to have them pointed out by somebody wiser than you, but you should test what that person says for yourself. Nonetheless, humans like to have authorities and human society is full of legitimisation systems, many of which work very badly.

This human sentiment provides the proximate cause that keeps the lineage system in being. When a great spiritual leader is dying, people want that person to appoint a successor. If the founder does so, people feel much more secure. Now we know whom to follow, they think. People like this because they do not like anxiety and uncertainty. It saves them having to choose.

The Buddha does not seem to have been in the business of turning people into sheep, however. When he was dying, they implored him to appoint a successor. He did not do so. If there is somebody who thinks he is wise enough to lead the sangha, then that person should make decisions like that, he said, and we can still detect the irony in his voice. He did not see himself as a power broker. Nonetheless, when he died, Mahakashyapa called the monks together and chaired the First Council. From this, some have deduced that he was the Buddha's successor. The Sthaviravada did not, however, regard him as such. They would have favoured Shariputra, if the latter had not died before the Buddha did. Pali texts in which the Buddha praises Shariputra, however, do not appear in the texts recognised by the Northern Schools of Buddhism. Clearly, therefore, there were disagreements quite early on about these issues.

The basic points, therefore, are that lineage is a legitimising device; that such a device is more necessary when other forms of legitimacy are less obvious; that it was not a device favoured by the Buddha himself; and that there have been disputes around it from an early age in Buddhist history.

One of the schools that places particular emphasis upon lineage is Zen. The *Platform Sutra* is an important text of this school. One of its prime purposes appears to be to establish the legitimacy in terms of lineage of Hui Neng who is thereby claimed to be the sixth patriarch of Zen in China. The stories of Bodhidharma are also an important foundation stone of this school's sense of identity. Bodhidharma is portrayed as bringing Zen from India to China and becoming the first patriarch in China. Zen eventually crossed to Japan and the various lineage lines have continued to be the basic organising structure of this church.

Why would the question of lineage be so important to Zen? In China, Zen made a radical break with older Buddhist tradition in a quest for acceptability. Many of the doctrines of Zen really owe more to Taoism, than to Buddhism. The tendency in Mahayana Buddhism as a whole to rest the whole structure of Buddhist thinking upon the idea of an eternal essence, identified with the 'essence of mind', a teaching alien to Buddha himself, reaches its finest development in Zen. Hui Neng or, more likely, his disciple Shen Hui was a genius of religious innovation in this sense. Although not Chinese himself – another reason for legitimacy problems – Hui Neng and his followers were able to transform this branch of Buddhism into a Chinese religion. After Hui Neng, Zen, or Chan, was popular in China as never before.

I suggest, therefore, that Zen laid heavy emphasis upon lineage because it needed some source of authority other than the authenticity of teachings and practice, precisely because the teachings that this school advanced were not obviously in accord with traditional Buddhism. The process of cross-fertilising Buddhism with Taoism had been going on for a long time. Shen Hui crystallised this process in a way that, as we say, hit the spot, with the educated section of Chinese society. Hence the *Platform Sutra* is an address to such people. You can imagine the question in their minds: we like the sound of this, but is it really Buddhism? Hui Neng's followers made the teachings Chinese so they then needed a way of asserting that they were still Buddhist – that they were actually even more Buddhist than the other schools. Lineage gave them this. The lineage that they drew up is, however, highly questionable.

Modern scholarship has come to the broad conclusion that many of the links in the Zen lineage lines are fictional. Thus, 'research into the history of Ch'an has irrevocably undermined the traditional transmission legends of Bodhidharma and the six patriarchs, as well as the traditional accounts of lineage transmission ... Ch'an did not come from India, much less Buddha's and 'Hui Neng, the alleged founder of the southern school, was perhaps no more than a useful alibi for his heir Shen Hui, and his canonization is as much a cover-up as an act of recognition'.' [6] Shen Hui really probably has a better claim to being the founder of a new school, or even a new religion, than he does to being the successor to the Indian form of Buddhism. A religious genius he certainly was. Whether it was Buddhism, however, depends how far you are willing to stretch your definitions.

THE NON-DUAL IN ACTION

In its autumn 1999 issue, *Tricycle* magazine published material about Yasutani Roshi and invited a number of his leading American successors and disciples to comment. They did so in a variety of different ways.

Robert Aitken Roshi, who received dharma transmission from Yasutani Roshi, offers something approaching a defence, or at least a substantial plea in mitigation, for Yasutani. In part this constitutes a counterattack upon Brian Victoria, the author of *Zen at War*, for having suggested that some of Yasutani's attitudes might have carried over to his disciples in North America. Aitken was a founder member of the Buddhist Peace Fellowship and when I met him in Hawaii where he lives, I found that our views on many social issues were similar. Our views on some of the underlying philosophical issues, however, differ and this has implications for the way we approach Buddhist training. Aitken's defence of Yasutani is, essentially, summed up in the question: how can you expect anybody to rise above their culture? Aitken is a sensitive and intelligent man who has worked hard for peace and humanity. This argument is hardly adequate, however. If a religion cannot help its leading exponents to rise above their culture, it is worthless. This would be enlightenment without crossing the river.

Bodhin Kjolhede, who received dharma transmission from Philip Kapleau, takes a slightly different line. He argues that there are many levels of enlightenment and he defines enlightenment as activity manifesting insight into the Non-Dual nature of reality. He says that Yasutani had some such insight, but it could not have been complete. As long as it is not complete a person will still be infected with defilements, hence Yasutani's delusions and warmongering. One has to ask, if a properly transmitted dharma heir can be this deluded, what is this transmission worth? Shortly after this, Kjolhede broke ranks with most of the Buddhist community in order to support NATO-armed intervention in Kosovo.

Lawrence Shainberg is a disciple of Nakagawa Kyudo who received dharma transmission from Yasutani's associate Nakagawa Soen. Shainberg takes the view that Zen is a practice and that this practice does not get rid of delusions – it just makes you acutely aware of them. One has the sense that Shainberg thinks gross contradictions are almost an inevitable outcome in somebody who gets deeply involved in Zen practice.

Bernard Glassman received dharma transmission from Hakuyu Taizan Maezumi Roshi who, in turn received it from Yasutani Roshi. Glassman is the founder of the Zen Peacemaker Order, an organisation that figures significantly amongst contemporary engaged Buddhist groups and has done some wonderful work helping the homeless and oppressed. Glassman's view is that all beings are already enlightened and all beings are one body. This means that all life – the good, the bad and the ugly – is all included in the one Buddha body of universal enlightenment. Within this one body, each individual has his or her particular stains and limitations. A lifetime can be a short time. Not much may change in one lifetime. That is why continuous practice is necessary. Enlightenment is a realisation of the oneness. Practice, however, goes on indefinitely. We are all enlightened and we are all addicted to our egos – we always shall be.

Of these four, Glassman is surely the most consistent and logical and, to my way of thinking, the most clearly wrong. He has my respect because here there are no excuses, no shilly-shallying. Glassman is willing to say that if your definition of enlightenment does not allow for anti-Semitism within enlightenment then your definition is not big enough. For Glassman, himself Jewish, to say such a thing is, in one sense, big-hearted. I acknowledge Glassman's big heart. Nonetheless, I assert that he is wrong. My definition of enlightenment does not have room for anti-Semitism. I do not think that the Buddha's definition of enlightenment had room for anything similar either. The Buddha had compassion for bigots, but he did not think they were enlightened. In this sense, Glassman is a better successor to Yasutani – he has understood the essence of what Yasutani believed. The fact that it manifests in a quite different way in Glassman is by the way. This is the fascinating point. Both Yasutani and Glassman are compassionate men who have done much good in the world. Yasutani has also given his support to some iniquities and Glassman here gives his to a wrongly conceived idea. People are neither all good nor all bad. Our task at this point is not to label them, but to try to discern the better philosophy, and there clearly is a weakness in the philosophy that these two share and have both advanced.

On the basis of oneness, both can feel compassion for beings irrespective of how they are manifesting – as concentration camp guards or as humanitarian activists. On the basis of oneness, Yasutani can believe in the importance of destroying the enemy for the sake of the harmonious realm. He can advocate killing the enemy at the same time as feeling compassion for the enemy. This is the 'special way of understanding the precepts'. It may be special, but it is not Buddhist. The Buddha had a similarly all-encompassing compassion, but he did not arrive at it on the basis of oneness and so he did not draw the same conclusions. Buddha did not partake of Glassman's enlightenment any more than he did that of Yasutani.

Buddha's compassion was formulated precisely as a compassion for those who were not enlightened. Some were enlightened and some were not. In this sense, the Buddha was dualistic. The Buddha did not teach the Non-Dual, whatever that is. The

Non-Dual was invented by later generations who wanted to accommodate Buddhism to the prevailing spirituality of their times, first in India where the idea of Non-Dual meant Brahma and then in China where it meant the Tao and the unity of the empire. Buddha rejected the whole structure of Brahmanical ideas and would no doubt have rejected Taoism and Chinese imperialism as well, had he known about them.

Why did Buddha renounce the structure of Brahmanical ideas? After all, the notion of a transcendent oneness is popular and some people have used it to constructive and compassionate ends. Even some great Buddhist reformers whose practical work I greatly approve have sometimes favoured the idea. A recent example of the latter would be the late Reverend Gyomay Kubose who helped to establish a wonderfully inclusive approach to dharma. Oneness is popular and can be a useful vehicle for some teachers. However, it has serious drawbacks if pushed through to its philosophical conclusion. If all is really one, it ultimately becomes difficult, if not impossible, to make choices. It can just as well support oppression as liberation. Although the theory of oneness has an immediate superficial appeal, uniting all beings within one ultimate, beneficial, transcendent reality, it also underpinned the Indian caste system, just as it did later the Japanese one. In the quest for universal harmony and compassion, something can go badly wrong. This something is the erection of a transcendent Non-Dual something or other that somehow makes all the actual manifestations of life all right.

Buddha began his teaching with recognition that some things are not all right. Most people are living in a state of delusion and this is not all right. There is a need to do something about it and there is a need to differentiate. Buddha would have had no hesitation in demanding that Yasutani cease to misrepresent him. Delusion, to Buddha, did not mean a failure to see the Non-Dual nature of things – it meant a failure to see that things like anti-Semitism are not all right. Society is shot through with greed, hate and delusion, said the Buddha and this must be changed. Where there was greed, hate and delusion, let us create generosity, benevolence and wisdom. This is a duality. In this sense, and it is the sense that matters, Buddha was a dualist.

This does not mean that he believed in transcendent dualisms, like heaven and hell or god and devil. His metaphysics, if they can be called that, which is doubtful, were flat not hierarchical. They were flat precisely because he did not rely upon a transcendent reality either behind, above or below this one. Meaning is not given to life from outside, neither from above nor from below. It is for us to give meaning to our own life. This is a choice.

LINEAGE

How does all this relate to the question of lineage and the instance of Yasutani? The answer concerns the nature of enlightenment. If enlightenment is a matter of recognising the Non-Dual, then it is a non-obvious state. It therefore requires certification. Only another person who has recognised the Non-Dual can tell if the disciple has really done so, apparently. Lineage may, therefore, be an appropriate way of legitimisation for the transmission of that kind of enlightenment. Yasutani and Glassman may thus, therefore, both be appropriately transmitted and legitimate representatives of the school of enlightenment as realisation of the Non-Dual. This school, however, is not the school to which Shakyamuni Buddha belonged. It is also clear from this example that realising the Non-Dual is absolutely no guarantee of anything in the sphere of ethics or social compassion.

In the Pali texts[7] there is the story of Mahanama who comes to see the Buddha to ask about why unwholesome states of mind still afflict him. Mahanama is the brother of Anuruddha and Ananda who have both become renunciant disciples of the Buddha. Mahanama lives a good life and is much praised, but he has chosen not to go the whole hog. He prefers to continue living the home life. The Buddha said to Mahanama: 'Yes, you are right that there is something you have still not got free of in your life – you can see that from the fact that you choose still to live a worldly lifestyle.' He did not say: 'The trouble with you Mahanama is that you have not realised the Non-Dual.' If Mahanama had realised the Non-Dual, he could probably have kept his worldly lifestyle. After all, you can realise the Non-Dual nature even of wars of extermination, as Yasutani did, so you can certainly find the Non-Dual nature of the life that a good soul like Mahanama was living. No, the Buddha said, the matter is more obvious.

Lineage, therefore, is not relevant to the school of Shakyamuni Buddha except in the quite different sense that the Buddha stood in the lineage of all those, of whatever religion, who, from remote antiquity, had opened their eyes to the exploitation and cruelty that is in the world and resolved to do something about it. These were the past buddhas. The school of Shakyamuni Buddha is not a school for realising the Non-Dual. It is a school for realising nonself. We can see if a person acts selfishly or not. If a person writes tracts praising their race at the expense of other races, they are not enlightened in the school of nonself. If a person arranges their life around acquisitiveness or power seeking, then they are not enlightened in the school of nonself. It is obvious. It is also dual. Some do and some do not stand within this kind of enlightenment, and that is reality. It is hard and factual. It is not esoteric and solipsistic.

The spread of the Non-Dual type of enlightenment is dangerous because it unhooks enlightenment from ethics. Shakyamuni Buddha did not have any tolerance for that kind of unhooking at all, as is plain from innumerable incidents in his life. There has grown up an idea that you can be enlightened and still immoral. That kind of lineage-supported enlightenment is not the enlightenment of Buddha.

As for the lineage system itself, it has been a strong contributory factor in almost every significant scandal in the Buddhist world in recent years, not just in the Zen School, and it should be regarded with great caution. The test of legitimacy in things spiritual is behaviour, and the test of behaviour is intended and actual consequence. Know them by their deeds.

Lest this chapter be taken wrongly, let me clarify some of the things that have been asserted and, I trust, demonstrated, and some that have not. First, it is not asserted here that Robert Aitken, nor Bernard Glassman, nor other contemporary Western Buddhist teachers are or are likely to become Nazis or anything of the kind. These men are well loved and primarily known for their virtues and good works. What this demonstrates, however, is that the lineage system can throw up great disparity of persons and it is, therefore, questionable whether it guarantees anything. Since its function is supposed to be that it offers a guarantee, this means that it does not do what it is supposed to do. A guarantee that is so manifestly unreliable is no guarantee at all. Lineage as an authentication system is not the system founded by Shakyamuni Buddha, and he would not have approved it in that form. In the realm of things spiritual, the principle has to be 'let the buyer beware'. It is, however, perfectly possible for the buyer to beware. Buddhism is hindered, not helped, by unnecessary mystification. Considerable doubt is here cast – as in several other chapters of this book – on the philosophy of non-duality. It is asserted that the New Buddhism needs a better theoretical basis. This is because non-duality can be used and has been used to justify just about anything. It offers no useful guidance and since the purpose of philosophy is to guide rather than to mystify, it does not do the job. We would be better to return to the philosophy of Buddha that did assert the necessity of choices, that asserted the importance of those choices being ethical, that had no place within enlightenment for paths that were not ethical, and that expected us to make judgments on what is wise and what is not and to live accordingly.

People do not become enlightened without spiritual teachers. Enlightenment is not, however, a condition of spiritual dependency. These points will be amplified in the next chapter. The point at issue here, however, is that if the teacher-disciple relationship is reduced to a system for awarding credentials, then it is being misused. If, even worse, such credentials are then granted to people who are associated with views that are pernicious and non-Buddhist, then one of the main foundations of Buddhist training method is discredited and rendered ineffective.

Finally, the divorce of religion in general and Buddhism in particular from social concern is an error of great magnitude. In the summer of 2000, Jiun Kubota, the Third Patriarch of the Religious Foundation Sanbo-kyodan founded by Yasutani, published an apology for his teacher's expressions of support for war. This apology was, however, equivocal. With one voice, it was an apology. With the other voice it states that dharma and political ideology are two separate things and that Yasutani's disciples were only interested in the dharma and not in the ideology. This is an important argument, and again it is one that this book rejects. To be a dharma teacher is not simply a profession like being an architect. An architect might still be able to design good houses even if he did hold pernicious political views. The task of a dharma teacher, however, is to impart values, vision and inspiration that touch all aspects of the disciples' lives. The doctrine that says that dharma and social attitudes are unrelated is surely not the Buddhism of Shakyamuni Buddha.

The Teacher-Disciple Relationship

REAL AND FALSE AUTONOMY

The purpose of the teacher-disciple relationship in Buddhism is not that of providing credentials for the disciple nor of aggrandising the teacher. There has, in recent years, grown up an unfortunate culture in the West of preferring credentials to substance. People now frequently go on training courses as much in order to acquire the status of the qualification-awarding body as out of any genuine desire to learn. In terms of spiritual practice, however, this attitude leads nowhere. It is, rather, part of a system that seeks to keep the genuine inspiration of spirituality under the control of bureaucratic procedures. The question – Are you enlightened? – has been replaced by the question – Are your papers in order? This, however, is not a system that cultivates autonomous people. It is, rather, a means of keeping people in childlike dependency.

Buddhism contemplates the reform of the whole world. It acts upon that contemplation. To do so it trains people. This training aims for genuine spiritual autonomy. It has a sudden aspect and a gradual progressive aspect. The gradual aspect is character building. The sudden aspect may be called a change of heart. It does not necessarily involve spiritual pyrotechnics. If there is a change of behaviour supported by a change of heart, then there is something reliable. This training is carried out through the medium of a teacher-disciple relationship. The common course of this relationship is that it is one in which all the trainee disciple's habitual patterns of dependency – inadequacy, blaming, pride, stubbornness and so on – encounter the teacher's unwillingness to cooperate with inauthenticity. This means that in many cases the would-be disciple goes away frustrated – sometimes repeatedly. Being a disciple is not an easy matter. Many of the greatest teachers in Buddhist history had very few disciples – though they may have had many who aspired to be so.

Modern people have particular difficulties understanding this relationship. They easily swing to extremes. Either they dismiss the whole idea in the name of individualism – 'Everything I need to know is already inside me, therefore I need nobody'. Or they fall into a slavish, irresponsible adulation – 'My guru is everything and I am nothing'. Neither of these attitudes is adult. The former is a kind of arrogance that makes the Buddhist method unworkable and the latter leads to passivity and abuse.

Buddhist training is a matter of realising true autonomy. Put simply: it is a matter of growing up. When a person is in their adolescent phase, they are in a position of false autonomy – and people can stay in this phase all their life – if, indeed, they get this far. The adolescent experiments with autonomy by adopting a pose of rebelliousness. If the parent thinks X, the adolescent thinks not-X and so on. This, of course, is a position of dependence that has some superficial appearance of autonomy. If the parent thinks not-X, the adolescent will start to believe X. It is automatic, not really chosen.

Clinging to false autonomy is a barrier to the attainment of real autonomy. Modern people frequently cling to a form of false autonomy. This form revolves around the desire to be selfish. The thought is that if I pursue my own pleasure, then I am being independent. This is not generally the case. The person who is selfish in this way only makes him or herself increasingly dependent upon possessions, circumstances and fashions over which they have very limited control. Their life becomes increasingly inflexible and they feel more and more lonely. Selfishness leads to loneliness and the limiting of options.

Since modern materialist civilisation has been built upon this philosophy of selfishness, it is full of lonely, alienated people. These people have few real choices. Society no longer needs slaves since people nowadays willingly buy into wage slavery. Their lives are soon completely encompassed by 'economic necessity'. Of course, the things to which this phrase refers are mostly not really necessary at all, but they seem so, and that is enough to keep the person imprisoned. That is the nature of delusion.

Individualism is promoted as a freedom. To a large extent, however, it is simply a social structure that keeps people vulnerable and available to do the bidding of the state, substitutable for one another and powerless because isolated. The Pure Land cannot be created by people who are not free. To become free, one needs the faith to step out of one's bonds, however gilded the cage.

RELATING TO AN OTHER

The mistake in selfishness, as it is commonly practised in the modern world, lies in the ideas of material independence and control. Each person thinks that they have to be materially independent and tries to be in control of his or her future. Neither are possible. Such people, therefore, do not live in the real world. One of the first things the Buddha did with his disciples was to get them to give up these two ideas. The bhikshu (the Buddhist mendicant) accepts that he does not know where his next meal is coming from.

When each person seeks material independence, each has to have a complete set of everything: one's own house, one's own vehicle, one's own washing-machine and so on. This means that one lives increasingly alone and one's time is more and more taken up with servicing these material possessions – earning the money to finance the house to keep them in. It also means that one finds it increasingly difficult to relate to others since one defines oneself by the choices one makes. Three people in one house who all define themselves by their personal taste are incompatible. Even two people. I once met a mother and daughter who lived together. The mother had her taste and the daughter had hers. In true democratic fashion they had agreed to decorate two walls of each room each. The result was a most incongruous house that pleased nobody. This is where modern life gets us – an incongruous world that pleases nobody.

Spiritual autonomy does not mean becoming a slave to taste. Out of taste arises craving and clinging. Out of these come projects of separation. An identity is born. From that separated identity grow alienation and loneliness and a wasted life. The Buddha calls this 'death-ness' (*mara-na*). Spiritual autonomy, alive-ness, is a matter of being in real relation with the real world. It means relating to a true other.

People come to life spiritually when they are in a certain kind of relation to something that is other – other than self, that is. When the Buddha saw the morning star, he was in a state of awe. We could say that there was nothing there but the star. He really saw it. There was nothing coming from his side – such as 'I want one of those', or 'It would be better if it was a bit further over to the left', or 'I wish I had got my camera' . . . nothing that would trivialise or deaden. We can say that he was empty – that would be one kind of language for describing the situation, or we could say that he was in a state of purity or awe, that he was completely given to the situation, completely in the experience. This would be a second kind of language. A Sanskrit word for this state is the word *prasada*. When the word prasada is applied to water, it means that the water is completely clear – transparent to the bottom. When the word is applied to a person, it is quite commonly translated by the English word 'faith'. This is not the kind of faith that indicates assent to a belief system. It is the kind that allows us to entrust ourselves completely to the present moment. In Japanese, the word is *shinjin*.

The slightly more technical way we can talk about this is that we can call it the state of relating to a pure other. In a sense, the other is always pure. It is impure only insofar as some distortion is imposed from our own side. When the Buddha saw the morning star he imposed nothing from his own side, so the star stood there purely. We are here constructing a language – a way of talking about something. What we are talking about is a certain way of relating. In order to describe it we need a language. There are a number of different languages in circulation, so it is as well to understand how they differ, since some are less confusing than others. It is possible, for instance, to say that when there is a pure other, there is a pure self. This is not wrong – it is simply a particular usage. Buddhism has, however, been wary of such language because as soon as attention is fixed upon the self the situation rapidly becomes impure and the star, as it is, is lost sight of. It is, therefore, less confusing to say that when the other is pure, self disappears. This is the basis of the Buddhist doctrine of nonself.

I hope you can understand from this discussion that the art of enlightenment lies not in the construction of a certain kind of self so much as in the manner of relating to what is other. If one can come to the point of seeing the other as real, one will have taken a major step towards spiritual maturity. This is what Buddhism is for. We have a duty to perform to a real world. We will not perform it until we encounter that world. While the world remains unreal to us, we will tend to retreat into quietism or lash out in frustration, but real compassion will not occur. Compassion is a feeling for something else. If the something else is not real, there is no compassion.

It is, therefore, not so much how we cultivate ourselves that matters. It is how we see the world that has effect. We have to get ourselves out of the way. We see the world item by item, so it matters how we see each separate thing. The person sitting near you is real. That person is as real as you like to think you are. He (or she) fears hurt and death. He has longings and fears. There are things he feels smug about and others he is ashamed of. He is just like you or me in humanness, yet is unique and different in a thousand specific ways too. We need to appreciate the person in both these aspects. The other is different and it is OK.

We can see that this process of learning to see the other as real is exactly the opposite of what happens in wartime. Then there is strident propaganda to see the different people, the enemy, in as stereotyped a manner as possible. In other words, to make them unreal. If all people learnt to see the reality of others, it would be much more difficult to kill them.

Much immorality arises from the failure to see the other as real. We see the other things and people in our world as so many commodities – as items that are useful, useless or boring. It is failing to see that they are real that enables us to exploit and destroy them. We need to learn a new way of relating to what is other. In Buddhism, this training is done through relating to a human other – the spiritual teacher.

We can say, therefore, that all others are our spiritual teachers. This tea cup on my desk is a spiritual teacher. If I can appreciate it as it is and not just think of my own possession or use of it, then my life will immediately become much richer. Cultivating the attitude of seeing spiritual guides in all things and in all people is thus an immensely valuable spiritual practice. The power that will liberate one is the power that lies in otherness.

THE NATURE OF SPIRITUAL DISCIPLESHIP

A person may have several different kinds of teacher. Most of the great figures of Buddhist history have had more than one teacher and frequently the different teachers came from different schools of Buddhism. This is wise. Each has something different to offer. One disciple might stay all their life with one teacher.

Another might have many teachers over a period of years. The relationships will be different. Some teachers have thousands of disciples and others only have one or two. Obviously, in the former case, accessibility may be a problem. It is difficult to have a genuinely personal relationship with a teacher if you are one of 1,000 disciples. The queue will be long. The fact that a teacher is famous, therefore, may not always be an advantage.

A disciple is not just a student. The word disciple implies discipline. Students take what they like and leave the rest. The student's relationship with the teacher is nowhere near as intense as that of the disciple. A student, in this sense, is still in the mode of using the teacher – treating him or her as a convenience or commodity. One can learn some things – a particular teaching or technique, say – as a student, but the important thing will be lacking.

On the other hand, a disciple is not a slave. The discipline of the disciple is self-discipline. The teacher gives an example and gives instruction, but the disciple remains fully responsible for his or her life and his or her sense of this responsibility grows. A disciple is emphatically not a robot. Indeed, the whole point of the training is to emancipate the disciple from robot status. The ordinary selfish person is largely a robot. That person is already bought and sold. His life is run by his attachments. Real encounters do not occur because nothing is clearly other for them. In some spiritual traditions there is a lot of talk about surrender. The disciple is supposed to surrender his or her will to the guru. The Buddha, however, did not operate like that. He wanted people to grow up. The disciple seeks to win through to a real life in a real world.

Why do we need a spiritual guide? In what ways does one help? First, this is a relationship in which there is sufficient intensity to generate change. We do not change until we experience something compellingly intense. In this sense we may make a comparison with falling in love. A young person might be sitting looking glum and you ask what is the matter and she (or he) says that their life is going nowhere and they have no future and no choices and so on. It all sounds quite convincing. A month later you meet the same person looking quite different and enquire what is happening. You are told that your acquaintance has fallen in love and is now planning a quite different life and career in a different city and so on. An intense relationship has great power to liberate us from our self-manufactured despair. The person who falls in love is liberated for a short time and then the attachment inherent in the relationship itself starts to become a bind. The spiritual guide is not so clinging, however. The disciple who enters into such a relationship finds him or herself entering into ever greater freedom.

Secondly, the spiritual guide provides an example. Human beings learn from example. We do not believe something is possible until we see it and often we do not know how to do something until we are shown. Relating to a spiritual teacher, therefore, is inspiring. It provides the demonstration, not just the theory.

The teacher is also a mirror. The relationship is not just a one-way street. Initially, people who enter into discipleship tend to do so in the old frame of mind. They think just to get something from the teacher. They do not think so much about participating in a two-way relationship. The teacher, however, is simply living naturally. The teacher does not respond to the disciple in quite the ways that the disciple habitually expects, but respond he (or she) does. Sometimes these responses give the disciple a jolt. There is a famous story about the Buddha's encounter with a brigand called Angulimala. Angulimala became a disciple of the Buddha. Later on, Angulimala was asked why, when he and the Buddha met, he had not killed the Buddha. 'Well,' said Angulimala, 'you see, he did not act the way I expected. When people saw me they usually acted in one of three ways, so I always knew what to do. One sort of person ran away. I ran after them, caught them and killed them. Another sort of person fell on their knees and pleaded for mercy. I spent some time taunting them and then when I got bored with that, I killed them. The third kind of person would try to fight me. I always won the fights and then I killed them. So life was predictable. I knew what to do. But the Buddha did not act in any of those three ways, so I did not know what to do. He just kept walking calmly as though I was not a brigand at all, so we fell into conversation . . . and that is how I got involved.'

Although the pattern of life of Angulimala might seem extreme, we can probably see that most people have something similar. Each person has a set of routines worked out. As soon as another person acts in a certain way, we fall into one or other of our routines. We are like robots. Somebody pushes a button and we are off. In a sense, by entering our routine, we do kill off the other person. The spiritual teacher aims to help us break up this pattern and discover the freshness of life. Instead of being triggered unconsciously, we will have real encounters that are new and different each time. When we do so we will have a lot more life.

The teacher is somebody to practise on. She (or he) is somebody that the disciple can gradually learn to love, trust and respect. Later the disciple will discover that this process has deepened their ability to love, trust and respect other people. They will love, trust and respect more and more people until they can do it with everybody. When this state is reached, it will be because all others have become really other for that disciple. One cannot respect something that is not really other. If I realise that that person who lives in the next house is genuinely other, it means that I see him as living his own life in his own way, just as the tree in the garden lives its own life in its own way. The fact that that man has different habits and values to me is only natural. If I realise that he is real and that he is not me, then I can respect him as he is. I can respect that he has made his own choices for his own reasons. He has his suffering and his joy. He is not me. I can trust him to be what he is. I can love him in his very difference.

Nowadays there is much talk about loving, trusting and

respecting oneself, but this is really rather irrelevant. There is no need for it any more than there is a need to hate, distrust or abuse oneself. What matters is how one regards the world. If one learns to treat the world well, then the personal stuff will take care of itself. It will no longer be a big deal. This problem of self-worth arises largely because of the way we regard our past selves. In the past I did this and that. Some of those things were not so good. Can I forgive myself? I will not forgive myself. I will only be able to forgive when I realise that the person who did those things is somebody else. That person is not the person I am now. The person I am now is different. This person might make new mistakes, but this person would not do what that old person did. When I feel like that, the problem of forgiveness takes care of itself. While I believe that I am still the same and still liable to reoffend then the priority is not to forgive, but to find some genuine contrition and reach a change of heart. Working with a spiritual teacher gives one such confidence.

So the work of spiritual training is work upon the problem of how to regard the other. It is about achieving a real relationship – a real encounter. The word prasada that we earlier met as meaning clarity and faith, could also mean encounter.[1] Encounter is what happens when we meet the other in a clear way, entrusting ourselves to the meeting. Much Buddhist poetry seeks to capture the simple freshness of a moment of encounter – when a leaf falls or the first splash of rain is felt. It is about waking up. This is not a waking up to a supernatural or transcendental reality. Nothing supernatural has half the awesomeness of this real world in all its fresh wonderfulness.

We have had a lot of discussions about the nature of the disciple-teacher relationship. Is it like a child and parent? Only in some ways. Is it like a servant and master? No, not much. Is it like an audience and a film star? All too frequently – but it should not be. What then? The best analogy I can think of for the moment is that of the relationship between a sports person and his or her coach.

The sports coach helps the sports person to improve her (or his) game. He is experienced, but he is not necessarily always a better player – though he probably was once. He has a certain authority – 'I'd like to see you out on the track at eight tomorrow morning – so not too late to bed tonight'. But the sports person still has to go out and run the race or win the match. At the end of the day, it is the disciple's performance in life that matters, not the coach's rightness or reputation, and finally the player is responsible for that herself. The relationship between the two can be intense, challenging and eventful. A spiritual guide is a coach in the art of living a life that will benefit all sentient beings. The responsibility for actually doing so remains with the trainee. The test of whether such a life has been lived is whether beings were actually benefited.

Qualities of the Teacher and the Trainee

What qualities are required of the spiritual guide? What qualities are required of the disciple? I have here a list of a dozen of each. It is not exhaustive. I hope this gives some idea of what this relationship is about and helps those who might consider entering upon such a course.

The teacher, whether male or female,

- provides an example – has crossed the river;
- is not proud – nothing is beneath him (or her);
- is established in the ethical precepts;
- is himself experienced in discipleship;
- has experienced spiritual awakening;
- is experienced in life's trials;
- has disciples who are not clones of himself;
- is not rigid, but is open to new learning – will take advice and acknowledge mistakes;
- knows his province – he can give worthwhile advice on spiritual and ethical matters;
- shines with devotion to the Buddha, dharma and sangha;

- is a path finder;
- is a living embodiment of the altruistic spirit.

The Buddha provided a wonderful example. He walked all over India living a simple life and helping everybody. He was not proud. He begged for his food. He wore only a patched robe. He did not indulge in luxuries – not even ones that many people today consider necessities. He was well established in ethics, not just because he understood the subject, but because he 'trembled for the welfare of the least of beings'. He had himself been a disciple of other teachers and so he understood what it was to be a trainee and to learn. He had experienced spiritual awakening and he continued to do so. The Buddha's vision continued to grow throughout his life as the sangha developed and the Buddhist movement grew. He was experienced in life's trials. His mother died when he was born. Life in the palace cannot have been as idyllic as it is sometimes made out to have been. After leaving, he went through all manner of hardships before he realised the true path and after he found it he suffered several severe betrayals and losses. These trials did not defeat him. He had many disciples and they were extremely varied characters. He did not treat them all the same and he did not expect them to be all the same. Each had something different to contribute. He helped each to bring out their strengths and to overcome their weaknesses. He was not above changing his mind. The procedures for admitting new members to the sangha were changed several times as new circumstances were encountered. The Buddha frequently reversed a former rule when it was found to have deleterious consequences. He was not rigid. He knew his business and he knew his limits. He could pronounce authoritatively upon matters pertaining to the discipline, the training, the life of the sangha and the goal of the spiritual life. On matters of speculative philosophy he kept silent. On practical matters beyond his province he was simply a layman like anybody else. Attributing omniscience to him is unnecessary and inappropriate. He shone with devotion. His presence had immediate impact upon many. It was his aliveness that gave most eloquent testimony to his truth. He was unstintingly devoted to bringing the wisdom into the world and establishing the wholesome life of the sangha and of all beings. In this he was a great path-finder. He was always pushing ahead, breaking new ground. As such he was a living embodiment of the altruistic spirit – open-minded, big-hearted, broad-shouldered and engaged in the great work. The Buddha was a spiritual teacher. If you find a spiritual teacher who has these qualities, follow and learn.

The disciple:

- is willing;
- is free from other ties;
- becomes established in the precepts;
- has a personal motive for training;
- is devoted, faithful and free from cynicism;
- recognises the two-way nature of the relationship;
- supports, participates in and continues the teacher's work of compassion;
- is willing to let go of old identities and enter a new life;
- works to overcome hindrances;
- becomes part of a team or community;
- has faith in Buddha, dharma and sangha;
- has a will to benefit all sentient beings.

This person is training to become one who can minister to others and help to bring a brahma vihara – a divine environment – into being. This training begins with an act of renunciation. Unless one sees that something needs to change in this world, that there are aspects of this world that are to be renounced, then one will not start, or, if one does start, one will have no staying power, because one will not understand why it matters. Training is not something that yields a desirable worldly status. It is something that yields the ability to be of service. If one sees that this matters, then one will be willing – willing to learn, to work hard, to change, to grow, to experiment. One will feel that this matters more than one's old attachments. The commonest reason for people giving up on spiritual training – in the Buddha's time just as now – was and is the unwillingness to let go of the attachments that stand in the way. The attachments that stand in the way are both attachments to things and to people. The things that stand in the way are those that we are so attached to that we arrange our life around grasping and keeping them. The people that stand in the way are those who do not want to embark upon the spiritual life themselves and resist the attempts of others to do so.

The ethical basis for training is essential. All spiritual training takes place within an ethical framework and the precepts and vows that a disciple makes become important teachers. It is not that every trainee keeps every precept perfectly all the time. It is rather that the sincere attempt to do so itself throws up into sharp relief just how far short of perfection one is. This is both humbling and guiding.

People generally come into spiritual training with a personal motive. This will have its roots in their history. It may be a personal suffering they have experienced. It may be a doubt that gives them no peace. It may be contrition that they feel for something done. It may be a longing for something they have never had or had once and lost. Whatever it is, people who enter spiritual training generally suffer from some kind of desperation and this provides the driving force for the work of personal reform that they undertake. Some people make slow progress precisely because they are not desperate enough.

The disciple is devoted to the teacher, of course. This is a practice in learning to love and care for another person. The teacher does not rely upon this devotion. The teacher simply lives his or her life doing what reality sends along to be done. The teacher is engaged in a work of compassion in the world and the disciple finds herself drawn into it. Other disciples too find the same. This means that much of the training can, in effect, be a matter of being part of a team. It is through working with others in a cooperative spirit that we learn most. A new world is actually created in this way.

In France, the Amida Trust has a small retreat centre – an old farmhouse in the countryside with a little land. Last New Year a small group of us gathered there to practise together and see in the new millennium. In December there had been storms. When we arrived we found there were holes in six of the roofs, some of them quite large. The work of the retreat became roofing. We worked together as a team. Also, this retreat was struck by an epidemic of influenza. So each day there were some people unable to work. We ran a sick bay.

From the common worldly perspective, passing the holiday period in a primitive house, in wet weather, with a third of the party sick, and spending part of the day sitting still in a meditation hall open to the elements and the other part climbing on roofs several metres above the ground putting back tiles, does not sound attractive. However, this was an excellent retreat. Caring for the sick is dharma work. That is what we are learning to do. Repairing the roof is dharma work too and doing it as a team we all learnt much: about our abilities, about cooperation, about the collective spirit, and also, by simply experiencing it, about the Pure Land. On the night of the last day of the year we had a beautiful ceremony of lights and, in traditional Buddhist style, rang the bell 108 times. We had spent much of the day reflecting upon our lives over the past year. In the ceremony we burnt tokens of what we were leaving behind. Immediately after midnight we held a vow ceremony, admitting two new members into the Buddhist sangha – probably the first Buddhists of the new millennium – and renewing our own commitment. It was a wonderful experience.

The work of Buddhist training is designed to help us change and those changes are designed to equip us to create a Pure Land – a genuinely harmonious community. When we reflected upon the week of retreat, I felt tears pouring down my face. The experience of being with people in such an excellent spirit in conditions that most people would not choose somehow made it compellingly obvious that war in this world is not necessary. Peace is possible. A Pure Land can be made. We experienced it together.

BECOMING A TRAINEE

There are probably as many different ways in which a person becomes a disciple as there are people who do it. It is a mistake to think that one can control this process over much. We might shop around, going to different Buddhist centres to find out which one seems to suit us and then attach ourselves to one of the teachers there. This may work for a time or it might not. The problem is that what suits one may not always be what is most useful. Equally the opposite – following somebody because you find them difficult – cannot be counted on either. There are many stories in Buddhist history about this kind of difficulty. The most famous, perhaps, is Ananda who studied with the Buddha himself for virtually the whole of his life and still did not really understand. He became enlightened under Kashyapa, the Buddha's successor. Ananda and Kashyapa did not get on half so well as Ananda and the Buddha, however. What is comfortable is not always what is most enlightening.

Nonetheless, by some chemistry, the process happens. We might mysteriously say, 'When the disciple is ready, the teacher will appear'. There is some truth in this, but, again, one would be unwise to let any such an adage lull one into a sense of complete passivity. The Buddhist principle is more properly expressed in the idea that by creating the right conditions one will give rise to an appropriate outcome.

What conditions can one create? One can begin where one already is and start trying to put the Buddhist ideal into practice. First one begins by learning to be of service to others – to one's community, to guests, to the needy, to animals.

One can practise making one's life useful and see whom this activity brings one into contact with. If one devotes oneself to making one's life more useful and productive, then it will be easier to see who is actually most helpful and who is simply putting on a show. The best Buddhist teachers do not necessarily have a neon sign above their door declaring their wisdom, nor adverts in the press inviting disciples, nor acolytes walking round behind fanning them. They do not live their lives posing good photo-opportunities. In fact, these might well be the kinds of signs that would make a wise seeker beware.

If you find somebody and think that they may have something to teach you, then consider this possibility seriously. Work with that person for a time if you can. Supporting their work will certainly do no harm and may do a lot of good. You might seek the teacher's advice and see if it is good advice. More importantly, you should observe their life. Is the teacher proud? Are they ethical? Look too at the existing disciples. Do they keep the precepts? Are they helpful and kind? Are they clones of the teacher, simply repeating his words and not thinking for themselves or do they seem to have achieved a genuine integration of understanding for themselves? Are they different from one another? Are they strong personalities in their own right? The Buddha was surrounded by strong people.

STAGES OF BUDDHIST COMMITMENT

Traditionally, one becomes a Buddhist by a ceremony called 'Taking Refuge'. The actual ceremonial form varies from place to place, but the core of the ceremony consists of saying the words: 'I take refuge in the Buddha; I take refuge in the dharma; I take refuge in the sangha.' Thus one dedicates oneself to the Buddhist path – one becomes a member of the sangha – the republic of enlightenment. One becomes a refugee from the world of conventional cruelties and comfortable exploitation. One becomes willing to embark on an unconventional future.

Becoming a refugee is usually followed by affirming one's intention to keep the five basic moral rules of Buddhism: Not to take life. Not to steal. Not to become involved in sexual misconduct. Not to slander nor lie. And to abstain from alcohol and drugs. By this formal commitment to Buddhism one becomes an *upasaka* – somebody who takes Buddhism seriously and undertakes to purify their own one life at least. Some contemporary schools of Buddhism have watered these rules down. If you want weak medicine, that is up to you. Beware, however. Many have been made immune to the real message by being immunised – i.e. by taking a watered-down version. The new world will not be made by weak water, nor by flaky fashions.

This ceremony is taken in front of witnesses, with a preceptor. The preceptor does not necessarily become one's main spiritual teacher by this act, but taking somebody as one's initial preceptor does create a basic bond or contract of a kind. If you take Refuges and Precepts from a preceptor and then act against them, you are letting the preceptor down as well as yourself. Also, if subsequently you have moral dilemmas, then you should be able to go back to your preceptor and discuss these with him or her.

This first step of taking Refuges and Precepts is common to many schools of Buddhism. Taking them with a particular school does not tie you to that school for life. It simply means you are formally a Buddhist. You can go to any Buddhist temple of any denomination anywhere in the world and say: 'I am a Buddhist – this is my temple – these are people of my faith.'

Beyond this first step there may be other steps you can take. These vary more from one school to another. You might take bodhisattva vows or higher precepts. The basic idea here is that having taken the five precepts one has set about doing something about oneself. Taking the bodhisattva vows declares an intention to do something to help others. It represents a shift of priorities. A person who takes bodhisattva vows may still not have a personal spiritual teacher, but in most cases, by this stage, they will have one. Taking bodhisattva vows does not necessarily mean leaving behind a conventional life in society, but, for some, it might do so. The essence of the bodhisattva vow is to put others first.

Beyond that there may be further stages of commitment. These further steps generally involve leaving the conventional life behind in a more total way. They demand a radical change of lifestyle. This may take the form of becoming a monk or nun or entering into a ministry role in the world. In the Amida Sangha we have evolved the role called an *amitarya*.[2] These brothers and sisters are dedicated to going anywhere and doing whatever is needed for the benefit of sentient beings. They are thus committed to lives of service – lives that are mobile and simple and that are filled with devotion and humanitarian activities. Other Buddhist orders each have their own systems. All these formalities, however, are to be seen as aids to practice. They are not ends in themselves. They help to strengthen our resolve. They ask for the support of the community. They dedicate us to good purposes.

· 13 ·

Vision and Reality

THE ARGUMENT SO FAR

The New Buddhism is being formed in a sea full of cross-currents. On the one hand, there has been the reawakening of Asian faith in Buddhism and the association of that reawakening with the struggle for social as well as personal liberation, as in the case of the Indian untouchables. On the other hand, Asian Buddhism can also become a reactionary force emphasising conservatism and reburying the spirit of the Buddha under centuries-old accumulations of cultural accretions. There has been direct condemnation of some of those traditions, by the Critical Buddhists and others, in terms of their pernicious social consequences, and this has led to a deeper questioning of what is to be considered truly Buddhist – a questioning to which this book aims to contribute. As Westerners have become involved, there have been the effects of modern liberal institutions that have liberated at least some Buddhists from those accretions and once again released the Buddha's original, intrinsically internationalist vision. On the other hand, modernism also brings the effects of secularisation that make it possible to mount a defence of such figures as Yasutani Roshi on the grounds that religion has nothing to do with politics.

In such a situation there is a serious need for a stronger theory base for the things that the New Buddhism stands for.

Without this, engaged Buddhism can too readily become simply a modernist, progressive humanism dressed up in a little Buddhist terminology. Many who are attracted by the idea of engaged Buddhism hope that this strong base can be found in the principles of Buddha Nature and interdependent co-arising. Our investigations here, however, cast substantial doubt upon whether those ideas will really prove to offer more than a useful rhetorical gloss. The problem is, essentially, that many people, including many engaged Buddhists, still see Buddhism as primarily a path of personal salvation and they do so because they see individual enlightenment as the final goal.

If Buddhism is first and foremost a path of personal salvation, however, then any defence of engaged Buddhism is going to be peripheral to the main theory. It will inevitably be a weak apology rather than a strong rationale. The Tibetans have a concept that can be usefully adapted here. This is the concept of teachings of lesser and of greater scope. A teaching of lesser scope is one that still has a substantial element of selfishness about it. This element makes the teaching narrower. Teachings of lesser scope are not useless, but they can be improved upon. The improved teachings are those of greater scope in which the element of selfishness has been reduced or removed.

For example, the teaching that good people go to heaven could be said to be a teaching of lesser scope. It is not a wicked or useless teaching. Yashas, the first lay person recruited by the Buddha believed in a heavenly afterlife and the Buddha did not disabuse him of the idea. A person who is convinced by it and lives his life accordingly will become a better person (unless he was already following another teaching of greater scope). It is, therefore, a legitimate religious teaching. On the other hand, it clearly depends for its effectiveness upon selfish consideration. If I live a good life so that I get my reward later, I am, to that extent, still selfishly motivated. A teaching of greater scope might teach me that it would be a good idea to tend the sick because this will help them, rather than because it will help me, for instance.

Now, the theory of interbeing – the idea that I am in you and you are in me – is, on these terms, similarly a teaching of lesser scope. It suggests that the reason for helping others is that others are not separate from oneself, so helping them is helping oneself too. Altruism is thus converted into enlightened self-interest. As before, this is not a wicked or useless teaching. A person who is convinced by it and lives his life accordingly will become a better person and it is, therefore, a legitimate religious teaching. However, it is still centrally concerned with benefiting oneself and so is not really a full expression of the Buddha's original injunction to abandon self-interest. Spiritual maturity lies in the direction of seeing others as other, not in the direction of expanding oneself to encompass everything.

When we reviewed what the different schools of Buddhism have made of the idea of enlightenment, we saw that there is a great diversity of ideas. This diversity is all attributable to this dilution of the message into teachings of lesser scope. All the different forms of enlightenment on offer in the 'Buddhist supermarkets' are essentially selfish in concept. They are the reward that an individual gets for his or her faith, effort or surrender as the case may be. Their prime purpose is the reward of the practitioner. They stand firmly in the tradition of Buddhism as a path of individual salvation. If Buddha had only wanted that, however, he would not have gone forth in the first place, because once he was enlightened there would have been nothing further for him to do.

If one starts from the axiom that Buddhism is primarily about personal salvation, then the idea that we are all part of one another does offer a way of rationalising social action. It suggests that social action will further my personal quest for enlightenment. This, however, is a lesser-scope teaching and as such falls into the weak apology category.

If we are going to find a strong rationale for engaged and social liberationist practice, we will need to look to teachings of greater scope. These will be less metaphysical and more existential. They will be about nakedly committing oneself to an altruistic path, whether there is anything in it for oneself personally or not. The Japanese Pure Land teacher Shinran said, 'I cannot know for sure that this path I am on does not lead me directly to hell, but that is not the point. I proceed in faith'. This sort of faith is something far more robust than the kind of calculation that by helping others I am really helping myself.

Now there can be greater-scope and lesser-scope versions of the same concept. If we take the concept of Buddha Nature, for instance, the objection to it is primarily that it leads people towards a comforting complacency. 'Everything has Buddha Nature' is not too far away from 'All is well with the world'. Also, Buddha Nature can become individualised into my Buddha Nature and your Buddha Nature, and when this happens it comes close to reinstitution of the concept that the Buddha rejected of souls to be saved. These, however, are all lesser-scope versions. The greater-scope version of the concept of Buddha Nature is to be found in the teaching that, since Buddha was human and we are human, we have the same basic nature as Buddha. There is, therefore, no fundamental reason why we cannot make just as positive a contribution to life as he did. In this form, the teaching is anything but complacent.

The strong rationale, therefore, is to be found in rejection of the idea that Buddhism is a path of individual salvation. This is a more fundamental step. The path of personal salvation is a path of escape – of personal liberation, ultimately into some kind of extinction. That cannot be the goal for the New Buddhism. It was not the goal of the original Buddhism. This has to be the view of the New Buddhism. New Buddhists cannot rest their case upon a weak apology for modernist social commitment as a justifiable substrategy along the path to personal enlightenment. They have to take a stand upon the assertion that the Buddha's intention was – and remains – the creation of heaven on earth and that this goal requires giving up personal salvation as a motive.

The role of the teacher-disciple relationship should be seen in this light – as a path that enables the disciple to give up lesser-scope ideas as quickly as possible and get involved in the important task. The role of Buddhist training is to befit those who undertake it for the work of transforming this world by living exemplary lives themselves and reaching out to others. This is not something that can be achieved on one's own. Up to his enlightenment, the Buddha followed a path that led him into ever greater isolation. That was the path of lesser scope. As soon as he was enlightened he reversed this behaviour. He stopped thinking about himself and his own salvation. He immediately went in search of helpers and quickly built up a team that soon generated a widespread social movement.

We see from this that in Buddhism spiritual insight and social action are closely related. The former leads to the latter. There is no need to seek far, therefore, for the rationale for engagement. Engagement is the purpose of the spiritual path. That is where it led the Buddha and that is where it should lead his followers.

MYSTICISM AND FALSE DICHOTOMIES

Because the New Buddhism is involved in socially engaged work and in 'going forth for the benefit of the many', it is sometimes assumed that it must be opposed to the practice of Buddhism as a mystical discipline. Nothing, however, could be further from the truth. I was taught by my Zen Master that 'Service to humanity is another name for Zen training'. For 'Zen' one can read 'mysticism'. I am here, of course, referring to mysticism in its proper sense. We are here talking about the deeper experiences of the spirit that arise through the discipline of religious meditation.

A hallmark of Buddhism is the bringing together of these two dimensions of religious life – the socially engaged and the direct seeing into the heart of reality. Tearing these two apart does profound damage to the human spirit. Nonetheless it is common and many people fail to see how the two come together as one. One key to this mystery is provided by a reflection upon the subject of human longing.

King Bimbisara was a friend of the Buddha. He was overthrown by his son Ajatashatru who had been egged on by the Buddha's disaffected cousin Devadatta. The usurper had his father starved to death in a prison. He also imprisoned his mother, Queen Videhi. The Buddha visited Videhi during her incarceration. Queen Videhi said to the Buddha, 'What must you and I have done in previous lives to have such awful relatives in this one?' Betrayal is one of the most painful things that can happen to a human being, whether they are a queen, a sage, or anybody else. When a parent is betrayed by their child or a teacher by their disciple, there is a great grief.

Buddhism begins with recognition of this grief, which does not just pertain to these two situations but permeates the whole of life one way or another. This recognition is the first Noble Truth. It is noble to recognise this grief. From this grief springs an equally great longing. Videhi has such a longing. By the power and sincerity of her longing, the Buddha is able to reveal to her a great vista of Buddha worlds. In other words, she enters into a vision of the Pure Land.

Because this longing for better worlds is one of the deepest realities for a human being, visions of Pure Lands are generated. Because visions are generated, humans are inspired to actualise them. Religions come into existence as a result of a mystical inspiration. Buddha getting enlightened, Mahommed hearing the voice of Allah, and Jesus encountering and defeating Satan during his forty nights in the wilderness are all examples of this. What commonly goes wrong is that the religion is then appropriated and developed by people who do not have access to the vision. This is a bit like the builders not having access to the plans. Something gets built, but it may be only a distant approximation to the original intention.

The plan was not made simply to be worshipped. It was made

in order to be implemented. True mysticism gives inspiration for action. Mysticism and action need each other. After his enlightenment, the Buddha did not retire to a cave or commit suicide. He went forth and for forty more years lived out the inspiration that came from the vision that had come to him. Religion in its true sense is precisely that – the living out of the vision in the real world.

When people hear the word vision, they are often inclined to think that something escapist or fantastic is being described. The Buddha, however, had his feet on the ground. His mysticism sprang from the hard experience of open-hearted living. He taught his disciples an approach to meditation that began with deep reflection upon their material nature. Meditation upon the earth element was generally the first topic studied in Buddha's meditation class.

The guts of the Buddha's message is this: the deepest experience of life is not to be obtained by escaping from concrete reality but by entering more deeply into it. To train in religion as Buddhism understands that term means to enter into a deeper and more intimate relationship with concrete reality than most people have even dreamt of. It is the purpose of spiritual training to bring one to this point of intense encounter.

Such intense encounter is what Buddhism means by faith. To live the Buddhist faith is to live in direct, intense, intimate encounter with reality. This is more than bittersweet, it is simultaneously bliss-inspiring and heart-breaking. It is to know and feel in one's bones how every moment of life partakes both in the great grief and in the wonder of ever-fresh awakening. This encounter is assisted, not impeded, by the imagery and symbolism that Buddhism provides. In modern life we have made a mistake by convincing ourselves that imagination and reality are opposites. We have imagination in order to help us meet reality in a more vital manner.

When a Buddhist trainee learns to meditate upon the figure of Quan Shi Yin, a mythical figure representing compassion, this is, at first, artificial. In due course, however, this practice becomes deeply meaningful. The imagined figure become a catalyst for a process of personal change, because it helps the practitioner to let go of old habitual perceptions, both of self and of the world around. In terms of iconography, the figure of Quan Shi Yin originates in depictions of the Buddha. Over the centuries, however, the imagery has diversified and Quan Shi Yin now generally appears as a woman, though there are male versions in Tibetan Buddhism. One may imagine Quan Shi Yin in many different forms. First one might imagine her standing in front of you. In this first practice, one can enter into a kind of dialogue with her. One can make some account of one's life. Later one might learn to identify with her – to become Quan Shi Yin oneself. In this second practice, one can go into the world in the role of a celestial bodhisattva of compassion. This is role training of the highest kind. Or again, one might learn to see Quan Shi Yin in all events. Each thing that happens can be seen as the work of Quan Shi Yin. Instead of seeing what happens in terms of selfish priorities, everything becomes a blessing or a lesson. In this kind of training, one knows full well that one is employing one's imagination. This use of the imagination, however, brings us into more intense contact with reality by helping us to sidestep the habitual patterns by which we commonly dull or deaden everyday experience. The psychology employed in this practice is really little different from that used in the Western psychotherapeutic procedure called psychodrama. It leads to an enhanced vividness of experiencing. It is quite different from the use of imagination as a means to escape.

Most people, fearing the intensity of such a life, prefer retreat into the defences of ego, which are the opposite use of imagination – the use of it to keep reality at a distance. This, however, is also a function of imagination, only, in this case, a less benign one. Ego is the creation of a false, make-believe life, one or two or several removes from reality. In the make-believe world of escapism one can live voyeuristically. One can convince oneself that, by mentally replicating something, one has done the real thing. One can pretend that one's mood and sentiments are profound when they are merely selfish, and so on.

Buddhist training repeatedly turns the trainee back towards reality. It may be the reality of a beautiful sunset. It may be the reality of a cat killing a mouse. It may be the reality that the teacher also farts sometimes. In any case, it is the reality of Quan Shi Yin appearing 'on the street, and in the shops'. It is the Buddha lifting his foot and stretching out his arm. When the trainee knows in his or her bones the stretching out of the arm and the lifting of the foot, he or she will be plunged into a spiritual free fall from which there is no possibility of rescuing even a shred of the ego's carefully constructed defence system. This is a fall into a place that is as terrible as it is wonderful. It is the place that Videhi went to when, in the full knowledge that her son was, right then, in the process of killing his father, she saw the Pure Land.

Nobody should enter into Buddhist training lightly. It is not a hobby. Nor is it a business of building up a successful club or institution. Who, having not seen the plans, can build? No wonder the spiritual scene is full of jerry buildings. But do not doubt that there is indeed something wonderful to be had here, for those with the stomach for it. The word bodhisattva means one who has the courage (*sattva*) of the enlightened (*bo*) vision (*dhi*).

The task for the New Buddhism is to bring the enlightened vision into the light of day, by transforming the vision of the Pure Land into action in the real world. Every person has at least a glimpse of some bit. Each worker on this building site may not have the whole plan, but everybody does have a piece of it. The love and compassion that he or she finds in his or her own heart represent that piece. If each of us acts on that, although the individual may not have the whole plan yet, the pieces of the jigsaw will gradually add up. If you take part in the attempt wholeheartedly, one day, when you least expect it, the whole pattern will suddenly become clear. That is Buddhist mysticism.

Engagement inspires vision and vision inspires engagement. Going forth is what makes us realise how much work we have to do upon ourselves. Doing work upon ourselves inspires us to go forth. Mystical experience does not come from chasing after it. It comes as a by-product of carrying out the Buddha's original intention to the best of one's ability. If we do so, the larger picture will in due course dawn upon us. Everybody can have a part in this. Those who wish to do it wholeheartedly, however, should not be lulled into thinking that it is an easy road. The ego is not built for nothing. The world beyond the ego is a much higher energy proposition.

The primal longing is that which arises in us as a result of encountering the affliction in the world (*dukkha-samudaya*). This longing is not an imperfection. It is a Noble Truth. Generally it runs to waste in the sands of distraction, the ego and oblivion. The Buddha, however, offers the alternative of garnering and cultivating it (*dukkha-samudaya-nirodha*) so that it matures into a higher intention, an aspiration and finally a vow. This vow can take hold of one's life and set one upon the right track (*marga*). This track leads to *sama-dhi*, the consummate vision.

We should not allow such visions to go stale. They were made to lead us back into a total involvement with life. Mysticism is vibrant aliveness. If you come to Buddhism for visions, therefore, think first what they may get you into and consider whether you are ready for that and, correspondingly, if you come for engaged activism, ask yourself first if you are willing to undergo the religious training that will genuinely ground you in universal compassion and the Buddha's true intention.

EVERYDAY TRAINING

Buddhist training makes a person more useful. An arrogant person does not want to be used. A Buddhist, however, does want to be useful. In this, there is to be no ulterior motive. There is, therefore, a need to arrive at a rather straightforward, practical outlook. This outlook recognises that there is suffering in the world and this in itself provides the motive for doing something. In the process of helping relieve the suffering that one encounters in others, one becomes a worthier vessel oneself. By working upon becoming a worthier vessel, one becomes more useful.

How does one become more useful? First, by attending to little things. When one takes off one's shoes to enter the meditation hall, one learns to put them straight so that they are not an offensive sight to others. The Buddha Mind does not reside in some abstract place, it resides in the practice of cleanliness, simplicity and tidiness in the details of life. It resides in courtesy and small kindnesses. It resides in patience at some times and in hard work at others. It resides in good humour.

These details are the building blocks of Buddhist training. Attending to them inducts us into an appropriate gentle discipline and shows us what we need to do inwardly. While the inward work needs to be done, it should not, however, be the first concern. We need to overcome our neuroses in order to become more useful. If we become so obsessed with pursuing our neuroses that we become less useful, then we are defeating the object.

A trainee develops an evenness of attitude towards what needs doing. It does not matter whether what is required is to bake a cake or clean the drains, mend a roof or sweep a floor, compose a newsletter or speak at a public meeting, make tea for a guest or sit beside a dying person. The trainee's aim is to be versatile and not to raise personal obstacles to what needs doing. It is a life without unnecessary fuss – a life of diversity and many encounters.

Thus a person becomes reliable and steady. One begins to have confidence that such a person will not become hysterical when under more severe difficulties, but will remain composed and keep calm.

This kind of training is generally undertaken in a community. Life in a community is a valuable training ground because the other people naturally provide the raw material. There are meals to cook and everyday jobs to do and everybody has their own preferences. In order to live in a community, these preferences have to be relaxed. If everybody is thinking that things have to be done their way, then no progress is made and the community falls into strife and chaos.

In order to live as a community, a degree of ritual is necessary. People gather for meals at a certain time. If each person were to live by whim, then the cook and the diners would be unsynchronised. Perhaps a person used always to have lunch at twelve o'clock and the community eats at one. This person learns to adjust.

In a community there are thousands of such small adjustments going on. This process of adjustment involves noticing the feeling that has come up and letting it go again. This is a process of relinquishing narcissism. Every time it comes up, that is an opportunity to let a bit more go. This is what Buddhist training is like.

In such training there needs to be balance. Each trainee is taking responsibility for pushing back his or her own boundaries. Sometimes this means deliberately provoking one's own devils. The person who gets irritable when lunch is an hour later than he prefers perhaps takes on a practice of fasting for a few days. This enables him to look more deeply into his attitude towards food and his attachment to meal times. The person who is attached to sleep perhaps joins an all-night meditation session.

Such considerations may also affect choices of work. The person who is frightened of heights might gradually work up to joining the roofing team. Men who have been used to traditional roles might find a place in the sewing room and women on the building site.

It can be seen that there may be considerations in a Buddhist community that take precedence over efficiency and convenience. A Buddhist community is also a training ground. Its purpose is to help people to become fitter vessels, to become more useful. They need to acquire skills and attitudes that will stand them in good stead when there are people to help.

A community of this kind is likely also to be open to guests so

there will be people to attend to. Looking after guests is a particularly valuable aspect of Buddhist training. Each person who
comes has common human needs and, usually, some particular
needs. The trainee assigned to look after these is, thereby, learning.
This is not a matter of just getting a job done. This is the activity of
a buddha.

Training requires that every task be regarded as something
special. It is a levelling up rather than a levelling down. If one is
washing up, one sees the washing up as work worthy of a buddha.
This does not mean that one becomes absurdly precious about it,
taking half an hour over each plate. It means that one works evenly
and with care, not disparaging the task in any way. Every task is
a good task. Disparagement would be to side with Death. Death,
for Buddha, meant whatever negativity creeps into everyday life.

TRAINING FOR WHAT?

In the later Buddhist writings one comes across the notion of
endless training. In the earlier texts, however, training has a rather
different significance. Initially, training was not an end in itself.
We have already come across the Pali terms sekha and asekha.
Sekha means a person in training. Asekha means a person who is
no longer in training: no longer in training because the training
is complete.

It does appear that something has gone missing from the
writings of many Buddhist schools. What was this training for?
The idea is widespread that the training is to bring you to a state
of enlightenment and that this enlightenment then guarantees you
the sublime reward of becoming extinct when you die. Even were
we to accept that becoming extinct after death were a desirable end
and one difficult of achievement, this still leaves us with a picture
of arhats accumulating, with nothing to do except twiddle their
thumbs until the karmic residues that are still keeping them alive
run out.

The absurdity of this idea is then somewhat obviated by the device of making enlightenment so perfect a condition that nobody is ever likely to complete their training, so the problem of what to do with redundant arhats will not arise very often.

Surely, we do not have to believe this nonsense. The Buddha trained people for a purpose. That purpose was to work to relieve the suffering in the world. That was a noble thing to spend your life doing, he said. It is also something that you need training for. That training is not endless. It is training for a job. You will need a top-up fairly regularly, and we will provide that on the regular summer retreats. The main purpose for which you are being trained, however, is to get out there and help people.

Training of this kind is not so very different from training for any other job. These people were being trained to minister to others. Such training does not arrive at an abstraction called perfection. It arrives at something demonstrable called competence. Asekhas were competent arhats. They knew how to do the job.

If we think thus about initial training and ongoing training, we can make a lot more sense of what the Buddha was founding. He was setting up an order of people who could minister to the many sufferings that are in the world. They would conduct this ministry in practical and spiritual ways. They would give advice and they would give care. They would do so in a selfless way. They would not allow personal traits like shyness, inhibitions, prudery, arrogance, greed or the like to stand in the way, so the initial training had to include measures to overcome these and acquire the necessary degree of dispassion.

This dispassion, however, is not a condition of quietude. These people were not dispassionate in that sense. They were passionate about what they were here to do. 'Be impassioned for peace,' said the Buddha. This was a mission. It was an attempt to take the message to the masses and to find ways of helping the ordinary people of the world.

It is easy to see how such a group of people dispersing across the countryside would start to have an effect. This would be a network of trained people – asekha arhats – going forth in twos, threes and sometimes larger teams, to create a grassroots revolution by the simple method of helping people. This help was sometimes practical and sometimes inspirational. Soon there was a network of people in the towns and villages inspired by these wanderers. The locally based people got projects going and the arhats came and inspired and supported.

This approach would do a lot of good. One can see how, also, after a period of time, the growth of such a movement could become unsettling for the authorities. The empowerment of the poor is unsettling for those who hold power in a society. There would eventually be pressure to domesticate these wanderers – to pull their revolutionary teeth. There would be inducements offered to the Buddhist sangha to buy into establishment positions.

Initially, this might seem attractive. Instead of homespun, person-to-person help and support, there might now be the prospect of state-funded welfare systems. There would be hospitals. There would be rest houses for travellers and relief for the poor and so on. The Ashokan regime set up a welfare state. Was it for this carrot that the sangha gave up its independence and became an arm of the state? Probably. There may have been some less noble motives too. After all, the arhats would not now have to tramp around the dusty countryside any more. They could work in purpose-built offices.

This is the way that the heart is ripped out of a revolutionary movement and once it is out it can be difficult to put it back in again. Buddhist training is not training for its own sake. It is not interminable – except in the natural sense that any person with skills needs to keep topping them up. The goal of this training is to be a competent contributor to the great work that the Buddha had in mind of combating the sufferings of all the people in this world – calming disputes, lifting oppression, feeding the hungry, tending the sick, ministering to the distressed, and helping all these groups to become helpers themselves in their turn.

14

Declaring the Republic of Sukhavati

A PEOPLE NOT A TERRITORY

If Buddhism envisages the transformation of the world, then this transformation will be achieved by people. The people concerned in effecting this transformation need to be trained for the task. In the last few chapters we have looked at some aspects of this training. Training and purpose go together. In principle this is no different from any other major undertaking. The people who are going to take on an important task need to be trained.

The purpose of the transformation is to overthrow those aspects of the world that are rooted in greed, hate and delusion. This means changing the system that keeps large sectors of the world population in poverty while other sections become fabulously and purposelessly rich, and it means doing so without resorting to wars of terror – doing so by constructive rather than destructive action.

This happens by building the new in the midst of the old. This principle is to be distinguished from 'working within the system' on the one hand and violent revolution on the other. It is a policy of renunciation: of nonviolent noncooperation on the one hand and constructive humanitarianism on the other. We can build a culture of awakening. We can only do so, however, if those involved are able to withstand pressures and short-term temptations. The traditional Buddhist name for this new awakened society is Sukhavati. We can think, therefore, in terms of the creation of the Republic of Sukhavati as a country without territory.

The citizens of Sukhavati are a tribe dedicated to and held together by a particular history, values, culture and commitment. There have been and still are other such tribes. When the values of such peoples are positive ones, they can have a profound effect upon the life and culture of all the people of this planet. For many centuries, the Jews were such a tribe. They had no homeland, but they bred much wisdom and many geniuses.

The Jews always longed for a territory to call their own. They always dreamt of returning to Palestine and becoming a nation in the conventional sense once again. As the state of Israel, however, they are likely to have a less valuable influence upon the world. Once one becomes attached to territory, that attachment siphons off much of the energy that formerly might have gone into other more creative purposes. A state apparatus is in fair degree an apparatus for greedy, deluded oppression. It is poisonous.

The Buddhist ideal, therefore, knows no particular territory and it is important that those who truly represent the dharma path not succumb to the lure of territory. Buddhism in practice has been weakened when it has become territorial. As argued in an earlier chapter, there is a sense in which Buddhism has never really recovered from the time when, around 250 BCE, it bought into the conventional system by becoming a state religion. Since then, there have been too many compromises.

Buddhism as an established religion is a contradiction in terms. Buddhism is the perennial revolution. The dharma wheel never stops turning. Establishing some kind of Buddhism as state orthodoxy is just an attempt to stop the wheel – to corrupt the Buddha. This revolution is never complete.

We should never forget that the Buddha gave up a kingdom and never went back. To go back would have been the victory of Death. Legend says that Death followed the Buddha on all his travels, but the Buddha never gave in to Death's invitations. 'Why not just become a powerful person in the world? Then you will be able to help the poor and the oppressed far more.' 'No,' said the Buddha.

The Buddha would never have become involved in a war to defend territory. He would simply have picked up his robe and bowl and walked away. When people tried to kill him, he was not abashed. But, then, he would just have become a refugee, you might say. Well, yes, that was precisely what he was. The citizens of Sukhavati are all refugees. The act of becoming a Buddhist is the act of becoming a refugee.

Successful refugees have a number of important characteristics. They are patient and tolerant. They share with one another and help each other. They stay true to their basic values while being flexible enough to learn from the other cultures with which they have dealings. They do not resort to force and they are content with what they receive while still working hard to improve things. They enrich the cultures they enter. They appreciate little things. They stay good-humoured and are appreciative of the beauty and sweetness of life while remaining in touch with its basic existential aspects – impermanence, loss of fixed identity and hardship.

All these factors are explicit aspects of the Buddhist path. The person who becomes a Buddhist trains to become a successful refugee – in heart a stateless person whose home is everywhere and whose brothers and sisters are all people. Such a one is alert to the suffering and affliction that is found everywhere in the world, yet is not thereby corrupted into hatred, greed or egotistical fantasies of their own.

The Buddhist way, therefore, is not really a path of individual salvation. It is a movement that aims to subvert the processes of corruption and oppression. This requires courage and perseverance and a willingness to refuse to buy back into the dominating system – a willingness that sometimes requires great firmness.

THE IN-BETWEEN LAND

If the Pure Land is not a territory, where is it? In the time of the Buddha, as we saw earlier in this book, a change in political organisation was underway. Republics were giving way to monarchies. What we need to understand in order to make sense of the Buddhist social agenda is that, in terms of the Buddhist analysis, the modern nation state, for all its democratic pretensions, is really more of an heir to the early monarchies than it is to the early republics. In order to understand this, we have to shift our attention away from the manner in which governments are selected and focus it upon the type of society that they exist in. The really salient feature is that pluralistic societies were giving way to monistic ones. Representative democracy and kingship are both institutions of monism.

The changeover from pluralism to monism has happened repeatedly in human history. Such changes are usually painful. In Europe, something similar happened in the creation of the Roman Empire. The Roman Republic, a pluralistic society based on tradition, gave way to the imperial government of Octavian, its most successful general, who thereby became the Emperor Augustus.

Augustus reformed his society in a radical way. He was a general. His model was the army. An army has a command structure. Its general has absolute authority. In effect, Augustus swept away the power of all the intermediate structures based on tradition, kinship, religion and accidents of history, with which Roman society had until that time been richly endowed. Rome ceased to be a community of communities and became a sovereign power populated by individuals. This is the model that has come down to us. It is the model upon which the modern state is based. We now have elected prime ministers and presidents, but they are kings by another name. They have sovereign authority while they hold office. Whichever way you vote, you still get the same centralised power structure.

Let me put this another way. Before emperors, like Augustus in

Europe or like the kings of Magadha in the India of the Buddha's time, came along, the cohesion of human society was provided by a matrix of traditional institutions that were, by comparison, much more local in their scope. If we think about society as having layers, then the bottom layer is the single person. In the old type of society, the person was part of a variety of small groups, of which the extended family or clan was generally the most potent. Most of the power and authority in such societies resided at this level. The head of a family was a powerful figure. In many societies there were only these two levels. If there was a higher level, then it was not very powerful. The overlord or the priest-king in such circumstances performed ritual functions that were prescribed by traditions that he could not change. A council of state of some kind might meet from time to time, but it did not have a lot of business, since everything that mattered was decided at the family or clan level. There have been many societies of this kind in human history.

The danger to such a society is that it can fall into feuding. Families can maintain bitterness towards other families and conflict can grow. Conflict grows into war. War calls for emergency measures. Armies are created. Eventually the army is a mightier power than any of the other institutions of the old society and a military pattern comes to be imposed on the whole society. This is what happened in Rome. Imperial power was better than civil war. It was the lesser evil. In the new arrangement, the third tier becomes massively more powerful, and the second or intermediate tier is emasculated. Its functions are appropriated by agents of the central power who owe their position not to tradition, nor to those that they have power over, but solely to the central authority. With this loss of local power, the person ceases to be controlled by and looked after by kin and friends and becomes, instead, an individualised citizen directly accountable to the agents of the central authority. The person can be directed by the central authority and this authority does not readily tolerate intermediate powers. The person becomes individualised as the traditional elements of society are stripped out. Society becomes simpler and more ruthless. It becomes monistic.

Some such political analysis as this seems to lie behind the distinctive form of Buddhist social life. It suggests that there are two types of society, one adapted to peace and one to war. The latter is characterised by a strong, central, national authority and an individualised citizenry. People are concerned about their self and about their nation. They have ceased to be concerned about their community. In the society that is adapted to peace, the intermediate layer is rich and diverse and the central authority is weak or nonexistent. People are much concerned about community and little concerned about self or nation. This is a more satisfying, healing and nonalienating way of life. This type of society will degenerate, however, if certain virtues are not upheld. As long as there is greed and hate, there will be a danger of war and of a flip over into the other kind of society. If greed and hate can be reduced, then the pluralistic society can be stabilised.

Buddhism is devoted to peace. Buddhists, therefore, are in the business of creating a society adapted to peace rather than one adapted to war. This means creating such a society – a society called a sangha – and it means inculcating the values that will keep such a society stable while it evolves and grows. This means that Buddhism offers an approach to social life that is at odds with the monistic society. In contemporary circumstances, therefore, it is subversive.

The central authority of a monistic state, of course, is invested in a quite different set of values. Greed and hate are essential to its survival. It, therefore, cultivates individualism and competition and, under the guise of fairness, it seeks to pit all against all. The natural, organic structures of society are systematically replaced by artificial, rational structures. We are no longer to trust one another, but must rely upon procedures. Justice replaces compassion as the highest virtue and a harsher world ensues. In such a world there are many alienated people, but this alienation helps to keep the system in being.

Buddhism as a social movement, therefore, has often been a force persistently trying to restore the in-between level of society – the level that is commonly called community. There is, however, an extra twist to this analysis. Buddhism is not simply attempting to return to the kinship type of society. It seeks a pluralistic society, but on a sounder footing. We cannot simply put the clock back. The Buddha saw how vulnerable the republics of his day were. He did not want simply to shore up the old. He wanted to create a new type of pluralism.

He saw that while greed and hate remained dominant forces in society, they would create the conditions for monistic societies to keep coming into being. They bring war. A society based on families was almost certain to run into this fate. In English, when we think about community, we talk about kith and kin. The term kin is still used. It refers to our family relationships. The term kith has fallen out of common use. It refers to friends. The Buddha created what we might call a kithship society rather than a kinship one. Friendship is the basis.

We are talking here, therefore, about voluntary association. A revolutionary regime, like the Jacobins, or an absolute monarch like Augustus, might forbid voluntary association for a time, but it is almost impossible to repress completely. As soon as the paranoia dies down it becomes possible for people to meet in various forms of peaceful association. This is the beginning of sangha.

We can see that throughout history, therefore, there has been an ebb and flow between monistic and pluralistic types of society. This is true in all parts of the world, whether they have been influenced by Buddhism or not. What Buddhism offers are the ingredients that can make a pluralistic society flourish.

SANGHA GROWING

The ideal sangha is a group of enlightened people acting together for the benefit of the world. The elements of this are:

- join a group;
- become enlightened;
- act together;
- benefit the world.

Sanghas form a matrix. There are groups within groups. To create a Pure Land, there must be a great richness of connections between groups. It would be a mistake to think that this means that the groups should be uniform. Quite the contrary. The secret of creating a better world is to create cooperation within diversity. Harmony implies contrast not sameness. To be enlightened does not mean to have found the one right path, nor to have penetrated to the one singular underlying reality. It means to appreciate 'what is'. And 'what is' is diverse. 'What is', is the arising and falling of beings.

Traditionally we say that a sangha needs four people. When four people gather together for the purpose of contributing to the creation of a Pure Land, there is a sangha. Now we know that people in the ordinary, common mentality gather together in groups too, but these are not sanghas. They are not sanghas because such groups are self-seeking. Being self-seeking, they are inward-looking.

Many Buddhist groups also have this self-seeking quality. We are human after all. This, however, is what we must seek to overcome. It is not by perfecting the purity of one's own tradition that one becomes a sangha. It is by opening one's heart to others. If you want to understand the pinnacle of spiritual achievement, pervade the four directions with compassion, says the Buddha. One's compassion and friendship should not be limited to those one agrees with. If we can only be friends with 'our kind of people', there will never be peace.

Nor should we think that belonging to one sangha excludes relations with other sanghas. Such an attitude is death to the greater enterprise. What is needed is the creation of matrices of intersecting cooperative connections. In the contemporary world this process can be greatly facilitated by technology. We are now able to communicate with people on the other side of the planet with ease. We should do so. It also, however, means adopting values that cherish diversity. We need to learn to enjoy discussion with people who think differently from ourselves. We need to learn to see the different characteristics of each person as a contribution rather than as something to reject. We need to learn the skills appropriate to life in a more organic kind of society where structures are more fluid and dynamic. Buddhism teaches us how to live with impermanence and how to stop identifying with fixed social structures, that then imprison us. In reality, social structures are impermanent. They rise and fall in endless succession. They branch out. Some branches branch again. Some merge. There is cross-fertilization. Some wither away, temporarily or permanently. Some are reborn.

When I was young there was a good deal of optimism around. It was thought that the relatively new disciplines of psychology and sociology would gradually enable us to create a more perfect world. The term social engineering was coined. New towns were built. There was an interest in planning. It was wonderful to experience the optimism, but it was misplaced. Many of the new towns came to be regarded as undesirable places to live in. The plans came unstuck. Why? The reason, surely, is that these plans were mechanistic rather than organic.

The same is true with the work environment in which most people spend large parts of their lives. It is constructed to a large extent upon mechanistic principles. It is bureaucracy. The basic principle of bureaucracy is to give responsibility for a task to one person (or committee) and that one then logically subdivides the task into a number of roles. People are then recruited to fill those roles and rewarded for doing so. This creates a logical structure. The logic in question, however, is not the logic of human nature. It is the logic of machines. In effect we create human machines. We even sometimes call them this.

Bureaucracy is the structure used by a monistic society to fill all the gaps that have been created by the destruction of the intermediate layer that is the main substance of societies that are not the product of war. It is a top-down arrangement.

A society that runs like clockwork, however, is not fulfilling. If we are to create the good life, we need a different metaphor from the machine. Plants provide a better metaphor. Sanghas are not constructed – they grow. And if they flourish, then that growth becomes complex and even tangled. When we look at thriving vegetable life, we see a tangled profusion. Within this profusion there are many different species. Even in areas where first appearances suggest that nature has created a monoculture, closer inspection reveals something else. If people deserted England for 200 years, most of it would revert to oak forest. An oak tree, however, supports over 100 other forms of life and an oak forest goes through cycles that create shifting areas of clearing in which many other complex ecologies arise and disappear in succession. This kind of complexity is a much better model than the purpose-made machine, if we are looking for guidance upon how to bring about a better world.

Modern societies are unduly clean and lean. There is just not enough to them. The Protestant spirit that permitted no priest between a man and his god has also brought a society in which there is precious little between the citizen and the all-powerful, sovereign, central government. This state of affairs is maintained in the name of equality and justice. It is, however, spiritually impoverishing.

A sangha is, in terms of political theory, an intermediate layer. It detracts from individualism as a social principle. In a Western-style society, however, it is an uphill struggle to create a community and when a group succeeds in doing so, that group in turn then finds itself under great pressure to act as though it collectively was an individual, or to fall under the control of the central government. In the early modern period there were many debates about whether the state could afford to let people combine together for social and economic purposes at all. In the case of trades unions, this battle still continues. The compromise that was reached was, in many cases, to allow groups to 'incorporate'. This means that a legal fiction is created whereby a group of people can be treated in law as though they constitute one person. This arrangement allows the law to carry on as though only individuals exist.

Groups, therefore, all too easily find that they are in competition rather than cooperation and the system encourages them to become exclusive and self-seeking. This is a substantial challenge for Buddhist sanghas in the West. It requires a persistent courage, discipline and determination to go against the stream. This is, however, exactly what the Buddha asked people to do. He did so so that we can contribute to creating and maintaining the kind of society that is adapted to peace, not war.

For a group to be a sangha rather than a bureaucracy there must be congruence between ends and means. A bureaucracy does not do this. I used to work in a social work department. The department existed to deliver personalised service to clients. The organisation itself, however, was designed to be as impersonal as possible. The adoption of a community-centred approach to organisation would be a fundamental revolution in our Western way of life.

Why has society adopted a bureaucratic rather than an organic style of organisation? Because the former, like an army, is more efficient in the short run. It may leave human devastation in its wake, but it will deliver the goods in an emergency. It is, in fact, an eleventh-hour way of doing things. Western society is a permanent emergency. This is why there is so much stress in our culture.

As an illustration let us take the recent war in Kosovo. There were many refugees in Albania. Many humanitarian organisations came to their aid. These organisations, for the most part, were set up on the Western model. They were efficient at putting up tents and delivering loaves of bread. This is a benefit. Wars are not cured, however, by processing their victims as though they were commodities in a factory. They are cured by a change of heart and this requires something else. It requires a social fabric that is capable of receiving them as human beings.

A sangha is a community that aims to help people experience a change of heart. It therefore has to be a human, organic, growing, complex affair. It involves many single acts of person reaching out to person. A million loaves of bread delivered by a human machine do not touch the heart.

We need, therefore, to create a refuge for the heart. This begins with an acceptance of uniqueness. The other person is not me. She is whatever she is. For sure, she has the same basic human hunger and thirst as I do. She needs, however, to be heard and appreciated in her distinctiveness. This distinctiveness comes not from the possession of a unique soul. It comes from the fact that she participates in many different dimensions of human life, all of which go beyond herself. A person comes to fullness in going beyond herself in many different ways. Fulfilment, therefore, depends upon being part of a rich society – not necessarily rich in commodities, but rich in friendship.

A sangha, therefore, needs to be a place where people can laugh together, can tell stories together and can challenge one another within friendship. It is a place where a person can belong in many different ways. These different affiliations criss-cross. The sangha that the Buddha set up did not have a command structure. It seems to have been more like a rather complex and slightly anarchic family. It had a code of discipline, but its members were free to go where they chose. Members rose to prominence without the Buddha's say-so. Disciples spent much of their time in small groups. The composition of these groups was not fixed for all time. They travelled. Different groups met. Groups formed and reformed. A trainee might spend some time with a teacher learning what that teacher could teach and then go to another one, then, perhaps, go back. They were friends helping friends. When Buddhism moved from India to Tibet, China or Sri Lanka, other patterns of organisation emerged. To some extent these were shaped by the ambient culture of the country in question, but they remained communities based on sharing, friendship, training and a richness of communication.

THE WIDER SITUATION

Buddhist training has always to be seen in the context of the wider purpose. The Buddha's message has the potential to transform the world. The world today is in the grip of an orgy of greed. The rich become richer and the poor get poorer, and this is not new. The scale of it is new, however. I do not want to throw statistics around, but the fact is that the gap between rich and poor has never been so great in the whole of history.

Reforms of international commercial and trading arrangements are having the effect of transforming the whole world into a single market. In this situation, the scope for disparities of wealth have never been remotely so great as they are now, and the process is still accelerating.

Buddhism predicts that greed and hate follow one another. The periods of greed are long and the periods of hate are short, sharp and vicious. The current surge of greed contains within it the makings of war. The greater the greed, the more devastating the war to follow. It is ironic that the collapse of the Iron Curtain and the demise of communism has created in the world precisely the conditions, that Karl Marx predicted, in which the inherent contradictions of the world greed system would become ever more glaringly apparent.

If we do not want the world to be destroyed in a blood-letting orgiastic enough to compensate for the era of greed, then we need another way forward. The Buddhist solution to this is the creation and growth of Sukhavati in our midst.

To create a country without territory, however, means to create a community of values. To hold a community of values together requires steadfastness on the part of those who participate. The pressure to rejoin the greed system is considerable. The pressure to sell out to it *en bloc* is also a major danger. A number of times in history, Buddhism has done so. Each time has been a great loss to the world.

As times grow more difficult and dangerous, the need for courage and steadiness become greater. Such times will come. A Buddhist needs to be prepared so that the purpose will not be lost when the going gets tough. The citizens of the Buddhist community of values – the Sukhavati territoryless republic – need to be steadfast and that means that our training has to be thorough. The purpose of Buddhist training is not a kind of 'I'm all right and never mind the rest' salvation. The purpose of Buddhist training is to make Sukhavati a reality.

The elements of this training, therefore, are simple enough to understand. The new arhats need to unhook themselves from the values of the prevailing system, to eliminate their own dependence upon greed, hate and delusion and to create community in as many wholesome ways as possible.

MOBILITY AND SOCIAL CONTROL

The term vihara is often rendered into English as 'Buddhist monastery'. Originally, however, it meant a park. The original disciples of the Buddha did not live in monasteries, they slept in the park. In a hot country this was not arduous. Most villages had a park and generally a shelter in it where itinerant visitors could stay over. The Buddha's followers were mobile. Later some wealthy supporters purchased land so that the Buddhists would have their own parks in some cities as venues for the summer retreat. The Buddha allowed his followers to construct small huts in these parks, but the building activity was strictly limited and nobody owned a hut as personal property.

In the climate of India the monsoon season naturally became a period of retreat. It was during these retreats that the Buddha

gave many of his discourses. For much of the year most of the
disciples went from place to place. Then in the summer they
gathered together for a period of more intensive training.

The Buddha did not, therefore, establish cloistered monasteries. He did not lock his arhats up. In later centuries, monasteries, in some countries, became a way of confining these
dangerous people lest they become too effective in unsettling
the powers that be. The Buddha, however, sent his followers
forth through all the land. They travelled.

We should not forget these original principles. Buddhist training in the modern world must prepare people to go forth, not
just to retreat. The arhat is not attached to particular places.
Patriotism, nationalism and attachment to territory have no
place in Buddhism. Sukhavati has nothing whatsoever to do
with territorial boundaries.

From the perspective of conventional society, renunciants are
dangerous. Their act of defiance consists in the fact that they
refuse to participate in competition, accumulation, exploitation,
patriotism, militarism and so on. They are willing to live without
the transient benefits that such participation brings. They thus
become difficult to control.

Most of the population of a modern Western country can
be controlled through the debt system. Instead of slavery, we
have mortgages. It works just as well and requires less overt
oppression. Nobody has to be whipped or crucified any more.
People, of their own free will, apparently, spend their whole lives
doing work that they do not believe in and do not like in order
to service their debts, their mortgage and pension plans. The
renunciant has no or only minimal involvement in this system
and so has nothing to lose. This makes them dangerous.

Monasteries can be a base from which to go forth into society.
They can, however, also, sometimes become an encumbrance.
Becoming propertied was the price that Buddhism paid for
respectability. It is, therefore, important, if the dharma is to have
something more to offer this world than simply a relapse into

comfortable moralism, that Buddhism come out from behind the monastery walls. Leave the householder life, said the Buddha, but a monastery can also become just another territory to defend.

Many contemporary Buddhists realise this. Others do not. For some, Buddhism has become a highly conservative quest for personal salvation within an authoritarian institution. This is true for many who do not actually live inside monasteries, but have become members of Buddhist sects, in which the ruling mythology revolves around the idea of the guru's near-magical powers to confer blessings upon the devotees. All this has little in common with the founder's wishes. It was not his style.

Those who do realise the importance of not becoming institutionalised, however, all too easily then lose sight of the importance of training. The institution provides a discipline. Outside the institution, the discipline is often lost. It is here outside, however, that discipline and training are even more important and significant in their effect. The Buddha taught discipline precisely because his followers did not live in institutions. It was because they went abroad all over the world that they needed to have their boundaries well internalised. The discipline has to go with such a person, not be left behind. The boundaries of Sukhavati are not border posts with barbed wire and sandbags. The borders of Sukhavati are inside each of its people.

The Buddha recruited a host of people who were willing to live highly disciplined lives while taking the message to the masses. By doing so, they also brought the goal into the present. They were, themselves, the living example. When such people walk upon the earth, Sukhavati exists. By the way they walk, Sukhavati is seen to exist. When it is seen to exist, then it can become a haven for many others who would become refugees from the storms now and to come.

15

Going Forth

RITUALS OF PREPARATION

Buddhism has many myths. It draws strength from its myths. Myths have the power to inspire and move people. Between myth and reality lie vision and ritual. What we envision and rehearse is what we will create. The practice of envisioning the Pure Land is, therefore, a powerful and effective practice. It is powerful because the mind is such that action follows what is envisioned.

A traditional way to envision the Pure Land was first to bathe, then make offerings, then sit in meditation for a time, and then to use the imagination to send all the earth element of one's being scattering to the far horizon in one direction, then to send all the water element in another direction, then all the air element in a third direction, the fire element in a fourth, and the space element in a fifth, and then, experiencing a feeling of complete letting go of all that one is made of, a letting go that symbolises the willingness to die, to bring to mind a visualisation of the disc of the setting sun. When one does this, the streams of cloud that one sees tracing across the sun disc are said to represent those defilements to which one is still attached. The practitioner strives to see the sun disc become clear and white, but typically is unable to do so. He or she then weeps in contrition for the impurities that he or she has still not managed to eradicate and these tears are said to bring purity. The sun disc is closely associated with the image of the Pure Land.

This meditative ritual is similar to those carried out in shamanic societies both by shamans themselves and by warriors before an important ordeal. The warrior has to make every effort to start the work from a place of inner purity. This will give the greatest opportunity for outer success in the real world. His mind will not be unsteadied by the shadows of the past. His aim will be surer and his endurance more extended.

The Buddhist practitioner is sometimes called a *sramana* – a word closely related to the word shaman. The task of the sramana is to heal the world – to be a world shaman. This work may be presaged by ritual and sanctified by myth, but it is not intended to remain ensconced solely in the realm of magic. The ritual preparation is intended to set the practitioner upon the path in the right spirit and with the kind of inner preparation and protection that will bring courage and immunity to the perils that lie in wait. There is much wisdom in these procedures.

A follower of the Seer (Buddha) goes forth as a sramana to heal the world, willing to meet whatever peril there may be. The sramana envisages all the spiritual ancestors – all the buddhas, bodhisattvas, sekhas and arhats that have ever been – as gathered around, offering their protection and support. The sramana tells them what he is doing and asks them to stay in this world until the task is done. They are the family of power that assists him or her. There is, therefore, the idea that we are helped. If we believe in the Pure Land and act in that belief, then all the Buddhas, arhats and bodhisattvas that have ever been will help us. It is as though they have left their great vows in the world, continuing to work within the pattern of things. All this is part of the mystical element of Buddhism. Rituals of this kind are a preparation.

The structure of shamanic ideas is different from that of later religions. In the religions, other worlds have the function of offering a place of escape or punishment. After death, you can go to heaven if you are good, or hell if you are not. This is not the shamanic approach. In shamanism, the function of the other world is to be of use to this one. The shaman makes his journeys to the spirit realm in order to bring something into this world, not in order to escape from it. In this respect, Buddhism is more like shamanism. Spiritual practices are for the sake of this world, not for the next.

This world is a place where it is not easy to become enlightened nor to live a pure life. The task of the sramana is not to think of oneself in this situation, but to set about creating that better world where all will quickly awaken. If we envision it, then we will act on that vision. The mind, as the Buddha said, goes ahead of things. This means that what the mind envisions later becomes reality. The reality follows the mind just as the cartwheel follows the ox that draws the cart. Mind is our ox. Of course, it is possible to imagine things in an idle way that never then come to pass, but the power of a strong vision is very compelling.

This world seems too difficult. We cannot become enlightened here. Therefore we envision a better world. If we envision it, then we are much more likely to start to create it. If we create it, then more people will become enlightened. This is the kind of upward spiral that Buddhism aims to create. All Buddhist myth is like this. It seeks to serve the needs of real people in a psychologically and spiritually skilful way. This is not superstition. It is dramatisation. Through this drama, the mind is prepared and the energies of the person are aligned to the task. These procedures become superstition when it is thought that ritual alone is enough. That would just be magic. The Stone Age hunter prepared in this way, but he still had to go out and catch the beast. He did not think that the ritual would fill his belly, he thought it would prepare his mind and make him more bold and skilful on the trail. He was right.

Buddhism, therefore, is full of such myths to prime our minds. We have the myth of the bodhisattva who makes great vows and fulfils them. It is the same myth in a different language. Vows are visions. If I vow something, I envision it. I rehearse it in my mind. What I rehearse, I will perform. Sooner or later, what has been internalised will bear fruit.

Such envisioning is characterised and accompanied by passion. It is an act of sublimation. Sublimation is a good thing. Sublimation is the harnessing of raw human energy and vigour into the service of the sublime purpose. It is the act of putting the ox in harness. The ox is not put in harness in order just to stand there, however.

When we have faith in our visions, when they capture our passion, then they will transform us into a suitable instrument. There is no nobler task than the creation of a better world. That world will come from our actions and our actions will come from our mind.

THE STAINLESS IN THE STAINED

The first disciples of the Buddha made their robes from rags. They found these rags on the charnel grounds. When bodies had been burnt, there would be rags left around. These could be collected and made into patchwork. The patchwork cloth was then stained with ochre, thus giving it the bright orange colour that is associated with Buddhism. Buddhism is colourful. The robe was referred to by a word that also meant 'stained'. The disciple him or herself was expected to be of stainless character. Hence the phrase, 'the stainless in the stained', as a designation of the Buddha's follower.

It is an evocative phrase with many adaptations of meaning. In one phrase, it encapsulates a powerful myth. The disciple is a person of stainless character in a stained robe. They are also a stainless person in a stained world. They are also the representative – the living presence of – a stainless world in the midst of the ordinary one. The stainless refers to the Pure Land – to this Pure Land – that already exists in the midst of, or under the cover of, the ordinary one. The Buddha sent his disciples out in their stained robes, under the disguise of poverty, to bring a new kind of richness to the world

There are many ways to 'go forth'. In October 1998, in the community where I stay, we heard that another community with which we have connections was short of a worker. One of our members, Sister Modgala, volunteered to go to help. The community to which she was to go is in Eastern Zambia, one of the poorer corners of the underprivileged half of our world. Modgala is British and had never been to Africa. She had travelled very little at all. The group in Zambia were living in extremely primitive conditions with only two rooms for six people. This little group offers primary healthcare services to the surrounding fifty-eight villages. Four of the other five people in the project were Zambians.

The whole assignment was extremely challenging. The task was to enter a different culture and learn how to be useful. The first task, however, was to learn how to be among people without offending against their customs when you do not know what their customs are. African society is complex. There are numerous tribes with very different patterns. To a European it can be bewildering. Most Europeans, however, never even attempt to understand the local culture and do not bend to it. They simply continue to be white people and expect the local people to make allowances or even defer to them. Such is the caste system of this world. That, however, is not the Buddhist way.

In Buddhism we make much of the practice of bowing. More even than meditation, Buddhism should be associated with bowing. There are little bows when meeting people and bows right down to the forehead meeting the ground as a way of expressing gratitude to the Buddha, dharma and sangha. When among Buddhists, these practices feel completely natural and the most complete expression of Buddhist faith and devotion. When going among a foreign people a different kind of bowing is called for. This is the bending to local custom.

It took Modgala several months to gain a sufficient working

knowledge of the local mores. When somebody dies in that part of Zambia – and many people die since there is much disease – those who knew the deceased gather around the house where the body is laid and hold a kind of wake that goes on all night. Traditional manners dictate a place for each person – men and women, relatives by blood or by marriage and so on, all have their place. Modgala sat at many such gatherings, taking her place as a woman of the appropriate category and sitting for long hours through the night on the earth with the other women. This too is a form of Buddhist training. When she returned to England, she said that she felt that the highest accolade that she had received while in Zambia had been an occasion when a local woman had said to her that she had, for a time, forgotten that Modgala was white.

This adaptability requires a strength of character that in Buddhism is called nonself. Modgala was able to let go of her white self. It did not stain her. She found that it was only a patchwork wrap that she could take off. Learning to take it off is one of the most important aspects of Buddhist training. The Buddhist texts abound with the phrase: 'You are not that.' The Buddha says, 'See that you are not that. Abandon it. If you abandon it, that will be for your benefit and wellbeing for a long time.' This is the practical meaning of nonself.

This Buddhist kind of strength of character has nothing to do with establishing an identity that one can hold to. Quite the reverse. It is about never giving birth to such a thing. One relies, not upon one's identity, but upon something much greater. In the context of the Pure Land, all identities are simply stained robes. They are useful for the time being sometimes, but they are not you.

Going forth means having this kind of flexibility. The unstained is without a colour of its own. It is willing to take on the colour of the environment. Such a person can enter the society of others, willing to learn their ways and not wantonly offend.

At the same time, such a person does have something greater

to be held by. They will not be sidetracked by local attractions nor fall back into old habits, because they have faith in the larger purpose. They have faith in the myth and the method. Because of this, they can act with dignity and generosity, even in the midst of hardship. They can recognise the nobility of spirit in others. They can both accept and offer material and spiritual gifts, hospitality and friendship. They can help to build community even when they are not in the community from which they originate. The communities so created are of great value for they give people faith in the potential of the human spirit to overcome difference of background. These are seeds of peace.

THE GOOD HEART OF THE ORDINARY PERSON

Buddhist compassion is not something that has been invented. It is something that everybody has. However, it does benefit from refinement and training, just as a rosebush benefits from cultivation. Modgala returned from Zambia with a greatly strengthened sense of why Buddhist training is needed.

Around about the same time as she was in Africa, a tragedy was unfolding in another part of the world. Wars in the Balkans have been going on intermittently since time immemorial. In 1999 the war was in Kosovo. The TV screens were full of pictures of refugees and the newspapers full of debate about the merits and drawbacks of Western military intervention that seemed imminent and that in due course did come.

During the refugee crisis, in the first few months of 1999, I returned to Newcastle from a retreat in France one day, and checked the e-mails. There were, as usual, a lot of them. One arrested my attention, however.

The Amida Trust runs a number of training courses. Often these make considerable use of e-mail and students who may be scattered around the globe use this medium to get to know one another, to debate relevant materials and issues and to submit work. In one such e-mail group at the time, discussion had gone on to the issue of the day – the refugee crisis. Students were discussing 'What can a person do?' The problems of the world seem so vast, impersonal and interrelated, that the individual person feels incapable of making any useful response. The idea can grow that only experts can solve the world's problems – and they are not doing a very good job of it either.

If I digress for a moment, this belief in experts is a relatively recent development in British culture. When I was young, experts were frequently viewed with suspicion and there was a culture of respect for amateurism. To be a professional was regarded as not quite decent. The amateur was believed to be a person who did things for love and so did them conscientiously and whole-heartedly whereas professionals did things simply for money and could be expected to cut corners and to produce the work in a soulless way. How things have changed!

To return to the e-mail. There it was: a message from one student, who lived in Ireland, saying: 'I have been awake all night thinking about this crisis and I know that I have to do something personally.' She owned a van and proposed to fill it with clothes, toys, medicine and whatever else people would give her that might be useful and drive it to Albania.

This message had been put out several days before. I immediately picked up the phone and rang her. I discovered that the only response she had so far received had been words of caution or discouragement and she was on the verge of abandoning the idea.

This gave me pause. I find it rather shocking that when people speak out their compassion or when they clearly have the intention actually to act upon it, they do not get a surge of support. They all too frequently get no response, or one that speaks of cautious discomfort. What is the obstacle? What is it that stands in the way of people acting upon the best part of themselves and encouraging others to do likewise?

In the contemporary world we have become entranced by

size and daunted by our own seeming smallness. Living in an industrial age, we have come to think that ten widgets are better than one widget and ten million are better still. In fact, if there are less than ten million, they are not important. This is the logic of scale. Lives are treated in the same way. If only a few are killed it is not so serious as if many are. Of course, if you, or your child, is the one, then you know that this does not make sense.

We have also become entranced by the idea of impersonal services and efficiency. This is the same thing really. All problems have a mechanical, military-style solution. The one-to-one contact is not valued. Insofar as it is valued, it is coming to be provided as a service industry. Instead of friends, we have counsellors. We buy our friendship, these days, in the same way as we buy carpet – by the metre, rather than through a relationship with the carpetmaker.

Friendship is one to one. If one reaches out to one person, something real has been achieved. It is complete in itself. It is also a condition for good in the future. This is what is not seen in the logic of widgets, but is fundamental to the logic of Buddhism. One thing leads to another. There is a ripple effect. The initial gift does not necessarily have to be large. But the delivery has to be high quality. The quality will then multiply of its own accord.

There is a natural permeation at work. A loaf of bread feeds a person for half a day. The love that is given with it may continue to unfold for half a lifetime, or even many lifetimes. One Albanian fleeing from Kosovo said, 'We are the unwanted of the world and soon we shall all be dead.' People can endure hardship. They can walk through the snow and go hungry for days on end. They can do this and recover. They can do it and emerge as stronger, more compassionate people. But if they are made to feel rejected and unwanted, the conditions for future tragedies are already being sown, however many loaves are distributed.

I look back at my notes written at that time. I wrote: 'If one can look at this political crisis dispassionately, then one can see that there is a great likelihood that in twenty years time there will be another tragedy. Next time it will be Serbs being massacred.' I was wrong only in my time scale. It already comes to pass. We are only twelve months on at this time of writing and there are now more Serb refugees than Albanian ones.

We talked on the phone for a time and the venture seemed possible to me. It was clear that a co-driver would be useful, so I held the phone for a moment and asked one of the other members of our community who happened to be in the room how she would like to drive out to Albania. She said, 'Fine.'

From there on things started to fall into place. Aid was collected. Another friend told us about a convoy of vehicles that was going. In the event, the van went as part of the convoy. In the convoy were Sikhs, Christians, Buddhists, anarchists, socialists and others. The receiving agency in Albania was a Catholic nunnery. The beneficiaries were Muslim Kosovan refugees.

The Buddhist approach is basically friendship. It is not expertise. Certainly we learnt things from the experience and these would affect the way we went about another such venture. The person who goes forth also comes back. They come back and what they share contributes to the richness of the sangha community. Those contributions help the Pure Land to grow and mature. The core element in those contributions, however, is not technical expertise. It is the spirit of awakening. It is the spirit that is willing to go with the compassion that awakens whenever we open our eyes to the suffering that is in the world. It is the willingness to reach out to those who are different from ourselves.

TRAINING

People who have been on such missions know why Buddhist training exists. They have experienced the challenge that it exists

to meet. The training that we are talking about here is the cultivation of character that we call nonself. It consists of attitudes,
values and methods. It prepares a person to be patient and
to learn.

When you are driving a lorry-load of aid to a faraway country,
you arrive at border checkpoints. There is red tape. There is a lot
of waiting. You could be stuck there for several days. What are you
going to do? For a Buddhist, this is simply another opportunity to
meditate, to cultivate inner peace, to be compassionate to the people
one meets, to make new friends and learn from them, whether they
are drivers of other lorries, border officials or simply passers-by. The
Pure Land knows no territory. It is not in this place or that place
only. It can turn out to be a checkpoint where nobody else speaks
your language and they do not recognise any of the paperwork you
have brought with you. It is always in this place if we have the faith
to live it so. And there is always a stranger there that we can learn
something from.

Sometimes there is a comfortable place to sleep. Sometimes one
sleeps under the lorry. Sometimes there is tasty food. Sometimes
a meal does not arrive. Sometimes it is necessary to work fast.
Sometimes one needs endless patience and an appreciation of
the empty time. Sometimes one meets with success and it is
important not to get too carried away. Often one meets with
frustration and needs to see this as the occasion for enlightenment.
Repeatedly one must face one's own failings and weaknesses
and learn from them and grow. It is important to overcome.
All this is the product of Buddhist training. When one has
spent time going forth in the service of sentient beings, one
knows why.

The untrained person may believe that their happiness comes
from material circumstances. When my new carpet is fitted and
I am sitting in my new living room with a cup of tasty coffee in
my hands, then I will feel happy, one might think. This is the
sort of stuff that the advertising industry constantly indoctrinates
us with. It too is a myth and a method, but it is a completely

different one from that offered by Buddhism. I sit with my cup of coffee and the cat jumps up. The coffee goes flying and comes to rest in a remarkable pattern straight across the middle of the white section of the new carpet. That is the moment of enlightenment.

This Pure Land comes into view as a result of conditions. They are not, however, the conditions of indulgence. They are the conditions of inner work. They are put in place by the training in selflessness that the Buddha recommended. He did not offer this training as the means to get enlightened. He offered it in order for us to be able to build a new world. When we have tried some of that work, we know why he offered it. We do this training for two reasons. The first is that we have realised that we need it in order to do the thing that matters most. The second reason is gratitude.

BUDDHISM AND SOCIAL PHILOSOPHY

The Buddha organised a social movement. In many countries this movement has grown to a size and influence such that it has transformed the nature of the whole society, and this has not been an unintended consequence. In some of those countries, Buddhism subsequently declined. Part of the argument of this book is that the seeds of that decline were sown by the manner in which the ascendancy was achieved in the first place, and that we can learn from those lessons. I do not mean by this that we can find ways to consolidate gains made. I mean precisely that the attempt to consolidate is counterproductive. What is productive is repeatedly to give them away and move on. The problem is not that Buddhism sometimes loses ground – the problem is when Buddhism loses quality. This can happen when it compromises too far with other philosophies that are alien to it. To be accepting and tolerant and even protective of other philosophies is Buddhist, but to assume then that there is no difference between Buddhism and those other philosophies is a mistake. It is possible to be friends with people without picking up their habits.

Buddhism has been dissolved into Hinduism and into Taoism or Confucianism on occasion. In modern times it finds itself in company with new acquaintances. Apart from Christianity, Islam and Judaism, there are democracy, socialism and capitalism. There is also something a little vaguer that one might call scientism – a belief that technical progress will solve all human problems and that the paradigms used to explain phenomena in the natural world – relativity, evolution, and so on – can be applied directly to social phenomena too. There were attempts during the second half of the twentieth century to align Buddhism with each of the four secular philosophies mentioned. We should be careful not to get too seduced by such ideas.

Buddhism has a democratic aspect in that it does empower ordinary people. People of the most humble origins are regarded as just as much endowed with spiritual potential as anybody else. The Buddha often deliberately favoured the disadvantaged. Buddhism is not, however, a system of government by vote and it is wary of the tendency of democracy to create centralised power, wage wars and gravitate toward mediocrity. In Buddhism, status is supposed to accord with wisdom and kindness rather than popularity.

Buddhism has a socialistic aspect. Buddhism is good at creating communities and is critical of consumerism. The word that was used to designate the earliest disciples of the Buddha meant sharers. The sangha was a group within which private property was reduced to the absolute minimum. At the same time, Buddhism is not a system in which individual enterprise has no place nor one in which the need for virtue should be legislated out of existence. When Buddhism has aligned itself with the corporate state, things have usually started to go badly wrong. Buddhist egalitarianism is not based on envy. Socialism assumes that material possessions are benefits and so their distribution should be socially controlled, whereas Buddhism sees them as burdensome and advocates minimalism as a path to freedom.

Socialism is generally seen as the opposite of capitalism. Buddhism, however, has about as much in common with the one as with the other. Buddhism does not object to the capital necessary for the execution of beneficial projects being in private hands. Whatever institutional arrangements a society makes, there will be capital and it will be under somebody's control. Buddhism would prefer that it be used in ways that are wise and compassionate. There is no evidence that governments are universally wiser and more compassionate than individuals. Indeed, governments are capable of great infamies. So Buddhism shares with capitalism an acceptance of private property as an institution, but it does not see a race to maximise one's holding of property as anything more than a kind of self-imposed slavery.

Buddhism is not incompatible with science. In many ways, the claim that Buddhism is the most scientific religion is true. The basic attitude of science – a search for the truths and laws of this world – has always been a characteristic of Buddhism. They are both, in this sense, looking for enlightenment. Both are seeking objectivity about life and reality. When Western civilisation colonised South East Asia, it brought science and Christianity. The chagrin of the Buddhists in those countries who after a time were able to say, 'But our Buddhism is more compatible with your science, than your own religion is', was justified. Buddhists have no compunction about using the benefits of new technology for their own purposes, nor should they. Technological progress would certainly not stop if Buddhism pervaded the world. Nonetheless, scientism is often associated with tendencies that are either amoral or antimoral, and these Buddhism does reject. Society should not be dominated by a philosophy of survival of the fittest. In the moral sphere all things are not relative.

Because Buddhism has something in common with each of the above, there have been attempts to present Buddhism as a modernist social philosophy and the high point of this development could be said to have been reached in the state of Burma under U Nu shortly after Burmese independence. This social experiment was aborted by a military coup, however, and the future of Burmese polity remains uncertain. The analysis offered in this book, however, suggests that, even should the direction of the political wind change, we should view the prospect of a state-run, socialist, Buddhist nationalism with more than a pinch of caution. It would be better than military dictatorship, but there are many flaws in the twin ideas of Buddhism in one country, on the one hand, and Buddhism as an established state religion, on the other.

The reason that socialism has commonly failed is that when the state runs things, there is nobody left to arbitrate or criticise. Under socialism, the state becomes judge and jury in its own court. Any monistic polity contains an inherent tendency towards oppression. Although capitalism has many evident faults and manifests a glorification of greed and delusion, it does at least leave the state as an independent body that is supposed to have the role of referee. Capitalism, too, reaches its worst excesses when this mechanism breaks down. The problems that we are seeing in the world at the present time are substantially attributable to this factor. Some capitalistic enterprises have become rich enough to cheat. They are no longer subject to the disciplines of their own capitalistic system, because they are in a position to bring pressure on the referee.

Buddhism needs neither to merge with, nor polarise from, any of these modern ideas. It needs to preserve its essential qualities and advance them to everybody, just as the Buddha did. Irrespective of where the other is starting from, even if the other is a serial killer, there will be some point from which dialogue can be commenced, but Buddhist socialism or Buddhist capitalism or anything of that kind are things we should be wary of. Buddhism has its own treasures and should not be ashamed of them. Buddhism is the best hope for peace.

Each war is more devastating than the last war of similar scale. How long can we go on? A world of oppression is a world heading for war. The world moves towards oppression under the driving forces of greed, hate and delusion. It does so particularly quickly, however, when there is no check on the operation of those pernicious tendencies. That check is provided by moral leadership and that leadership sometimes has to be critical. The Buddhist sangha was created for precisely this purpose. The members of that sangha must, therefore, remain independent. The sangha is constituted to be a perpetual, critical opposition. It is a republic of good existing within the interstices of the polities and vested interests of the world. It exists to give perpetual witness to an alternative way. It was intendedly created as a purified sangha, a place where the people meet in counsel, not to discuss how to get the best selfish advantage for one's own group – which generally becomes the function of parliaments – but to consider what is right and good and to offer that to the world.

It follows from this that there is a dualism at the heart of Buddhism. Buddhism faces people with choice, and it should not apologise for doing so. There are the three poisons and there are their antidotes. What will you choose? Buddhism is not about 'not picking and choosing'. Buddhism is precisely about the fact that there is always, in every life, a choice to be made. This is why the infiltration of Buddhism with monistic ideas is dangerous, even if in the short run they have popular appeal. They ultimately provide a social philosophy that justifies, or fails to see, tyranny and oppression, and spells disaster for the world. While such ideas are held by a fringe group that has little real influence, they look radical and enticing. White people play with these ideas while they think that Buddhism is a game – a pastime that will yield them delightful spiritual experiences. Those who do so have not recently looked at the world.

ENGAGED BUDDHISM

New Buddhism is not really a new Buddhism. Social transformation is an intrinsic dimension of the original goal of the founder. It is not just an accident that Buddhism has, at numerous points in history, become a powerful force in changing or shaping society. Nor is it surprising that Buddhists should be involved in resisting the military government in Burma or should have burned themselves to death in protest at the war in Vietnam. On the whole, the role of Buddhism should be that of constructive humanitarian action. Nonviolent noncooperation does have its inevitable part to play, however, when situations of gross oppression arise.

Ken Jones[1] did a considerable service to the cause of New Buddhism by publishing his book, *The Social Face of Buddhism* in 1989. This stimulated publications from numerous other writers and has brought the idea of social engagement much higher up the agenda for many Buddhists around the world. The book has a wide remit and I shall only focus here upon its analysis of the dilemmas of the *sarvodaya* movement in Sri Lanka. The sarvodaya movement has its origins in Gandhism and its roots in Buddhist social principles. It started in an innocuous enough way in Sri Lanka with a programme of work camps, in which schoolchildren went to assist villagers with such projects as road repairs, irrigation works, preschool facilities and so on. Small beginnings are often the Buddhist way. The movement spread and grew and now involves thousands of villages. It receives a lot of foreign aid and it cooperates with government agencies on a wide scale. It undoubtedly does a lot of good. It certainly helps to restore the sense of community – the intermediate layer of society – and does so in an altruistic spirit.

One has a strong sense, however, that the radicalism at the roots of the movement has gradually weakened. The goals of sarvodaya do appear to have become, little by little, more and more coincident with those of Third World development projects in general. In other words, it has ceased to offer an alternative. This is not wholly true. There are still many values that are important in the sarvodaya movement that continue to run counter to the modernist paradigm. What I would like to do here is not to evaluate sarvodaya as such, but to use this as a jumping-off point for highlighting some dilemmas.

The concept of 'development' commonly implies that Sri Lanka will be a much better place when it works like New York. Few people probably really believe this if they think of it that way, but most people in power act on that assumption. Things that favour such a course are seen as good and things that stand in its way are seen as bad. The sorts of things that would effect this change would be large-scale capital investment leading to an employment-based, urbanised, profit-oriented economy. On this scale of values, Buddhism would certainly come out as bad rather than good. It is not that Buddhism is opposed to development, but that it sees that sort of development as misguided. It is not only misguided for the countries which are currently being initiated into it, like Sri Lanka, it is also misguided for the countries which already have it, like Britain and the USA. The world is, as Joanna Macy[2] says, divided into underdeveloped and maldeveloped nations.

There are, therefore, dilemmas for socially engaged Buddhism. Often there is a choice between being for something or being against something. For instance, should we assist people displaced by the clearing of tropical rainforests or should we organise a boycott of the companies that are doing the clearing? In principle, it should be possible to do both, but in practice, there are forces at work that make this difficult. If we choose simply to help the displaced people, then we will probably seek grants from governments and donations from individuals. We will probably also find that the governments that provide the grants are also the governments that are licensing the forest clearance. When we organise our boycott, therefore, we will find that our grant funding dries up. This sort of problem occurs over and over. The bigger sarvodaya becomes, the more dependent it becomes upon cooperation with powers whose values system is the antithesis of what sarvodaya stands for.

This problem is not new and it is not an easy one to solve. It means that those who enter the Republic of Sukhavarti have always to be willing to go back to the beginning and start again. The Buddha's followers were dependent upon the local people for food. At the same time they were expected to maintain and teach a moral standard that was much higher than that practised by the people who fed them. In order to do this they had to be willing, on occasion, to go hungry.

The Buddha himself started a movement by teaching high principles of life. People followed him and the movement grew. As such a movement begins to become influential, there will be some people who will join it for less than completely noble reasons. During the Buddha's lifetime there were already problems with people who joined seeing the sangha as a meal ticket. There were times when disputes arose between factions within the sangha and times when people no longer listened to the Buddha's teaching. The Buddha demonstrated that he was, if necessary, willing to leave his own movement. He was willing to go back to the beginning and start again, if it came to that.

Buddhism is a continuous revolution and there will, therefore, always be revolutions within that revolution. The kind of ethos that allows for debate, accepts difference and continues to go forward both when there is resolution and when there is not is, therefore, important. The more monistic our ideology becomes, the less room there will be for debate and the more splits we will finish up having. Monism seeks harmony through unity rather than through diversity, but this runs up against reality. We will not achieve harmony simply by outlawing discord.

Engaged Buddhism, therefore, involves a kind of asceticism and renunciation. It can be carried out most effectively by those:

- who are least dependent upon those forces in the world that will seek to compromise their purpose;

- who do not become attached to the idea of consolidating gains into worldly power; and
- who remain free and international in their perspective, willing to go wherever they are needed.

Those who accept that discord and struggle are part of the deal can carry it out most effectively. The Buddha did not come into the world simply to pour oil on troubled waters. He went forth in order to point out greed, hatred and delusion. He pointed them out so that something could be done about them and so that people could make choices with their eyes open. When we are enlightened, we are not waking up to the fact that everything is already fine – we are waking up to the fact that there is a job to do. When the Buddha was enlightened, it galvanised him to get on the road. Until then, he had been becoming more and more isolated and cut off from the life of his society. After he was enlightened, what did he do? Did he retire to a hilltop in order to contemplate the perfection of things? No. He set off for the city. He gathered followers and trained them. He talked to kings and to commoners. He advocated a change in the way people live at all levels of society. He established a sangha that would give an example of the ideal he advocated. His enlightenment was a vision of what could be, and that sent him forth.

16

Resurgence

A CRY FROM THE HEART

Buddhism is medicine for a sick world. It aims to cultivate peace, relief, sound ethics, reconciliation, good relations and happier lives. It is not simply an approach to individual happiness and salvation. It is primarily aimed at bringing these supreme benefits to the world at large. You cannot heal the privileged without emancipating the downtrodden, any more than we will be able to heal humankind as a whole without healing nature.

It, therefore, confronts us with choice. At the heart of the Buddhist message is the idea that people are what they do, and what they do has consequences. Since we have a life, and since that means we must act, and since actions have consequences, it matters deeply what we do. If our acts are carried out in ignorance of the great disease, we shall only compound the problem.

Buddhism is also a cry from the heart. The Buddha went forth from his palace because he could no longer stand to live in luxury while so many suffered disease, poverty and premature death. This cry, however, is not just emotionalism. It is also a wise and principled course that brings to the practitioner the knowledge of being on the right track as well as bringing benefits to the world.

Some say Buddhism is a religion and some say not. In the Latin sense of *religio* – that which ties things back together – Buddhism is certainly a faith in cooperation: an assertion of the desirability of harmony in diversity. Buddhism is not, however, exclusive, nor strongly institutionalised, nor guilt-ridden, nor overconcerned about the gods. It is compatible with science. It creates community. It is compassion without frontiers. One person may step into freedom. Others may follow. If many do so, then they will naturally cooperate. Buddhism is synergism.

In Buddhism, the responsibility for how the world will be stays with us. We cannot shuffle off our responsibility on to divine beings and metaphysical forces – whether these exist or not. What we can do is to transform ourselves. We can work together to create new and better worlds. These new worlds are not located in another dimension. Buddhism gives us visions for this life and for lives like this one.

In Buddhism, therefore, personal training and global intervention function together. They need each other. This book has situated Buddhist training in its most meaningful context, namely the healing of the world. It has been concerned to show how real transformations of the world are not possible without something like Buddhist training. These two agendas, personal training and global transformation, are here presented, therefore, as each only being meaningful and purposeful when linked to the other. The slogan, 'Think global, act local', is very Buddhist.

When personal training and global concern are operating together in practical ways we speak of New Buddhism, even though, in fact, there is nothing really new in this. It has become necessary to coin terms like 'New' and 'engaged' Buddhism because, over the centuries, there have grown up branches of Buddhism that have stopped being engaged and have become paths of individual salvation only. Individual salvation, however, does nothing about the real problem and can contribute to the very blindness that is the root of the world disease.

Individual salvation is that form of religion that operates upon the assumption that one person can be saved by their own effort, irrespective of whether others benefit or not. Thus there are forms of spirituality in which salvation is said to be attained by believing a certain idea or by having a certain experience or even by bathing in a certain river. The Buddha used to pour scorn on such ideas. If you can get enlightened by bathing in the holy river, then there must be a lot of enlightened fish.

The reduction of Buddhism to a path of individual salvation, common as it is, is a betrayal both of Buddhism and of the world we live in. This betrayal comes about as a result of Buddhists repeatedly becoming reinfected with the world disease and selling out to the established power in the societies in which they find themselves. They thereby buy back into the caste system – that most obvious and noxious symptom of the very disease that Buddhism exists to cure.

That they thereby perhaps make some small local gains for humanity is a small matter, compared with the loss occasioned by giving up the strategy of the founder. Buddha was steadfastly unwilling to buy back into the established power structure – something that he could have done at any time. There is a serious danger that white Buddhism is itself well on course to do exactly the same thing again. Respectability beckons. Many existing Western Buddhist groups are on precisely such a course, both because of the conditioned outlook of their members and because they derive their attitudes from Eastern groups that have already done so.

VISION, FAITH AND ACTION[1]

The name Amida has always been closely associated with the Pure Land project. The Buddha told a story of a bodhisattva of long ago called Dharmakara who created a Pure Land by fulfilling a series of vows to serve all sentient beings. By succeeding in this task, he became a buddha and received the name Amida. The idea of Amida has thus become a kind of rallying point for much populist sentiment in Buddhism – a symbol of the flowering of the lotus that the historical Buddha planted in humanity's muddy pool all those years ago. Amida's Pure Land, therefore, is an archetype of the Buddhist purpose and Buddhists have been calling Amida's name ever since.

As a word, *amita* (from whence Amida) means measureless and this indicates the scope of this vision. In one passage in the Pali Canon[2] the Buddha says 'lust is the maker of measurement; hate is the maker of measurement; delusion is the maker of measurement – if you do away with these three you will be delivered into the mind that is free of measurement'. Buddhism is about getting beyond the kind of mentality that is always keeping score or keeping count. The Pure Land will not be constructed by negotiating contracts.

Humans carry a measureless longing for a perfected world and if we do not work towards it we are betraying our deepest truth. Amidism, therefore, is not a denomination, not a creed. It belongs to no particular school. It is essentially a project for Buddhists of all religions. This project is the perennial revolution, rooted in compassion power and led by all those who both open their eyes to the condition of the world and show the courage to do something wise about what they see.

These are few. The great majority do not see. They stay in the white palace. There is complacency abroad. There is a sense, since the fall of communism, that ideals are out of place, that all the important battles of history are over, that consumerism has triumphed so it must be right, and there is nothing to be done. This lack of alternative breeds decline and casts a shadow over our future. Next in number are those who see that something needs to be done, and do something, but do it from a position of hate or greed. From the Buddhist perspective: 'All violence, indeed all anger and hate, is inherently counter-revolutionary, acting to powerfully reinforce the oppressive status quo.'[3] Then there are those who see as if from a great distance and do nothing. They see and despair. There are many sensitive people in the world who live in despair.

My Zen teacher, Houn Jiyu, told me that Buddhism is service to all sentient beings. She also gave me the dharma name Hakuun Homyo, which means White Cloud Dharma Radiance. Dharma names are given to provide inspiration – something for the recipient to aim for. She herself was engaged in bringing something of value into the world by founding a monastic order that now flourishes. My own vocation, however, lies in creating a sangha without walls and in this respect my way has come to reflect a different strand of the dharma work. Wherever we work, however, the task of disciples of the Enlightened One is to help beings through the creation of a Buddha field. This means making a different kind of world by the cumulative effect of acts of kindness, great and small.

When the Buddha was born it was predicted that he would either become a 'wheel-turning king' or a great sage. A wheel-turning king is a universal monarch who brings an era of peace and plenty to the world. A great sage brings virtue, liberation and enlightenment to people. The Buddha, in fact, became a wheel-turning sage, combining these destinies as one who brought not only inner awakening to individuals, but also a revolutionary vision of the creation of a heaven on earth through the lives of his inspired disciples.

The Buddha indicated the unlimited scope of this vision by using the Indian word amita – 'measureless', or Amida, as it has become. The Buddhist texts are full of stories of enlightened beings called Amitayus (measureless life), Amitabha (measureless light) or simply Amida.

Amidism, then, is not a school of Buddhism so much as a popular undercurrent within Buddhist history that is sometimes suppressed, sometimes languishes, but seems to well up again and again, reflecting the longing that ordinary people have for a better world. It is Liberation Buddhism. It carries forward the original intention of the founder of the faith who advocated a change that would both improve the lot of the poor and oppressed and heal their exploiters and oppressors.

It is the counterforce to the recurrent tendency of Buddhism – and any other religion – to sell out to an alliance with power, wealth, privilege and respectability. I did not come into Buddhism to help establish another system of oppression. Too often Buddhism in the East became the spiritual arm of autocratic secular power.

The earliest Buddhists, with their rag robes and shaven heads, deliberately aligned themselves with the poorest. Buddhism attracted followers from all sections of society, but its solidarity with the downtrodden was obvious. The Buddha refused to favour the well-off and in numerous conspicuous gestures made plain his concern with the lower strata of society.

Buddhism is strongly ethical. Those ethics, however, not being theistic, are not associated with authoritarianism, punishment or guilt. Indeed, true ethics undermine authoritarianism and are the surest antidote to it. As the degradation of ethics becomes more widespread or more severe, so the apology for tyranny becomes more convincing. The power of virtue, truth and compassion, on the other hand, is precisely the weapon with which the excesses of the rich and the powerful are to be opposed. Ethics, in Buddhism, are simply a function of facing facts. Acts have consequences. Good acts have good consequences. In the face of evil, we must mount a courageous demonstration of good. Tyrants are an evil – whether they were elected or not. In a world of inadequate ethics, however, they become a necessary evil. Let us make them unnecessary, therefore, and we will all be much better for it for a long time to come.

The Amidist tendency in Buddhism aims to implement the vision of creating a realm of virtue, truth and compassion in the real world as a bulwark against authoritarianism and cruelty. Ethics are the defences of the Pure Land. A tamed mind is a foundation for ethics. Hence the Buddhist prescription calls for a particular form of training for those who 'have but little dust in their eyes'. This training is not to obtain enlightenment for the individual concerned as some kind of personal reward in heaven, but to equip them to take on the work that needs to be done voluntarily and gratuitously.

A Pure Land is a realm free from the three poisons of greed, hate and delusion. That means, free from exploitation, war and oppression. The legend of Amida is the story of the creating of an enlightened world, a Pure Land in the west. Actually, Amida is not just concerned with the West. Amida aims to bring about a Pure Land everywhere. This story has become a light for those the world over who see Buddhism as a path to creating a better world.

The way of enlightenment, therefore, is full of stories, visions, faith and action. Buddhism is a faith rooted in real-life experience. It is a story that can be lived. It is not a belief in something unbelievable. We know that by changing the conditions, we change what happens. We know that the way we live has consequences. It is also clear that we cannot tightly control the future. To think there are no consequences is one extreme. To think we can control the future is the other extreme. The Buddha rejected these extremes and distinguished the middle position, called dependent origination or conditional arising. We know that all things depend for their arising upon conditions. Enlightenment itself is no different. We aim therefore to create the kind of conditions, the kind of world, in which enlightenment will naturally and universally arise. These conditions are all the things designated by the word compassion.

The principle of dependent origination – the Buddhist interpretation of karma – is thus very important and should not be diluted. Ethics are not just a personal matter. They are not something private for the individual. They are the safeguard of society against oppression. The more ethical people become of their own free choice, the less need there will be for rules and coercion and the less occasion for war.

This gives us a vision of the future and it is important to have such a vision. However, the vision is not just in the future. When people act upon this vision, trusting sincerely to it, it immediately begins. As soon as a group of people start to work together to make a Pure Land, a Pure Land exists. That embryonic land will grow. By having faith in this vision and acting upon it, we can immediately bring a new way of living into existence and create the kind of community that breeds harmony and enlightenment. It starts small, but this is not really a question of scale. It is not about measurement. When we are living the vision, we are living it.

In the Amidist way of going about things, one does not aim to become enlightened oneself first. One works with others to create the Pure Land. In the Pure Land people will have no difficulty getting enlightened, whereas in the ordinary world people find it far too difficult and so waste their lives on all kinds of sundry practices that are really just a pursuit of personal experience. Knowing that it is extremely difficult to become enlightened in the world as it is, Amidists aim to create a better world in which all beings will become enlightened naturally and easily.

Amida sanghas, therefore, consist of people who support or take part in this great work of creating a perpetual nonviolent social and spiritual revolution. This work requires personal Buddhist training to overcome the three poisons in oneself. This training is challenging. It includes a thorough grounding in ethics and the training of the mind through meditation and mindfulness. It is not aimed at achieving a personal enlightenment, but at making one more skilled and capable as a worker in the cause of bringing about the 'wheel-turning' change.

We say that the Pure Land comes into existence as soon as a group of at least four people start to work together sincerely towards this aim and with this vision. The Amidist revolution thus begins with small cells of people that network with each other. In China these small cells were often called White Lotus Societies or White Cloud Societies. These societies were mostly lay Buddhist associations that aimed to bring the Buddha Light into all aspects of social life including charitable, political and economic activities.

A revolution is created cell by cell. These cells can grow and multiply and the Pure Land thus grows. The purpose of such a cell is not to be inward-looking, but to work collectively for the benefit of other sentient beings, in practical, social, spiritual or psychological ways. The real activity of Amidists thus focuses upon education, personal dharma training, creating community and going forth into the world to do humanitarian work, and all this requires a process of personal reform to be going on alongside the engaged work.

This approach trusts in the natural synergism that comes from many separate, but similarly inspired, initiatives gradually flowing together. It aims to build a movement from which a Pure Land arises spontaneously. This is an application of the fundamental Buddhist theory of dependent origination. We cannot plan a Pure Land, but we can create the conditions that will naturally give rise to it.

These conditions are virtuous collective action and the exercise of the selfless will. All the practices of Buddhism become meaningful within this context whereas without this context they may just become self-indulgent. Practitioners of this approach have faith that if they do the Buddha's work, personal salvation will take care of itself without the individual concerned having to think about it.

Being Buddhists, Amidists regard the Buddhist refuges and precepts and the disciplines of mind-training and devotional life as a basis for their life. They do not differ fundamentally from conservative or salvationist Buddhists in the methods that they use. They differ from them in the context in which they understand those methods and in the use that they put them to. These methods provide the framework for a training that makes one into a better instrument of the great work.

Some may live regular lives in society and pursue the bodhisattva ideal of ministering to others through action in their local community in cooperation with other sangha members. Others may give up the home-holding life and become sekhas, training to follow the arhat ideal of becoming free to go wherever help is needed and wherever they are required for the work of creating a Pure Land.

Now Buddhism is spreading to new cultures in the West and the voice of Amida is beginning to be heard again. White Clouds are beginning to gather and the Dharma Radiance is beginning to shine in many corners of the world.

THE RIGHT SORT OF BUDDHISM

Buddhists of the modern age must study the mistakes of the past with care and ensure that the dharma we propagate is a force for peace and emancipation and not just the foundation for another repressive establishment in the future. Buddhism must not be allowed to become an opiate that allows its followers to feel smug. 'The truth should always disturb,' said Buddhist teacher Dogen. It should not be allowed to become just another private, other-worldly religion concerned solely with death and rebirth. There have been many varieties of such extinction Buddhism, but they all bear the mark of decline – the mark of Mara.

In the modern world there is a strong ideology of division of church and state. This is then taken to mean that religion should not concern itself with matters of public policy and that the religious should concern themselves only with their own salvation. This is a mistake based upon the perception of society as having nothing between the individual and the sovereign power, with the latter being able to tolerate no rival.

A church worth its salt is subversive of such an approach, not because it contends with the central authority as a kind of alternative absolute power, but because it works to create the strength of community that makes such absolute power redundant. Furthermore, it is not just an opposition in one country seeking that one country's selfish ends better than the selfish government. It is an international movement. It is concerned with the power of wise compassion to transform the whole world. It should be an unrelenting influence for friendship and internationalism. Those who support and inhabit it should be people without colour. When they enter the stream of enlightenment their colour is washed away.

It is understandable that people become seduced by power and conformity. It is understandable, but it is not Buddhism. It is not the spirit, the sattva, that Buddha tried to instil in his followers. It is not the spirit of bodhi, of enlightenment. It does not lead to the Pure Land. It does not take us to the brahma vihara.

What gives hope is the fact that the ideals of compassion, love, joy and peace are alive in the Buddhist movement. Buddhism has by far the best record of any of the major faiths on the great questions of war, oppression and good neighbourliness and this is what makes it worth its talk. This is what makes many people who belong to other religions support Buddhism. The right kind of Buddhism is not just for Buddhists. Buddhism is worthy of that support.

Nonetheless we are, as yet, far from perfect. It is crucially important that we learn the lessons of our own past. It is easy, when not much seems to be at stake, to allow a kind of laxity to develop that can be a source of corruption later. Buddhism is enjoying currently a window of opportunity and the dharma is spreading. It is vitally important to the future of the human race what kind of dharma becomes widespread. What is the right kind of dharma and what is the wrong kind?

Half the problem lies in the fact that many Buddhists do not know what to do with a question like this. One extreme is to fall into bickering. A second extreme is to adopt a blithe tolerance that implies that every kind is as good as the next and hurriedly sweeps the question under the carpet. A third is to say, 'That is not for me to think about – our guru knows everything, so who am I to ask such questions?' The Buddha would not have supported any of these approaches. He would not have supported them because they avoid the issue.

Buddhism is worth its support because there is a right kind of

Buddhism. The right kind of Buddhism is not the property of this or that sect. The right kind is not much concerned with sects and schools at all. The right kind is concerned with the willingness to serve the common good. There may be a million ways of doing it, and we may have many differences of opinion about the best way to go about it, but that is all grist to the mill. It is creative to have differences of opinion, so long as we let them lead us to new insights and to constructive action.

This book is an attempt to increase our willingness to look at our Buddhist heritage, including its mistakes. It is a good heritage on the whole. Buddhism has been a movement that has continued for twenty-five centuries to keep a light alive in the world. Although that has meant making some compromises along the way, it has remained remarkably intact as a movement for emancipation and universal compassion. This strength has come from the fact that Buddhism has always united inner and outer – the personal and the universal. Buddhism as a social movement has its roots in rigorous training of the person. We should not, however, forget that the training of the person has its roots in the highest ideals of social reform.

Aung San Suu Kyi is the leader of the nonviolent resistance to the military government in Myanmar. She writes:

> Paradise on earth is a concept which is outmoded and few people believe in it any more. But we can certainly seek to make our planet a better happier home for all of us by constructing the heavenly abodes of love and compassion in our hearts. Beginning with this inner development we can go on to the development of the external world with courage and wisdom.[4]

Perhaps it is time that this outmoded concept was reinstated. Without it, Buddhism lies impoverished, cut off from its original inspiration. As Buddhism comes West, it encounters an ideology in which religion is seen as a private affair and in which the concern of the spiritual person is solely with their own soul. In other words, the philosophy of individualism and selfishness has already invaded the spiritual sphere in the white world and the very ground where Sukhavarti should grow has been concreted over. It is important for the future of the world that Buddhism not catch the Western disease. The same thing is repeated at the group level. Religions are divided into sects and denominations that easily become dominated by the logic of self-interest. Diversity is a good thing. It goes wrong, however, when groups are incapable of cooperating with one another and spend much energy on defending 'their own turf'. We must avoid catching this disease too. If we catch it, we are no better than the other selfish organisations that dominate this world and corrupt millions of people. This world is full of nice people who go to work every day and think they have no choice other than to pursue the selfish interests of their group, their constituency, their shareholders and so on.

The architect of our modern world was Adam Smith. He believed, and has managed to convince most of the world by now, that if everybody is sufficiently selfish then an invisible hand will deliver the paradise on earth. It is a mistake. Smith was no doubt sincere, but he was wrong. The consequences of one person's mistake can be immense. The consequences of one person's enlightenment can, also, be similarly unmeasurable.

TOLERANCE OR CLARITY?

Buddha argued his case. He did not often get angry, though he felt passion enough. In the first chapter of the Buddhist Canon in Pali, the Buddha deals with the question of how one should respond to criticism. He says:

> If anyone should speak in disparagement of me, of the Dharma or of the Sangha, you should not be angry, resentful or upset on that account. If you were to be angry or displeased at such disparagement, that would only be a hindrance to you. For if others

disparage me, the Dharma, or the Sangha, and you are angry or displeased, can you recognise whether what they say is right or not?[5]

This gives us some idea of the man. Don't think, from this, that he lacked views. He was not one who thought that one view was as good as another. He did not say these things because views do not matter. He said them because it is vitally important to arrive at the truth. Arriving at the truth is obstructed by anger, so anger has to be set aside. This does not, however, lead to a wishy-washy incertitude. He argued forcefully and decisively against the views that he did not agree with. Later in this same sutra, he systematically demolishes sixty-two views advanced by a variety of his contemporaries – views of extinction and views of eternalism and so on – that he regards as misguided obfuscation that only serves to draw people's attention away from what really matters, which, as he always said, is the affliction in the world.

Buddhism has a reputation for tolerance. Strictly speaking, this is a false impression. A Buddhist should not be tolerant. A Buddhist should not cooperate either overtly or tacitly with what is wrong, bad or harmful. A Buddhist should not be afraid to use the word 'should'. A Buddhist should be willing to say 'No', and mean it, and be willing to take the consequences. Refusing to be tolerant should not, however, mean becoming violent or oppressive. Where is the line? Let us look at some examples.

Question: Should Buddhists tolerate non-Buddhists living in the same town?

Answer: Buddhists should protect people of other religions and defend their rights. They should do this not because one religion is just as good as another, but because it is a Buddhist principle to serve all sentient beings and protect their safety. It is Buddhist to cherish diversity and pluralism as contributions to the strengthening of community.

Question: Should Buddhists be willing to argue that other religions are misguided and mistaken?

Answer: Yes, definitely. Interfaith cooperation is a good thing in some circumstances, and not a good thing in others. Where two groups share a common purpose, they can happily cooperate. Where they do not, they cannot and should not. For example: Buddhists should cooperate with Christians in feeding the homeless and probably have a few things to learn from them in that respect. At the same time Buddhists should oppose those Christians who believe that animals were put here by God for human consumption. Buddhism is not served in the long run by cultivating the idea that all religions are the same. If we look at history, we see that where that kind of idea has gained ascendancy, in India and later in China, Buddhism has gone into terminal decline.

Question: Should Buddhists tolerate the huge prostitution industry that goes on in one of the most solidly Buddhist countries in the world, namely Thailand.

Answer: No. Considering the number of Buddhists in that country, it should definitely be possible to do something to change this situation. This is precisely the kind of problem that could be overcome by direct nonviolent action. Surely, Buddhists should, through organised intervention, systematically disrupt this so-called industry, until the time is reached when children are no longer bought from poor families in the countryside and sold by the hour to provide sexual services to affluent foreigners. It is a scandal that one of the most Buddhist countries in the world is also its prime haven of child prostitution. This is an area in which Buddhism should be massively intolerant and this intolerance should be converted into direct social action. Why does this not happen? In part, because such action would be illegal, and Buddhism in Thailand has become too tied up with the state. Being tied up with the state means also being tied up with monied interests and prostitution is a big money earner.

All this is part of the question, what is Buddhism for? Buddhism is supposed to be for the welfare of all sentient beings. Buddhists should be campaigning for animal rights, not wondering how to water down the precept against eating them. Buddhists should be combating alcoholism, not watering down their own precepts against drink. Buddhism should be a moral force that does not get compromised by alliance with power and money. It should be a perennial opposition.

There may be Buddhists who would see it as success if Buddhism simply became the established religion in more countries. Any such dash for respectability would be a mistake. Respectability is not the same thing as moral integrity. In an ambience of democracy, there is a tendency to think that what the majority wants must be right. Actually, the Buddha's philosophy predicts that what the majority wants is almost invariably wrong. The world is not inherently enlightened. Most of the world is not enlightened at all. Many things that are popular are wrong. If democracy is that system in which the majority is always considered to be correct, then Buddhism is not basically democratic. There is another kind of democracy, of course. In that other kind people feel empowered whether they are in a majority or not.

The Buddha was a rebel. Buddhism exists to oppose as well as to construct. It is a moral force or nothing. If it allows its moral integrity to be diluted in the search for converts, it will dig a hole for itself that will be difficult to get out of. It should seek converts – it should seek to convince people – but not by watering down its message. There is a strong current running in the white world that presents Buddhism as nice and cosy. This is popular. It is not going to serve either Buddhism or society well in the longer run, however. Some of the characteristics of this cosy Buddhism include the abandonment of moral requirements and the adoption of philosophies that are vague and transcendental. One of its concomitant features is the emergence of Buddhist churches increasingly invested in real estate. There is a relevant joke told about a politically unstable country in which the deputy president said to the president, 'What should we do about the rebels?' and the president shrewdly replied, 'Give them a building. In ten years they will have become conservatives.'

I, therefore, assert that Buddhism should be more robust. If we are more combative, then we will be criticised, of course. If we are criticised, then we will be challenged to live up to our ideals. Perhaps we do not want to do so. Perhaps we would rather be cosy. If so, would we not be better joining the local church of the dominant faith in our area? What is the point in being Buddhist if we intend just to carry on as before and disturb nothing? Buddhism should not be seeking respectability, particularly, and certainly not at the cost of a loss of moral integrity – which often is the asking price in the contemporary world.

Buddhism does not favour a particular political system. Buddhism aims to create, offer and sustain alternative leadership in societies of every kind, and to restore community. Whatever the political constitution of a country may be, Buddhism establishes its own sangha republic within whatever space there is and from that base offers moral leadership by example. In order to do so, its own leaders and members need to be ever-vigilant in regard to their own practice and integrity. There are many such Buddhist leaders in the world today and not a few of them have won the respect not only of the Buddhist community, but also of many people from other faiths. Some Buddhists have become deeply involved in politics. There are forms of involvement that are compatible with the Buddhist life and there are forms of involvement that would not be. An interesting case in point is Aung San Suu Kyi, who has already been quoted with approval in this chapter. In opposition, she represents a courageous rallying point for the forces of virtue. There are, nonetheless, many dangers in her alignment of Buddhism with democracy and nationalism, especially the latter. Suppose she were successful. What then? Nationalism has much to answer for, the world over. It seems important to this writer, therefore, that Buddhism remain an international rather than a nationalistic force.

FINAL WORD

This book offers a recontextualisation of Buddhism. It highlights the this-worldly purpose of the founder and its continuing relevance. It sets out his social philosophy that renounces property and territory and takes away the occasion for war. It shows how he tried to introduce a new kind of leadership into society – a new republic. It outlines the kind of training that people need in order to participate in that venture. It declares the Pure Land, the brahma vihara, on this very ground, not far away in the sky. It does not favour this or that Buddhist school, but points out constructive trends and destructive dangers that all face as Buddhism enters the materially privileged yet spiritually impoverished Western world.

The enlightened person is not the sort who just talks without actually doing anything. The Buddha did not just sit, he also walked. He walked all over northern India from country to country teaching, building a new kind of community and offering an alternative form of social leadership. He mediated to avert war. He tended the sick. He worked with criminals. He elevated the oppressed. He saved animals from cruelty. He supported the bereaved. He cured the mentally ill. He was a practical man. He organised.

He called people of goodwill. There are people who long for a better world. Acknowledging that longing is a crucially important first step. To 'call Amida' is just one way of acknowledging that longing. Longing alone is not enough, however. There also needs to be method. There has to be a means. Defining the goal is a lot less important than creating the right conditions and having faith that the goal will reveal itself in its own way. The best possible definition would, in itself, do little to aid its achievement. What is far more important is to know and use the means to attain it. This is the basic meaning of the Buddha's foundational teaching of dependent origination. If we want to create a better world we will do it by putting the right conditions in place now. If we do so then the better world will grow of its own accord.

Quality is more important than quantity. It is more important that the Pure Land exists in Aung San Suu Kyi's sitting room, even if there is a guard with a gun at her gate, than that a million people attend a lecture by an Eastern guru and then go home and chat about it over a few beers. The latter process – the outreach to the masses who as yet know little, is also important, but it is less important than the purity of the source. We, therefore, have to ensure the health of the movement for an enlightened world, by putting enlightened and courageous individuals in the field. The field may be sites in the so-called Third World or may be the cities of the West. If the Buddha's personal example is a guide, then he did both with some bias in favour of the latter. If change can be achieved there, it will affect everybody.

Buddhism, therefore, is a means. It was always conceptualised as such. Buddhism is not an absolute truth. Buddhism is a raft to carry one across the stream, not something to burden one when one reaches the other shore. Get across that stream as quickly as possible, was his message, there's work to do on the other side. Buddhism is peaceful revolution. Buddha tried to get as many people across as he could and then passed the job on to us. We are mistaken to assume that the other shore is far away. The other shore exists wherever a few meet to turn this wheel together. Start today. Renounce the alternative and find a new refuge.

Buddha crossed the river because he was unwilling to cooperate any longer. He realised that it is a spiritual sickness to live in affluence in the palace while the world suffers. He sought a different way. Now Buddhism is coming to the palace of the modern world – the coalition of materially rich countries that remain rich by exploiting the rest. How will Buddhism fare? What will it teach us? Shall we learn its lessons or shall we corrupt it? If we can grow in the practice of truth and in the power of compassion, undoubtedly, we shall overcome, and the Pure Land will grow to encompass all the dispossessed of this world. This is the manifesto of the New Buddhism.

Notes and References

2. Creating a Buddha Field

1. *Amnesty International Annual Report* (Amnesty International, 1997).
2. UNHCR, *The State of the World's Refugees* (Oxford University Press, 1997), p. 24.
3. For a discussion of this interpretation of the Four Noble Truths, see my book, *The Feeling Buddha* (Constable, 1997).

3. A Critical History of Early Buddhism

1. D. B. Bakroushin, *A Buddhist Christian Synthesis* (Vantage Press, 1995) p. 19.
2. *Digh Nikaya* 17.

4. Schism in the Buddhist Revolution

1. The etymology of the word that also reveals the meaning 'foe destroyer'. In this case 'foe' refers to greed, hate and delusion.
2. James Washington, *A Testament of Hope: The Essential Writings and Speeches of Martin Luther King Jr.* (HarperCollins 1986), p. 286.

5. Liberating Buddhism

1. *Samsara* means 'the going round in circles world' i.e. self-defeating behaviour.
2. D. Chappell, 'Engaged Buddhists in a Global Society: Who is being liberated?' In S. Sivaraksa *et al. Socially Engaged Buddhism for the New Millenium: Essays in honour of Ven. Phra Dhammapitaaka (Bhikkhu P.A.Payutto) on his 60th birthday anniversary* (Sathirakoses-Nagapradipa Foundation & Foundation for Children, 1999).
3. A similar point is made in S. Sivaraksa, *Seeds of Peace* (Parallax, 1992).

6. Varieties of Enlightenment

1. In Europe, 'E numbers' designate artificial colourings and preservatives added to mass produced products.

7. Chinese Enlightenments

1. L. Hanlon & E. Heau (editors), *Meeting of Minds: A Dialogue on Tibetan and Chinese Buddhism* (Dharma Drum Publications, 1999).
2. Hanh's statement of the theory of interdependent co-arising can be found in N. Hanh, *The Heart of the Buddha's Teaching* (Parallax, 1998), pp. 206–32.
3. *Majjhima Nikaya* 21.

8. Utopian Studies

1. E.F. Schumacher, *Small is Beautiful: A Study of Economics as if People Mattered (Abacus, Sphere, Penguin, 1973).*

9. Critical Buddhism: Part One

1. N. Hakamaya, *Hihan Bukkyo* [Critical Buddhism] (Daizo Shuppan, 1990).
2. S.K. Hookham, *The Buddha Within* (Indian Books Centre, 1991).
3. *fo-hsing*.

10. Critical Buddhism: Part Two

1. J. Hubbard & P. Swanson (editors), *Pruning the Bodhi Tree: The Storm over Critical Buddhism* (University of Hawaii Press, 1997) pp. 30–55. This book provides a valuable anthology of writings covering the spectrum of opinions about Critical Buddhism.
2. Sally King, in Hubbard & Swanson, *op.cit.*
3. *Majjhima Nikaya* 24, verse 2.

11. The Corruption of Lineage

1. Philip Kapleau, *Three Pillars of Zen: Teaching, Practice and Enlightenment* (Rider, 1965).
2. Brian Victoria, *Zen at War* (Weatherhill, 1997).
3. Yasutani, *Zen Master Dogen and the Treatise on Practice and Enlightenment* (in Japanese) (Fuji Shobo, 1943).
4. Kapleau ([1695] 1980) *op.cit.*
5. P. Lusthaus, in Hubbard & Swanson, *op. cit.*, p. 41.
6. B. Faure, *The Will to Orthodoxy* (Stanford University Press, 1997), p. 10.
7. *Majjhima Nikaya* 14.

12. The Teacher-Disciple Relationship

1. I am indebted for this important insight to Reverend Taira Sato, of Three Wheels Temple, London.

2.   From amita = (measureless, or, 'of Amida') + arya (= noble).

15.   Going Forth

1.   Ken Jones, *The Social Face of Buddhism: An Approach to Political and Social Activism* (Wisdom, 1989).
2.   Joanna Macy, *Despair and Personal Power in the Nuclear Age* (New Society, 1983).

16.   Resurgence

1.   These thoughts emerged from the dharma talks and dharma discussions that took place in France upon the New Year Retreat 27 December 1999 to 4 January 2000.
2.   *Majjhima Nikaya* 43, verse 35.
3.   David Edwards, *The Compassionate Revolution* (Green Books, 1998), p. 159.
4.   Aung San Suu Kyi, *Heavenly Abodes and Human Development* (CAFOD, 1997). This is the text of the 11th Pope Paul VI Memorial Lecture written by Aung San Suu Kyi and delivered by her husband Dr Michael Aris on 3 November 1997 at the Royal Institution of Great Britain, London, she herself being under house arrest in Myanmar.
5.   Maurice Walsh (translator), *The Long Discourses of the Buddha: A Translation of the Digha Nikaya.* (Wisdom, 1987), p. 68.

Index